D0130681

NEW
SOUTH AFRICAN
PLAYS

edited by Charles J. Fourie
with a foreword by Gcina Mhlophe

Rehane Abrahams
Sibusiso Mamba
Beverley Naidoo
Ashwin Singh
Mike van Graan
James Whyle

WOOLWORTHS

AURORA METRO PRESS

We gratefully acknowledge financial assistance from Woolworths Pty, S.A.

First published in 2006 by Aurora Metro Publications Ltd. info@aurorametro.com

Production Editor   Gillian Wakeling

Editorial Assistant Priyanka Handa

With thanks to: Claire Grove, Beverley Naidoo, Olusola Oyeleye, Adi Drori, Jacob Murray, Mannie Manim, Diana Franklin, Yvonne Banning, Michelle Knight, Africa Centre, South African High Commission

ISBN0–9542330-1-8   Printed by Ashford Colour Press, UK

Foreword

This country of mine – I do not remember a time when I did not love it. From early childhood, when my grandmother used to say to me, "There is a bigger world out there", I loved my little corner of it. From a time when she told me the ancient stories of my people, stories that taught my imagination to fly, images and songs and chants that were to stay with me all my life. Wisdom of our ancestors came through great sayings and idioms that are so African and yet so universal. My Gogo would say, "Hammarsdale is a small town; Durban, our city, is a small place in South Africa; South Africa is a small place in the continent of Africa and Africa is just one continent in a bigger world."

In our South Africa, there are so many people who look at us and see only our mistakes and weaknesses. They see the drought-stricken land and rivers that have so little water most of the time. They look at the inequalities that have been inherited from a long merciless chapter of our lives and top it all with the levels of illiteracy and the newest monster to devour many of our young people, our very future – AIDS. What hope is there, they ask? One must long for the Americas, Australia and Europe – run there to the houses on top of the hill. Houses with golden windows, houses with tons of food, endless joy, free-flowing cash, possession and wide rivers.

I say this land of mine, South Africa, is the place for me. I see the golden windows in the eyes of my people. I see the fountains of hope in the energy that encourages us to keep on living, no matter how hard the times. I hear the engine that drives us, in the song of my people. I see the spirit of our ancestors in the faces of the community builders who have so little and yet find it possible to build and uplift others. I feel the love of my creator in the heat of the midday sun on a winter's morning, and in the power of the ocean's waves that surround us; the uniquely diverse natural beauty that is only South African. And I know this little part of the world is where I want to be.

Politicians and big businesses are doing their part. But my inspiration comes from everyday people.

Again, I turn to our ancient wisdom: *Umuntu ufunda aze afe*, simply meaning – a person learns until she dies. I am one who believes that we will keep on learning to do things in new ways. Yes, we will embrace modern technology and new democracies and the works. We will tackle the

AIDS monster with even more vigor, more determination, than we used to fight Apartheid. It has been slow but I feel the momentum building.

But we will also find strength in the ways of this continent, ways that can guide us to strive for a better tomorrow, every single day. We are a nation of fighters and builders. And because we do not give accommodation to hatred in our hearts, we have come this far. Hope shines in our eyes and it shines like young love. Some people may wonder how we Africans can wake up and laugh with the sun, after all the rivers of tears we have been through. Easy – Hope, that's the undying light that keeps us here.

In these past few years of our relatively new democracy, it has seemed like we are losing our focus at times but I know from experience that the road is steep and we are struggling. Some say the struggle is never over. I know too that it is small people with very little resources who are working like mad to improve the lives of their families, their neighbors and communities. I have been impressed by the 'ordinary people who do extraordinary things'. Their invaluable efforts are the essential oil that turns the wheels of South Africa, my land, here at the very southern tip of the African continent. I look at them with admiration and from them I ask for the fire to light my own efforts.

Thank you.

Gcina Mhlophe
Extract from *South Africa My Land*

Contents

Introduction

Charles J. Fourie

An attempt to briefly reflect on the totality of South African theatre writing would lead one along diverse and never-ending paths. South Africa is as much a cultural prism as it is a rainbow nation, and this is true also of our theatre heritage which has seen many a season of change during the past few decades.

Our culture of resistance, which characterised the social and political landscape of the apartheid-years, mirrored these changes in many of the plays staged since the late 1950s. South African writers have consistently resonated the turmoils of our collective history in an attempt to awaken our social and political conscience.

Plays from this early era by writers such as Barney Simon, Athol Fugard, Gibson Kente, Bartho Smit, Andre P. Brink not only reflected the inner turmoil and conflict experienced by themselves as individuals, but also that of the diverse communties from which they came. As these writers explored the hopes and dreams of a people longing for freedom, they also voiced their fear, anger and frustration.

Censorship was the order of the day with many a playwright's work banned because it dared to criticise the then ruling National Party regime, or otherwise ignored the laws of segregation which prohibited people of colour from performing on stage.

Plays performed at state-run theatres were surreptitiously submitted to a censorship board who literally 'cleansed' the scripts before they were allowed to perform them in front of an audience, forcing playwrights to compromise their work or suffer the consequences. This led to further resistance from these playwrights, who in turn sought out alternative venues to stage their works.

The Market Theatre in Johannesburg (started by the likes of Barney Simon, Mannie Manim and Vanessa Cooke) was to become home to many of these playwrights, who felt the need to be heard and seen beyond state control. Other initiatives such as the Space Theatre in Cape Town under the auspices of Brian Astbury, staged challenging work from daring writers such as Pieter Dirk Uys.

And, albeit far from the mainstream, protest theatre took on a momentum of its own in the townships, where playwrights like Gibson

Kente devised much of their work, performing in community halls despite the lack of skills and infrastructure, offering audiences a chance to hear and see their own stories, performed by their own people.

To date, the works of Athol Fugard remain the most well-known South African export, but it would serve to note that other writers such as Paul Slabolepsky, Pieter Fourie, Mbongeni Ngema, Matsa-mela Manaka, and Maishe Maponye wrote seminal plays that wait to be discovered beyond our borders. So too, the works of Deon Opperman and Reza de Wet.

As the struggle for liberation drew to a close with the release of Nelson Mandela and the unbanning of the ANC in 1990, a new generation of playwrights would emerge whose aim it was to forge a common identity for all South Africans, and whose work one could describe as 'voices of reconciliation and reason'.

The plays collected in this edition by no means aim to reflect the complete, and one might add, prolific output of new works by our playwrights over the past decade since the 1994 democratic elections. Other ground-breaking and important plays have been written by young playwrights like Brett Bailey, Aubrey Sekhabi, Sabata Sesui, Malan Steyn, Saartjie Botha and Harry Kalmer.

This explosion of new writing could not only be ascribed to the birth of our new nation, but also to the enormous growth of arts festivals. My guess is that at the Grahamstown National Arts Festival and the Karoo National Arts Festival alone, some twenty new plays are staged each year.

Other initiatives such as the Baxter Theatre's *Playground* series of staged readings, the Market Theatre Laboratory and the Collaborations Festival at Artscape, have greatly contributed toward the development of our emerging playwrights. Three of the plays in this collection have their origins at such initiatives.

The opportunity for at least three of the plays included in this collection to be heard on radio for the first time, has also contributed to their further development. It is my firm conviction that if a play can succeed in holding an audience's attention within the strict confines of radio broadcast, so too will it succeed on stage.

The Plays

Mike van Graan's *Green Man Flashing* started as a radio play titled *The Reunion* and was later adapted for the stage as *Slippery Slope*. Collaborating with director, Clare Stopford, after a period of rigorous rewritings, the play finally made its way into the mainstream, where it played to instant success. Digging under the skin of contemporary South Africa as van Graan has done in previous plays, *Green Man Flashing* goes on to explore themes of sexual harassment, political loyalty and finally, accountance to truth, which has made it one of the most talked about plays in recent years to be staged in South Africa.

James Whyle's *Rejoice Burning* is a powerful and humane drama which brings the issue of AIDS to the foreground as a universal theme, and one relevant to contemporary South Africa. In a subtle juxtaposition of black and white – the old world and the new converge around the tragic circumstances that face each of the characters. One is left with the question – who is to blame? – when prevention would have been so easy.

Sibusiso Mamba's short play *Taxi* also had its orgin as a radio drama and was first broadcast on BBC Radio 4. Renowned South African actor, Sello Maake ka Ncube, played the role of Mzee in the orginal broadcast portraying a taxi driver who drifts the highways and byways of Joahnnesburg as he reflects on his life. His dreams and aspirations of getting himself out of debt and setting up his own business, is a reminder of the harsh economic reality that faces the majority of working-class South Africans today.

Beverly Naidoo is better known as a novelist and her work covers a wide range of themes relevant to the transformational processes we have experienced as South Africans over the past decade. Her play *The Playground* (based on a short story *Out Of Bounds)* tells the story of Rosa, a young girl, who is sent by her mother to be the first black child in an all-white school where many parents remained hostile to Nelson Mandela's new integration laws. As Rosa's world collides with that of Hennie (the white boy whom Rosa's mother has looked after since he was a baby) both are forced to overcome their fears and show the courage to face each other. In Naidoo's own words: "it is not the writer's task to find solutions to 'issues' but to tell a story well". With this play Naidoo succeeds in giving us a poignant and humane angle on the difficult process of integration that has become so relevant to our lives.

Ashwin Singh's *To House* was a finalist in the 2003 PANSA (Performing Arts Network of SA) Festival of Reading of New Writing. Set in Durban, within the confines of a multi-cultural sectional title development, the play becomes a clever vehicle to explore the lives of a diverse group of characters, who each come to terms with their own prejudices. In the end, the cultural divide remains and we realise that a long journey toward the integration of our cultural differences lies ahead.

Rehane Abrahams is better known as a vibrant young actress. Her play, *What The Water Gave Me* is also a product of the Cape Town Theatre Laboratory's Collaborations Festival and was further developed since its first performance. Fusing traditional storytelling, Indian Classical dance and Physical Theatre, she explores the roots of Java slave history in an attempt to manifest her own struggle toward identity. As theatre critic Yunus Kemp puts it: "Coloured identity is almost as mythic a concept as white superiority. The struggle by the coloured nation to establish one, is mired in the inability to fully recognise and acknowledge ancestors brought to these shores in chains by the colonial masters."

As South Africa shakes off the chains of oppression and a new history evolves, the tradition and task of socially and politically aware writing still has a long journey ahead. New themes replace the old and old themes become relevant again in our society. The realities of social and economic development in our country have become more important than political issues. A new generation of playwrights will emerge in the next decade, and as we forge a culturally integrated society which respects the rights of different communities and individuals, theatre will once again be the mirror we hold up to ourselves and the rest of the world.

Charles J. Fourie

Charles J. Fourie staged his first play as a drama student at the age of 19 at the Windybrow Theatre and went on to receive the Henk Wybenga Bursary as most promising student in 1985. Since then, he has written over 40 works for the stage. His plays have mainly engaged contemporary South Africa over the past two decades with hard-hitting productions like *Big Boys, The Parrot Woman, Vrygrond, Crimebabies, Stander* and more recently his award-winning play *Vrededorp*. He has also ventured beyond South Africa's borders with plays like *Goddess of Song* about the life and times of the American opera-singer Florence Foster Jenkins, and *Demjanjuk* concerning the trial of John "Ivan the Terrible" Demjanjuk. *Big Boys* was staged in London in 2002 and was a *Time Out Critics' Choice*.

He has also been actively involved with promoting plays by young South African playwrights abroad and collaborated on 'A Season in South Africa' staged-readings at The Old Vic. His play *The Lighthouse Keeper's Wife* was presented at the John Caird 'New Director's initiative'. He has been awarded the Amstel South African Playwright of the Year Award twice, the SACPAC Award, and more recently in 2005 the KKNK Nagtegaal Award for Best Play.

Three of his plays have been filmed as television feature films to be broadcast in 2006 in South Africa. He is currently the producer of a multi-media poetry collection for Litnet.

Jayloshni Naidoo and Teboho 'T-Bone' Hlahane in *To House*
Produced at the Catalina Theatre, Durban

Doreen Webster and Frances Simon in *The Playground*
Produced by Polka Theatre, Wimbledon

Peter Mashigo and Errol Ndotho in *A Man Called Rejoice*
Produced by BBC Radio 3

Rehane Abrahams in *What the Water Gave Me*
Produced by the Mothertongue Project

Jennifer Steyne and Tshamano Sebe in *Green Man Flashing*
Produced at The Baxter Theatre, Cape Town

THE PLAYS

Playwright's Note:

What the Water Gave Me is about my connection with the Mothercity, Cape Town and thus intimately connected with my relationship to the Sea. Cape Town is on a peninsula surrounded by Ocean, the Atlantic on one side and the Indian on the other. The Indian Ocean is particularly meaningful for me and not just because the non-white beach was there, but because it carried stories of where we came from. I grew up different within, in a Cape Malay (Muslim) community with a mother from outside (Johannesburg, Christian). Apart from being not white or black, I was different from the other Coloured kids and different from the other Malay kids. My family was reeling from the 'forced removals' fracturing of their traditional extended family structures for most of my childhood. The geography I inhabited was one of fissures, fractures, cracks like my grandmother's body, scarred with the many keloids of open-heart surgery. My grandmother, Gawa Arend, held the stories of Cape Town for me. She told me *Bawa Mera, Bawa Puti*, which I later discovered was an old Javanese story *Bawang Mera, Bawang Puti* (Onion and Garlic). She told me that her people had come from the East, non-specific, mythic Java, Indian Ocean and Ships.

I believe that theatre can actively be used for healing. With this work, I put those beliefs to the test using my experiences of ritual and what I found to be common – the creation of sacred space, the invocation of the directions/elements and the closure or release at the end. I also attempted to work directly with my ancestors (particularly my grandmother) and began practically exploring Southern African shamanic techniques during this time.

Faced with the gruesome realities of sexual violence and abuse, especially against girlchildren and the constant awareness of violence in South Africa, this seemed the most potent means at my disposal. In Africa, these practises are not 'New Age', they are continuous, 'Age'-less techniques for the restoring of psyche amongst other things. They are effective.

The associations of water with healing, sexuality, fecundity, release and purification were called on to effect a process using the performer's body as point of contact/interdimensional interface/channel. It aimed to connect outward to the audience and community and inward to cellular memory and ancestral line.

Rehane Abrahams

WHAT THE WATER GAVE ME

Written and performed by
Rehane Abrahams

Produced by The Mothertongue Project. Directed by Sara Matchett. Soundscape by Julia Raynham. It was first seen at the Cape Town Theatre Laboratory's Collaborations Festival at the Nico Arena in November 2000. The Mothertongue Project also presented the show in April 2001 at The Sufi Temple, a geodesic dome in a garden. The play enjoyed a further run at the Baxter Sanlam Studio in Cape Town, July 2001.

CHARACTERS

AIR – Storyteller
FIRE – Taxi Time-Traveller
EARTH – Hip-Hop-Head from Heideveld
WATER – Little Girl

Note:
We have not included specific stage directions, as we feel it should be left to the discretion of the director and performer to invent/create their own physical narrative that runs parallel to the spoken text. We have also left the transitions from character to character up to the discretion of the performer and director.
      Use is made of Indian Classical dance, Physical Theatre and Storytelling as the action moves in all directions simultaneously interwoven. This is theatre with emphasis on transformation and the corporal. It is speaking the body/the body speaking.

The Set
The set is comprised of four 'stations' situated in a circle. Each 'station' is associated with an element and direction thus representing a medicine wheel. There are four characters and each one is connected to a 'station'.

AIR – (East) is represented by a yellow circle (approx 1 meter in diameter)
WATER – (West) by a blue circle with an empty enamel bowl
EARTH – (North) by a white circle
FIRE – (South) by a red circle

The performer enters as the audience enters the space. She is singing a Yoruba Chant in honour of the Goddess Oshun and is dragging a cloth bundle filled with various props. She carries a long stick, similar to that carried by Indian Sages. As she sings, she circles the 'medicine wheel' in a clockwise direction. As she gets to the water 'station', she takes out a plastic Coca Cola bottle filled with water and pours the water into the enamel bowl. She also places a toy doll (without any clothing) at this 'station'. At the next 'station' she empties a brown paper bag filled with earth onto the white circle and places a black woollen hat down; then she takes out a large candle and lights it at the Fire 'station' and places approx 30 unlit small birthday candles onto the red circle and a ball; finally she places a small tape recorder/dictaphone and lights an incense stick at the yellow circle. She places her stick down here and takes the cloth that was used to carry the props and winds it round her head into a turban. Thus transforming into the first character i.e. The Storyteller.
At some points the props are interchanged between characters, thus creating a sense that the characters embody aspects of one another. Again this is left to the discretion of the director and performer.

AIR *(the story is told using traditional Indian Bharatnatyam Mudras hand gestures)* Once there was and once there wasn't. Long ago and yesterday. Round the corner far away. In a land over the sea where the sun rises, lived three sisters. And their names were Bowa Mera, Bowa Puti, Taki Taki. The people and animals were their friends, so they went about freely all around the place that was their home. Their father was a fisherman and he was clever and strong. Their mother was beautiful and kind and she tended the garden, she planted and harvested and filled the air with the scent of flowers. Where they lived was lush and green, so they never lacked for places to play and they dearly loved to play. Sometimes they helped with chores, but mostly they played. Their favourite spot was down on the beach by the rock pools and little ponds. And they would sing, 'Daar onder by die dam, daar woon a Slamse man, Khadija bring die Kerrie Kos, die kinders se monde brand'. When the sun grew watery and began to set in the West, their mother would call, 'Bowa Mera, Bowa Puti, Taki Taki. Bowa Mera, Bowa Puti, Taki Taki'. Aah. By the third time they were always there.

Bowa Mera the eldest, was the prettiest of the three. Mera's face shone like a full moon on a clear summer night. Her hair was a waterfall of starfilled darkness and her smiles were cool jasmine scented breezes. Every creature stared when Mera walked by. Even the flowers blushed. As a consequence, Mera was slightly vain. She annoyed her sisters for she would leave off in the middle of an exciting game and gaze admiringly at her own reflection. Bowa Puti, the middle one, was the cleverest of the three. She was sharp and quick and knew a great many things. Already she could speak all the languages in the area, including insect and a bit of bird. She knew all the plants and trees by their formal names and could calculate the grains of sand in a bucket. At least that's what she said. She said a great many things. Mostly starting with: 'Did you know ... ?' And her sisters found this a little annoying. Taki Taki was the baby and something else altogether. She liked what she did because she did what she liked always. And no one dared stop her. So because she was the baby and so cute, her sisters let her have her way.

One day the sisters were playing by the rock pools. Mera was combing her beautiful hair and singing softly to her beautiful reflection in the water. Puti was observing the patterns of rock erosion, loudly. And Taki Taki was doing her own thing. So engaged were they in their separate games that no one noticed the strange man till he was right beside them. 'Ooh,' said Mera, 'You startled me.' The man flashed a dazzling smile, which Mera returned and he returned and so on until *boof*, Taki Taki's mud-cake hit him square in the jaw. 'That's rude', said Mera. 'So cute,' smiled the man. 'Naughty Taki Taki. Say you're sorry,' said Puti.

Just at that moment: 'Bowa Mera, Bowa Puti, Taki Taki!' But Taki Taki was already halfway up the beach running for home.

FIRE   I came back to this place in a pirate ship. It docked. They threw me overboard, thought I was dead. The pirates didn't rape me, but they wouldn't give me any rum. I tried to run away from here, from this town, but I was kidnapped. They brought me back. I stole a cutlass. I keep it well hid. I'm going to find out what it is that keeps me here, then I'm going to cut it out, then I'm going to eat it. I'm looking for a hole. A hole in my flesh. So I can spy on my blood. See where its been. Where its coming from. Sail in its currents.

Last night I met a man that told me about the walls. He's seen them too. Of course I didn't let on that I knew. Shall I tell you? There are walls invisible to the naked eye that rise up in all directions in concentric circles around the city. In the twilight when you're not looking right you catch glimmers, glimpses and the more you spy on them in this way, the more solid they become. I'm looking for a hole. Where was it? I want to get to the centre through the walls. In the centre there is a giant centipede. He eats greed. The man said.

You can't let on you know this. They'll try to destroy you. Got to be very hush hush. Undercover. *(she hails a taxi)*

Taxi. From City to Langa. From City to Sun. My friend who knew, she got found out. They knew she knew – was forced to suicide. I tried to find her. She was flying through the flaming hearts of suns. I couldn't follow. I use public transport.

On the N2 they spot me. The foetuses in the sewerage plant make me drop my guard. Abortions are very loud. Just here driver. I switch taxis to throw them off the scent. Mitchells Plein. Soon the sun will set. Voortrekker Road. The athaan from a mosque. Maghrib. Now the spirits come. Be very careful at crossing times. Dusk and dawn. Don't trip. Don't stumble. Spine Road. Robots. Thank you driver.

There's a field across the road. No grass. Just sand in a square. I must be there. Six women in hijab. Black tops, black cloaks, black scarves, pass me. They are not alive. They have no smell. They have no feet. They want me to go into the mosque. The wind rises. Six crows take off. The street is empty. The sun has gone to the western lands. Six crows follow. *(sings)* 'Black crow you're dead crow for staring at your shadow. Dead crow you're black crow for pecking at your shadow.' I cross the street. On the square of sand. The walls are here. They are pulsing and wet. Singing like drunk men dreaming of running away. It is dark. The walls threaten me. They say violation is my historical condition being as I am five generations out of Slavery and a woman. They are looking for a hole. A hole to put their violence in. Force entry into soft flesh with a word, blow, knife, cock, bullet. It is dark. I am not afraid. Porous, I am already full of holes. Drinking dreams I stand on the field. Nothing happens. Nobody rapes me. The sun is rising. My grandmother calls from the East. The night is over. I go ... *(she hails a taxi)* Taxi! Cape Town.

EARTH   The thing is right. *(long pause)* Is what it is. Is what it be like. OK, let me get to the point. When I was small, right, I couldn't eat neapolitan ice cream just like that. Sien jy, some people, they eat one colour at a time. Some people, they take like a bite of strawberry and peppermint on the same spoon. I can't. It goes against my nature. I got to mix it up. Till it's one colour, many flavours. And that's the difference, verstaan jy? Cos why? Neapolitan separated, chocolate, strawberry, vanilla, daai's coloured. Mixed up, its caramel. Cos you see, if you mix all the colours in the paint tin, you'll get brown. Caramel. What is caramel, you ask. It's the new flavour. Its mutation, aberration. It's the genetic confrontation of disparate information. It's the clash of warring civilisations on a genetic level. There's revolution and the colony dancing a symbiotic samba in its every cell resulting in a fierce cultural combustibility, of plat gesê, kloraheid.

With much respect to public enemy but on a point of correction, my brother, black man, white woman, brown baby, white man, black woman, still a brown baby, if I may be so bold as to paraphrase the prophet Chuck D – it's the fear of a caramel planet. Fear of a caramel planet and that is why the white man, his only option is to go into space. It's the tummy full of yummy. Fear of a caramel planet on a global scale. I mean, statistics are showing that California is already fifty percent caramelised and Europe, the white man's homeland is on its way. And how do you make caramel? You heat sugar. The heat is on, my brothers and sisters, the heat is on. So whitie's trying to escape the kitchen. Escape the contradiction on a man-made mad Mars mission in crafts of dire purpose. In a mechanised electrosised phallus, ek se, which rapes the purity of space. I mean, that's my body. That's my night sky, my Egyptian Goddess mother. Like this is Gaia, Earth, my Mother. NASA, stop raping my Mother. And the problem is, you can't get there from here. NASA won't take you there. Voyager won't take you there. You won't even get there on the Starship Enterprise. When you gonna realise you have to spiritualise, open up your third eyes, caramelise?

AIR   'Bowa Mera, Bowa Puti ... Aah here you are,' said the mother. 'We made a new friend today,' said Mera. 'He's very clever,' said Puti. 'Monster,' said Taki Taki. 'Oh Taki Taki,' they all said, 'you're so cute'. The next day the girls were playing at the rock pools when just as suddenly as the day before, the strange man appeared. This time Taki Taki didn't throw a mudcake. She went off and played by herself. Mera and Puti were having such a wonderful time with their new friend that when their mother called, 'Bowa Mera, Bowa Puti, Taki Taki!' they were reluctant to leave. But Taki Taki was already halfway down the beach. So they followed with their cheeks all flushed. On the third day, Taki Taki didn't want to play at the rock pools again, but her sisters solemnly promised sweets. So off they went.

Even though the girls were waiting for him, they still did not notice the strange man until he stood right beside them.

'Come with me,' said the man. 'I have something to show you. Now you all three come close together and lean over the rocks as far as you can.' They did as they were told and there reflected in the water they saw it. A face like wormy leather, huge red eyes rolling in hollow sockets. Sharp pointy teeth and a long black tongue. A hideous monster face. They opened their mouths to scream, but before any sound could pass their lips, quick as a flash the monster pushed them into the pool. Bowa Mera he turned into a beautiful red fish, Bowa Puti into a fascinating white one and Taki Taki into a little blue fish with bulgy eyes. 'Now you're all mine,' the monster growled. 'Bowa Mera, Bowa Puti, Taki Taki!' called the mother, but no one came. 'Oh dear,' said red fish Mera. 'Oh dear,' said white fish Puti. 'Told you,'

said blue fish Taki. 'Well,' replied Mera, 'soon a handsome prince will come and rescue us.' So she leapt about wiggling her fancy tail and flashing her shimmering scale so the handsome princes would be sure not to miss when they passed by. 'Mmm … ' thought Puti, 'there must be a logical explanation for all of this.' And she swum about in circles looking for a simple scientific solution. Taki Taki ate insects. 'Humpfk, humpfk, humpfk.'
By the time the moon rose, Mera was exhausted. Puti was confused and Taki Taki was fast asleep.

WATER *(singing and playing with the doll in the water)*
Miss Johnson had a baby
The baby's name was Tim
She put him in the water to see if he could swim
He drank up all the water
He ate up all the soap
And now Miss Johnson's baby has got bubbles in his throat.
Miss Johnson called the doctor
The doctor called the nurse
The nurse called the lady with the yellow mini-skirt
I do not like the doctor
I do not like the nurse
I only like the lady in the yellow mini-skirt

It was a game we played, most of the time under his mother's bed. Sometimes with clothes sometimes with no clothes. We always fight about who goes on top. He says the boy goes on top, but he doesn't really know what he's doing even though it is his game. The bad thing about going on top is your hair gets stuck in the springs of the bed. There's a potty to pee in; he says it's his Dad's. Why does he pee in a potty? Him and Carlo got a hut in the bushes, they say they got a lot of books there with pictures in. Carlo says I can see the pictures if I come to the hut. But I don't want to let him touch me, I don't like him, he keeps him big.

His brother, he's in high school, asked me to sit in the car with him. There's a lot of cars in their yard; they are mechanics. He said he would tell me a story. He has pictures with men and women with no clothes on. There was one with a man and a woman in a train.

The man was licking the lady there. He wanted to do that. So he took off my panty, but no one was supposed to see. Then he went to lick me but he said it looked funny so I put my panty on and I went home. I don't like playing that game with him. I like it with Sharief better. At least he's my same age. Not like the teacher, Mr Walters. Sharief has a lot of books with pictures in. Mostly it's ladies with no clothes on and licking their titties and touching themselves there. Sometimes there are men with the ladies. They were bodies that just played together like we do. And I just have to act like I know what's going on anyway and ignore the dead feeling. Besides, its normal. Everybody does it. Everything is as it's supposed to be. Nothing is wrong – just you're not allowed to tell.

EARTH   The thing is, right, it's like everybody wants to be a dog these days. Like the mongrels. They all want to go bow wow wow yippee yo yippee yay to the funk like bow wow wow. Is so. Without understanding the reasons. Like Snoop doggy doggy is a negative role model for the youth. Because why, he is uncouth. Did you see his hair at the Grammies? It was relaxed and put in rollers, so it made curls, like Christmas locks. But hair, it's not about hair. Like some people only think your hair looks nice if it's controlled. That dog catcher song and the mongrels. See, my friend, he's Ali from Mali, he rides taxi. His mense. Like back in the day they were visited by a being in a flaming craft and his name was Nomo and he looked like a fish. They draw him like that in the caves. And they say he had gills. This is real nè, and he taught them like, this ou Nomo, about the star system that had a direct link with Earth. This evolved mense that were in constant connection with us. Man, they were making an effort to reach out and touch. And this place was where Nomo was from. I know it's not where you're from, it's where you're at. But like this place was the dog star, Sirius, my broer. And anyway, he gave Ali the Mali's mense information about the constellation and taught them this dance to keep Earth tuned into the right channel so we can keep receiving the same signal. And then the white explorers told Ali's mense, 'No, you are wrong. There's not two suns in that constellation, only one. We saw it on the telescope.' But the mense were like, that fish ou, Nomo, came here and made us wys. So gwaan! And they kept dancing and then when the explorers telescope was more powerful, years later, he checked like, ja is so. The Ali's mense were right. And that tribe is called the dogon. So, our people always had the information already. Like before technology. So what I'm saying is, like technology is backwards. You don't need a cellphone to make a connection. It's like making us lazy to use our minds. And laziness is the work of the devil. Like the devil spelt backwards is lived, right? And dogon spelt backwards is like no god, right? So what does that mean? So is the devil bad?

FIRE   This time it's different. Men and women on their way to work dragging their sleep behind them. Nothing is true. Everything is permitted. 'Stop crying or I'll call Michael Jackson to get you.' The child stops. His eyes wide. He has a nightmare of a moon-walking ghoul attached to his left shoulder. The roof is full of them this time of morning. Soon they will melt in the combined smells of piss and frying meat that dominate this place. Taxi Rank. On the parade. 'Pantaloons, the devil wears pantaloons.' He tells anyone who will listen. No one understands. I do. It is a code, a formula for initiation into a mystery of this city. I have looked for the devil since I was a child. Starting in the places my grandmother told me. The mirror at night. At sunset she said. Under the kitchen table. Under the bed. In the drains of the Bo Kaap. Licking dirty feet while the child sleeps. Sleeping in the sun after Sunday lunch. I have looked for the devil in the hope of not finding him.

Good. People with places to go. Follow them. Inconspicuous. Change direction. Keep it random. Now follow that high heel. Now that one. Now a blue shirt. Black sports pants. White jack purcells. 'Pantaloons. The devil wears...' back to the Parade. Try again. Blue skirt for half a block. White takkies. Dreadlocks. Handbag. And back to the Parade. Following fashion is getting me nowhere. Deep breath. Launch carefully. Tweed skirt. Yellow blouse. Briefcase. Overall. Spandex. Tie dye. Kick flare. Green-market Square. *(she sniffs)* Ozone. The smell of time travel. There's the skipper. He thinks I'm dead. *(she ducks)* They are here. Recruiting probably. Strollers with special skills. Kidnap them like they did me. And if this is the portal for today, they'll probably go back too, for more recruits or supplies. That skipper has a fetish for a dark rum that became unavailable after 1887. He has to have it. The smell's getting worse. He's a creep and I hate him. Can't breathe. The cops all have deals with him. *(she falls)* Masonry is raining down on the Square. *(she becomes a radio)* In Istanbul today … *(radio sounds)* the rebel leaders are refusing … *(radio sounds)* a missile mistakenly fired … *(radio sounds)* the bodies of the hostages … *(radio sounds)* killing twenty-three and wounding twelve others … *(radio sounds)*

It's happening. They've spotted me. *(she runs)* The walls are singing. They're crumbling. *(she dives through one)* Everything's crumbling. *(she looks down)* Aaaahhh! Falling … I'm falling. One day, like Alice, I fell down a very large hole, and to my surprise discovered it was my own. Down down down. Will this fall ever end? *(she falls to the ground)* Sis. it's wet. Doesn't smell like a drain. Smells musky. Like insides. It's warm too. Heat coming from there. A tunnel. Another. More tunnels. It's too quiet. Got to move. Choose which one to use. Keep left. Underground. Under-ground. What's that sound? A hum? Like a generator. Coming from down there. The water's getting warmer. The tunnel opens up. A huge room with no floor. The hum's coming from down there. Louder and louder. The scent. The centre. The centipede. Flaming. Where's my cutlass? Hid it too well. It's massive. Segmented. Transparent. Made of heat. It eats people and purifies them in its digestive juices. I'm not afraid. I want … I want it to … Here Centipede … Eat me.

WATER   I'm thinking … I don't think I'm going to play with them anymore. Then Celeste comes and asks me to go with them to the hut cos Carlo's got new books. We went. The others were already there. Carlo's smoking a cigarette. 'I hear you want to tell your granny. Don't be such a doos. So, you want to be in the gang or what? Cos you can always go play marbles in your granny's yard…'

We were quiet. He turns the pages. It's a children one again. The children's eyes are scratched out with black felt tip. Sharief is there too. It's Ramadan and we are supposed to be fasting and being holy. I feel like Allah can see us but I just act like it's nothing but the feeling doesn't go away. Sharief doesn't like children, he says they not sexy. He likes big ladies with big titties. In one of the big pictures, there's a girl our own age, with make-up on and long black socks. Why she got socks on? Carlo says it's panty hose but there's no panty on. Her legs are open. It's a butterfly says Carlo. That's what you call it when it's open like that. It's the only photo that doesn't have that black felt tip on the eyes. So it's different. It's someone. Celeste says maybe they scratch out the eyes so you won't recognise the child. We went closer to look into the girl's eyes. She wasn't crying, but it looks like she wants to. Sharief says that's how you look when you are sexy. In the next photo, there's a man with the girl. He's got a long white beard like Father Christmas, but he's wearing a sailor cap pulled low over his face so you can't see his eyes or his face just his mouth and his beard. His hands have white hair on them. And his fingers are fat. And he's got a fat tummy with hair on, some of it white. You can see his penis it's very big with the hair like tummy and he's pushing it into in-between the girl's legs. She's wearing clothes now, a dress that's too babyish for her age. It's a Sunday dress with frills and the man's lifting it right up. She looked squashed and she's crying in this picture but her eyes are scratched out now. The man's got her arm like this. There's marks on her arm, red. 'Where's her mommy? Where's her friends?'

'What? Are you scared or what? Don't be such a doos. There's nothing to be scared of.'

It's just weird. In the other pictures with grown-ups it's different. What are these photos? Are they for us? Are they for adults? Celeste says, 'What do the grown-ups have to do with it? Children and adults can't mix, can they?' *(she gets up)* 'My granny's calling me. I'm going home.' The boys all laugh.

FIRE *(she wakes with a start)* What happened last night? I fell down a hole. And found the Centipede. It didn't eat me. So I wandered around the tunnels for a while. There were lots of dead people there. Then I met a little girl. She's lovely. She's wearing a pretty white dress. She has black hair in two plaits down her back. 'Take my hand. You can't stay down here. We have to leave through the Eastern gate.' I follow her for hours. It seems she knows everyone down here. They look at me as if I'm not there. There's a yellow light. We dip up through a drain, on to the street. 'Let's go to my father's shop. He's a tailor, there by Longmarket Street.' Which

world have I come out in? It's not the one I left. They're selling
vegetables on the square. The girl buys a mango with money from
her father. She holds out her hand. 'Walk with me. Walk the broken
past, named and not.' And by the big tree on the Square, women are
being sold. They are small. Like her. Like me. They are not bound.
But they are too afraid to run away. I feel shame spread through my
body. The women are taken off by large rough men. 'Walk with me,'
she says. 'Walk the plank, walk the discovered and what cannot be
discovered.' She has a long stride, though I am taller. Soon we are at
the harbour. There are ships that carry only disease. Others off-load
human cargo. Men and women. 'Walk with me. Walk the seen and
unseen. What can be rendered visible and what cannot?' We are at
the water's edge. The dock has gone. Just beach remains. 'Sit down
there and I will tell you a story. Then we can eat mango. Its lekker to
eat mango.' The sand is warm. She rises with her back to the waves
and begins. 'This is the story my Grandmother told me ... Once there
was and once there wasn't. Long ago. Yesterday. Round the corner.
Far away. Three sisters. And there names were ... *(sings)* Bowa
Mera, Bowa Puti, Taki Taki ... *(into story)*

AIR   'Where are those girls?' said the mother. 'Probably still
playing,' said the father. 'They've never been late before.' The
parents waited and called and waited and called till they could wait
and call no longer. All that night and well into the next day the
mother and father searched for the girls. They looked in the town,
they looked in the field. They searched for two whole nights and two
whole days without stopping for so much as a drink of water. On the
third night the father was on the sea scanning the waves for even the
bodies of his daughters now. His salt tears mingled with the spray.
The father was adrift on an ocean of tears. With the last of his
strength he stood up in the little boat and cried out, 'Ocean ocean
deep blue sea, send my daughters back to me!' And then he turned
to go home. On this same third night the mother was on the beach
listening through the songs of a million sea shells for one solitary
note, a laugh, a sigh or a cry from her girls. She sat on a rock
weeping with such anguish that the moon came out to comfort her.
The mother looked up and cried out, 'Mother Moon that shines on
all the waters. Help me. Help me find my daughters!' And then she

turned and went home. All this time the three little fish girls heard not a word. Trapped as they were in their watery world. Each day and each night the monster came and watched them. Disappearing as suddenly as he appeared. And he drank from them. Taking in large gulps of their laughter, their songs, even their little squabbles. He got drunk on their sweet young flesh and soft skin and sucked the light from their dreams. Mera's shimmering tail began to wilt. Her shining scales grew dull. Puti's lightning mind became sluggish and turgid and Taki Taki – she ate insects.

EARTH *(singing)*
Mama used to say, take your time mmmmmm,
Mama used to say, don't you rush to grow up,
Mama used to say, take it in your stride,
Mama used to say, live your life

Anyway nè, when my Mama, not my Mother, but my Ouma, when she used to tell me stories about a princess with long hair, or something like this ... I used to ask like – when the princess is in danger, where's the prince? When's the prince coming? And Mama used to say, 'Prince? Prince? Jy soek man, jy! Watter prince? My girlie, nobody's gonna rescue you.' Is so. When I was a lightie, nè, I wanted them to come down and adopt me. Come in the night and lift me out of my bed, because I couldn't really see a way in the world for me. So I tried to smoke the herb and I got as far as Zion, but I don't want to stay in Zion. It's too full of Rastas and Vegetarians. And buttons – they just put you out and they make you feel dirty man. And whatever you take, you always come back. Even if you take an overdose. I checked, naai, if I kill myself, I'll come back in another life and it will be worse, or even the same. Swak nè? And then I checked, even death won't rescue you and the aliens, contact them anywhere. So I looked deeply into the thing and I channelled this entity from an inner dimension. Like she's not even made of light, she's so different. She's got no form. She's like more than a feeling. So anyway, one day when I was swak, she gave me this. *(pulls a piece of paper from back pocket)* You want to hear it? 'I feel a premonition come upon me invoking the vision. In my heart there is a flower of sedition. I am cool electrical being. Uncorruptable. My flesh is

sensational. Retrieving the power to feel. Retrieving the power to
heal. My body displaces the priest. My body replaces the Imam. My
femininity becoming it's own divinity. I carry my pride inside. And
outside I won't hide. The beast of shame, don't know my name, or
even where to find me. In the positive-connectivity of my life I still
feel the knife changing shape. I feel the rapist and the rape. One
birth, one earth, one breath, one death. And still I flower with divine
intent. To the full extent. Petals soft. Open. And resilient.'
Its cool nè? I did that. Do you want to hear it again?

WATER *(running)* Celeste says adults and children don't mix. Adults
and children don't mix, don't mix. But Mr Walters says there's
nothing wrong. On a Friday when the big children from Standard
One up go to mosque, he chases us and then he catches us. He
catches me a lot. And then he makes me sit on his lap and draw. He
gives me paper and pastels and he says he will put the picture up in
his class. The Standard Five class. And I ask what must I draw. And
he says draw fishes. Sometimes he draws a fish and I colour it in. He
holds me very tight, so I can't get off his lap. And he takes his penis
out. And when he's finished, he says, 'Go.' Even if I haven't finished
the picture. When I check my panty in the toilet, it's wet and sticky.
He does it a lot. Chases us on a Friday. All the teachers are gone to
Mosque too. Some children are bachaing next door. There's a green
board in front of his table. So, the other children can't see under. I
went to tell teacher Bassardien. She said, 'You naughty. Don't tell
stories. And whosoever digs a pit, shall fall in it.' What pit is she
talking about? Mr Walters is the only Christian teacher in the
school, that's why she sticks up for him. Before I leave Mr Walters'
class, he hits me with a cane. Sometimes he buys me sweets or gives
me money. Sometimes when I scream and kick and one of the big
girls with periods walks past, he leaves me alone. I wonder, must I
tell Celeste about Mr Walters? Because sometimes adults and
children do mix. Maybe not.

AIR   That night when not a soul on earth or sea, not even the
         monster, was stirring, the moon looked down and called to the sea,
         'Oh Sea Star Sea!' 'Shoo!' said the sea, 'The saddest man I have
         seen.' 'Ooo!' said the moon, 'and I the saddest lady.' So moved were

they by the tender love of the father and mother that they resolved to help as best they could. The sea knew exactly what had happened to the girls, having witnessed the entire affair from the start. So the moon, using all her strength, tugged at the sea and together they made huge crashing waves that washed the fish girls right out of the rock pools into the open ocean. They were terrified, but the sea made little currents that kept them together all through the night. In the morning, the father on his boat, was casting the nets for the day's catch. He sat with a heavy heart and not a single thing had he caught all morning. As he was packing up to go home he noticed three little fishes in the bottom of the net. 'Very pretty,' he thought, 'but too small' and threw them back. Again he pulled in the nets and again there they were and again he threw them back. By the third time, he picked them up and took them home and gave them to his wife. The wife took them and put them in a pan on the fire. Just at that moment there came a loud bang, followed by another and another. Everyone was overjoyed and they had a huge party.

A few days later, the monster man was found drowned, half-eaten by a school of little fishes and everything was as before. Well, nearly. Mera was not quite so pretty anymore and Puti was not quite so clever and Taki Taki, though slightly plumper, was still cute.

The performer picks up a large bowl filled with rose petals and sprinkles them on the audience before inviting them on stage to engage in interactive rituals at each of the 'stations'. They can wash their own or someone else's hands at the water 'station'; leave a handprint in the earth at the earth 'station'; light one of the smaller birthday candles from the main flame and place it anywhere in the space at the fire 'station'; and leave a recorded message for any of the characters at the air 'station'.

The End.

Rehane Abrahams

Rehane is a theatremaker, playwright and performer (actor, dancer). She is currently based in Indonesia where she develops theatre projects and studies classical Javanese dance. She co-founded the Mother-tongue Project, a collective of women theatre artists based in Cape Town, South Africa and Teater Gelombang (Theatre of Waves) in Indonesia, which aims to develop arts exchange along the Indian Ocean Basin. This is her first play to be published.

The Mothertongue Project

The Mothertongue Project is a collective of women performing artists who are interested in exploring the sacred in and through performance. A major focus of their work deals with transformation and healing, thus empowering the audience to recover and discover their own resources for self-healing.

www.mothertongue.co.za

Playwright's Note:

I developed *The Playground*, my first stage play, from a short story I wrote after South Africa's first democratic elections. Each story in my collection *Out of Bounds* (Puffin 2001) takes place in a different decade, covering my lifetime and that of apartheid. *The Playground* is the first post-apartheid story. The idea grew from a news report about the first black girl to enter an all-white primary school in a rural town where white parents fiercely resisted the new laws on integration. Asked how she felt, the girl replied, 'They will want me when they know me!'

In 2000, I was invited by PAL, the Performing Arts Lab, to join a ten day Playwrights' Lab on New Writing for Younger Audiences. Asked to 'come with the passion of your heart', I chose *The Playground* as my starting point. It was a daunting process, breaking apart a tightly-constructed story and flinging my characters onto a stage. It forced me to dig deeper and wider. It gave my characters new freedom to breathe each other's breath, old and young, black and white, rich and poor.

Some months later, Vicky Ireland, then Artistic Director of Polka Theatre, asked if I would like to write a play about Nelson Mandela. I told her that I already had a first draft of a play, in which he wasn't a character, but a presence. A commission followed and, when I was free to pursue it in 2003, I decided to research and develop the play in South Africa. Workshops in schools in a North West Province town helped me check the pulse. The past was still present.

My director Olusola Oyeleye subsequently led a week of workshops with actor graduates from the Arts Media and Access Centre (Community Arts Project) and Project Phakama in Cape Town, with particular thanks to Yvonne Banning at the University of Cape Town. The South African High Commissioner in London, H.E. Dr Lindiwe Mabuza, found sponsorship for one of the group, Thabo Twetwa, to join the London production. Although Polka is a theatre for young people, the play brought in audiences of all ages. We were rewarded with a Time Out Critics' Choice for 2004.

Beverley Naidoo

THE PLAYGROUND

Beverley Naidoo

The Playground has its origins in a Performing Arts Lab at Bore Place, Kent in 2000 and was developed in South Africa in 2003 with particular thanks to Community Arts Project (Arts Media & Access Centre) and Project Phakama, Cape Town.

First presented at Polka Theatre, London on 23rd September 2004, directed by Olusola Oyeleye, designed by Phil Newman, with the following cast:

ROSA – a black girl	Frances Simon
MAMA – Rosa's mother (the van Niekerks' maid)	Doreen Webster
HENNIE VAN NIEKERK – a white boy	Alistair Moulton Black
MENEER VAN NIEKERK – Hennie's father	David Anthony
MEVROU VAN NIEKERK – Hennie's mother	Jennifer Woodburne
PRINCIPAL OF ORANJE SCHOOL	Jennifer Woodburne
MARIE – a white girl	Jennifer Woodburne
JANNIE – a white boy	César Ribeiro
REPORTER	César Ribeiro
PAPER BOY – a black boy	Thabo Twetwa
SELO	Thabo Twetwa
JOSEF – a worker at the van Niekerks' house	Thabo Twetwa
PRINCIPAL OF POLENG SCHOOL	Thabo Twetwa
'INVISIBLE' WORKER	Thabo Twetwa

Notes:
If possible, the roles of Paper Boy/Selo and Josef/Principal of Poleng School/'Invisible' Worker 1 could be divided between a younger and an older actor. The roles of the Paper Boy and 'Invisible' Worker as silent observers could then be expanded.

Setting
A flexible stage so that the action is continuous. The action takes place in a rural town in South Africa between the years 1989 and 2000.

Time
The play opens in 1994. It goes back to 1989 in Scene 3. From then on,
time is chronological. Scene 12 is a vignette of Scene 1.

Music
Some Setswana and other songs have been included in the script. Music
and traditional songs, including songs in other South African
languages, were threaded throughout the play in the premiere
production at Polka Theatre in London.

ACT ONE
Prologue ...
*Winter 1994. South Africa's first democratic government has begun
removing apartheid laws. An empty stage except for a newspaper
stand at the side with a poster:*
**'WHITE SCHOOLS MUST OPEN DOORS' – PRESIDENT
MANDELA**

*On the other side of the stage, the same news is headlined in
Afrikaans:*
**'WIT SKOLE MOET HULLE DEURE OOPMAAK' –
PRESIDENT MANDELA**

*A Paper Boy in a cap and faded T-shirt enters energetically. He tries
to sell his papers to members of the audience.*

PAPER BOY *Die Star! Die Stem*! White schools must open doors!
    White schools must open doors! ... Sweet news! Sour news! ... A
    paper, Sissie? ... Aiee, why do you never buy from me Sissie? ...
    Die Star! Die Stem! Cheap papers here! ... Big news, small news,
    all kind of news! ... Sir, you can read what President Mandela
    says! You don't have money? Hey, never any money! ... OK then,
    tomorrow! ... *Die Star! Die Stem!* President Mandela says white
    schools must open doors!

The Paper Boy settles by the newspaper stand and watches.

SCENE 1

Winter 1994. Early afternoon. A small rural town. A fence surrounds the playground of the whites-only Oranje Primary School – Laerskool Oranje. Rosa, age 10, in black school tunic and white shirt, enters. She is outside the fence. She carries a school bag and a plastic bag containing a kleinmeid's uniform. This is her first day coming into the town to work for the van Nierkerk family. She is both curious and anxious as she approaches the fence. Her journey is accompanied by singing off-stage.

Hennie van Nierkerk, age 10, barefoot, in khaki shirt and shorts, enters the playground with Jannie, age 9. They are absorbed in a game of rugby, cheered on by Marie, age 9. Rosa watches Hennie but he does not see her. Jannie falls. He spots Rosa. He whips himself up, making his hand into a mock pistol.

JANNIE   Pioouu! Pioouu!.... Hey, got her, man!

Rosa is startled. Her bag spills open. Explosion of laughter from Jannie and Marie.

JANNIE   D'you see that, Hennie! Jiss man!

Jannie and Marie go, laughing. Hennie glances uneasily at Rosa before he goes. Shaken, Rosa picks up the kleinmeid's uniform that has fallen out of her bag.

PAPER BOY Dumela Sis.

The Paper Boy lifts his hand in a furtive, sympathetic wave. Rosa acknowledges the gesture. The Paper Boy goes.

ROSA *(to audience)* Imagine ... That is the school Mama wants me to attend!

SCENE 2

Mama enters, singing 'Ntate roma nna'. Rosa runs to her. They hug. Hennie enters and Mama stretches out her other arm. He goes to her and Mama hugs them both. Rosa snuggles closer as Mama leads them towards the audience.

MAMA *(sings)*
 Ntate roma nna, roma nna (Father send me, send me)
 Ntate roma nna, roma nna (Father send me, send me)
 Ntate roma nna (Father send me)
 Roma nna ko ditjhabeng (Send me to the world/foreign land)
 (o) Ke tla go sebeletsa, sebeletsa (I come to serve you, to serve)
 (o) Ke tla go sebeletsa, sebeletsa (I come to serve you, to serve)
 Ke tla go sebeletsa (I come to serve you)
 Sebeletsa ko ditjhabeng (To serve you in the world)

Meneer and Mevrou enter.

MAMA   My children! Rosa, my daughter ... and Hennie, my son –
MENEER *(over-riding Mama)* My son.

Meneer claims Hennie. Mama continues to hug Rosa while each van Niekerk speaks their thoughts. They present themselves in front of the audience, as if for a family photo.

MEVROU *(puts her arm around Hennie)* Our son.
MENEER   He's a good little rugby player.
MEVROU   He could be our first Springbok in the family.
MENEER   That's if the blacks haven't taken all the places by then!
MEVROU   I like to think one day he's going to play for his country.
MENEER   Our country ... Suid Afrika!
MEVROU   It's not quite the same as it used to be. But it's still home.
MENEER   We are not running away anywhere, that's for sure.
HENNIE   Where could we go?
MENEER   We're not going anywhere. We are staying right here ...
     in the land of our forefathers.
HENNIE   When I grow up, I'll become a Springbok ... just like Ma
     says ... I'll make history! *(laughs)* I'll show Pa!

Roar of a rugby crowd as Hennie delivers a winning drop kick. Hennie glows in the limelight in a triumphant family image. The van Niekerks go.

MAMA   Mmmhh! Hennie! Always a happy child ... *(Rosa looks fed up)* You and Hennie! When you were little ... you played nicely
     together.

ROSA   That was a long time ago Mama.
MAMA   Mmmm! My two children.
ROSA   He has changed, Mama.
MAMA   He grew big ... and you grew big! But inside, he is still the same.
ROSA *(resentful)* When we were little, it was different!
MAMA *(playful)* You taught Hennie your Number One song! Remember?

Mama cajoles her, singing 'Bana ba sekolo' to the tune of Frère Jacques. Rosa gradually relents and smiles.

MAMA *(sings)*
   Bana ba sekolo (Children of the school)
   Bana ba sekolo (Children of the school)
   Tlong sekolong (Come to school)
   Tlong sekolong (Come to school)
   Utlwa tshepe ya lla (Hear the bell ringing)
   Utlwa tshepe ya lla (Hear the bell ringing)
   Ding dong belele (Ding dong bells)
   Ding dong belele (Ding dong bells)

The song takes us back in time to 1989. The stage is divided. While Mama is singing, Hennie, age 5, enters barefoot, singing 'Bana ba sekolo'. Mama and Rosa go.

SCENE 3
Five years earlier. July 1989.
A sunny winter's day. The stage is divided. Inside the van Niekerks' house, the garden outside, and the street beyond. The scenes are simultaneous and interweave. Hennie dances and chants in the garden. Cast sing off-stage. Mama enters and begins dusting inside the house.
At the same time, the Paper Boy enters and pins up the day's posters outside on the street:
'PRESIDENT INVITES PRISONER MANDELA TO TEA'
'PRISONIER MANDELA – TEE MET DIE PRESIDENT'

PAPER BOY *(to the audience) Die Star! Die Stem!* Mandela out of
jail! Aieeeee! Tea with the President! Aiee! Aiee! Then back to jail!
Aiee! Aiee! Aieeeee! ... Hot news! Cold news! *Die Star! Die Stem!*

*Paper Boy settles by his stand at the side. Rosa enters, age five. She
joins Hennie dancing and singing.*

ROSA/HENNIE *(sing)*
Bana ba sekolo
Bana ba sekolo
Tlong sekolong
Tlong sekolong
Utlwa tshepe ya lla
Utlwa tshepe ya lla
Ding dong belele
Ding dong belele

They pretend to get dizzy ringing the bell.

HENNIE   Let's play Tag now! Kom! Kom! You can't catch me!

*Their game involves tumbling, laughing, giggling. They move on to
playing a game of pebbles in the background where we can see them
but no longer hear them. Meneer enters side stage into the street.*

PAPER BOY *Die Star! Die Stem!* Hot news, sir!
MENEER   Give me a paper, boy! *(he goes off, reading)*
PAPER BOY Your change Meneer!

Meneer ignores him. Paper Boy shrugs and goes.
*Inside the house, Afrikaans music is playing softly on the radio in the
sitting room (something with an accordion and a strong dance beat
e.g. Die Laaste Dans). Mevrou enters with a vase and a bunch of
winter flowers. Mama assists as Mevrou arranges the flowers. Mama
plays the obedient servant but we sense her independent character.*

MEVROU   Haven't these flowers lasted well? Mooi, ja!
MAMA   Yes, Madam. They look fresh like when the Master
brought them.
MEVROU   I didn't think he would remember our anniversary this
year. All this trouble in the country. It's not good for business ...
(Mama shakes her head and makes sympathetic noises) ... No one
wants to build new properties these days.

MAMA   Shame, Madam. It's hard.

Josef, a worker, enters silently and begins polishing the floor.

MEVROU   Ag, it's a lot of worry for the Master. It's not just him, Ragel. If the work doesn't come in ... ag nee! His workers suffer as well. If he doesn't have houses to build, then he must lay them off. That's what the outside world doesn't realise ...! They complain our government is so unfair and they make our economy go down ...! and do you know who they hurt most of all ...? *(looks at Mama and Josef)* ... Ja! Your people ...! The black people they say they want to help! *(she sighs. Mama and Josef exchange glances)* ... Ag, that's what these criticisers don't realise.

Mevrou waits for a response but when she doesn't get one, she returns to her flower arrangement. She hums along with the music. Josef keeps his head lowered but sees everything.
A door bangs. They all look up. The sound carries outside and Hennie and Rosa stop playing for a moment.

MEVROU *(concerned)* Why is he home so early?

Mevrou switches off the radio as Meneer enters. He is holding a battered leather briefcase and a newspaper. He is tense, on the point of explosion.

MEVROU   Wat makeer, Willem? Is something wrong ...? *(looks at Mama)* ... Ragel?
MAMA   Excuse me, Master.

Mama goes. Meneer moves aside without acknowledging her. Josef continues polishing the floor.

MEVROU   What is it, Willem?

Meneer stares at Josef. Mevrou signals to him to leave.

MEVROU *(to Josef)* There's work to do outside ... Hurry now! Maak gou!

Josef goes outside and starts digging near Rosa and Hennie.

MEVROU *(solicitous)* Is it that headache again, Willem?
MENEER   Kan jy dit glo ...? *(shakes newspaper and begins reading)* 'ANC leader Nelson Mandela was taken from his prison cell last Wednesday to have tea with President PW Botha at

Tuynhuys ...' *(Mevrou looks shocked)* Our country is falling apart ...
riots, strikes, bombs ...! *(Hennie and Rosa hear his raised voice and
creep up to the window to listen, bemused, scared)* My own
business is falling apart ...! And what do our leaders do? Take tea
with the terrorist who started it all!

MEVROU *(persuades him to sit)* You're forgetting what the doctor
said, Willem! Your blood –

MENEER   They took tea together!

MEVROU   Ag, bokkie, you need some tea!

MENEER   God will punish them ... betraying His trust!

MEVROU   Please Willem, it's not good for you! I'll tell the maid to
bring you tea. Ragel! Bring the Master some –

MAMA *(has already entered from behind with a tray and two cups)*
Yes, Madam.

MEVROU   Oh!

*Mevrou takes the tea. Mama goes. The children run away from the
house. As the scene continues with the children playing, Meneer and
Mevrou remain on-stage, inside the house. Meneer pulls out a large
ledger from his briefcase. They pore over it together, worried.*

HENNIE *(loudly)* I don't know why my Pa came home early.

ROSA   Sshh! Let's go far away.

HENNIE   OK, race you to the bottom of the garden! Een – twee –
drie!

*Hennie and Rosa race and tumble over each other. Hennie pins down
Rosa.*

ROSA   Let's make a house!

*Hennie releases Rosa and they become engrossed in their imaginary
game. Rosa takes out a doll with a broken leg from her pocket.*

ROSA   This is where the baby sleeps.

HENNIE   This is the garage.

ROSA   The big sister sleeps next to the baby.

HENNIE   The brother keeps his bike here. So no one can steal it.

ROSA   This is the sitting-room where –

HENNIE   ... this can be the TV and ...

ROSA   – they have a sofa.

HENNIE But the brother only likes cartoons – and rugby.
ROSA The sister likes –
HENNIE The brother likes to chase the sister on his bike. It's a
racing bike! I'll show you, hey? You start running!

A noisy racing game. Near collisions. Hennie suddenly trips and falls.

HENNIE Einaa!
ROSA Hennie?
HENNIE *(rubbing his ankle)* Einaaa!

*Josef comes to examine Hennie's foot. Inside the house, Mevrou begins
gently massaging her husband's temples and shoulders to ease his
headache.*

JOSEF *(patting the foot, reassuring)* Daar's niks stukkend nie!
    (Hennie pouts and continues to whine)
ROSA Shall I get Mama?
HENNIE Jaaa!
ROSA *(running off)* Mama! Hennie needs you! Tla kwane Mama!

*Suddenly Rosa remembers she is near the house and claps her hand
over her mouth. Mama enters.*

JOSEF *(to Mama)* O rata ho kgomotswa ke Mme! He wants a woman's
    touch!
MAMA Mmmhh, basimane! Boys!
JOSEF Êê! *(returns to his digging but continues to watch)*
MAMA *(to Hennie)* Ah-ah-ah. What were you doing, Master Hennie?
    What happened?
HENNIE Something tripped me!
MAMA *(eyes Rosa)* Was it you?
ROSA No Mama!

*Mama examines Hennie's leg and pampers him with soothing noises.
Hennie whimpers, enjoying Mama's attention. Rosa watches, still
upset at Mama's accusation.*

MAMA There! Is that better now ...? A little more here?
HENNIE Mmm.
MAMA You must be more careful.
HENNIE Don't tell Ma or Pa, Ragie.

MAMA   See if you can walk now, Master Hennie. Come Rosa,
let's help him ... *(Mama and Rosa help Hennie stand)* There you
are! You must play quietly now. The Master is home early.
HENNIE *(mimicking his father, loudly)* 'Quiet! Quiet!'
ROSA *(very worried)* Shh! Shh!

Inside the house.

MEVROU *(stops massaging)* Any better, bokkie ...? Ag, let me get you
something for your head.
MENEER *(quietly)* It's the heads of our leaders that need sorting out.
If they don't bring order to the country, my business is finished.

Mevrou goes. Meneer presses his hands to his head.
Outside the house.

MAMA   I'll make a nice, nice drink of orange for you both ...
and, if you're good, something special.
HENNIE   Chocolate cookies ...? *(Rosa's eyes light up)* Bring it
here for us, Ragie! We can have it in our house!

*Mama nods conspiratorially, signals to them to keep their voices
down, and goes off.*

HENNIE   Hey! Let's water the garden for Pa!
ROSA *(shakes her head)* Mmmnh ... Mmmnh!
HENNIE   Let's turn on the tap! *(Rosa is still reluctan.)* Kom!

*Hennie grabs her hair band and runs. Rosa chases him. Hennie turns
on the tap and pretends the hose is a snake. Inside, Meneer looks out
of the window and observes the children.*

HENNIE *(showering Rosa)* Sssss!!!
JOSEF   Nee, my Baasie, nee!

*Hennie and Rosa shriek with laughter. Meneer strides out of the
house, catches Hennie and begins spanking him. Rosa backs away in
terror. Mama appears with a tray of orange drink and cookies. Josef
witnesses everything.*

HENNIE *(crying)* You're hurting Pa! Let me go!
MENEER   Wat makeer jy? What do you think you're doing?
HENNIE   Niks nie, Pa!

MENEER Running around like a savage? Half-naked with this pikkenien?

HENNIE Nee Pa! Nee!

Mevrou comes running.

MEVROU Willem? Hennie?

MENEER Is this how you're letting him grow?

MEVROU They were just playing, Willem. Just children's games.

MENEER It's time he learnt to be a proper boy.

MEVROU Look how you've frightened them.

MENEER It's time he knows he's a white boy.

Meneer marches Hennie away. Mama waits silently. Rosa continues sobbing.

MEVROU Ag nee! Ag nee! *(awkward, almost apologetic)* ... It's best you take the child home, Ragel. Don't worry about coming back today. I'll manage – and tomorrow – you better come alone, nè?

MAMA Yes, Madam.

Mevrou takes the tray from Mama. She hurries after her husband and son. Josef takes the tray from her, as she goes. He glances sympathetically at Mama and Rosa and goes. Mama hugs Rosa.

MAMA Sorry, my baby, sorry. Tla kwane.

Mama sings to Rosa to comfort her. The Cast sing off-stage. Rosa goes reluctantly, still sobbing.

SCENE 4
Next day. The stage remains divided inside and outside the van Niekerks' house. The two scenes are simultaneous and interweave. Outside the kitchen, a wooden bench with two enamel mugs of tea. Mama takes one and drinks.
Inside, Mevrou enters the sitting-room with Hennie. Hennie sits on the floor with a comic while his mother reads a magazine.

MAMA *(to audience)* Sometimes it's so hard to know what to say to a child ... You don't want to put all these heavy things on top of them. She will have to carry these burdens when she's older and you pray

she will grow strong ... So I told my little girl that Hennie's Pa had a
bad temper. What else could I say?

HENNIE *(whining)* When are you coming to play with me, Ragie!

MAMA   I'm coming soon, Master Hennie!

HENNIE   Hurry up Ragie! Hurry up! I'm bored!

Josef enters and joins Mama on the bench.

JOSEF   How is Rosa, Mma?

MAMA   Very quiet, Rra. Quiet – quiet. Her tongue was stiff
all night.

JOSEF   Êê.

MAMA   This morning she didn't want me to leave her. She never
saw someone mad like the Master was yesterday.

JOSEF   Tell me, Mma ... how many years have you looked after
this family?

MAMA   It's ten years now.

JOSEF   Tchaa! Maburu a! My wife says you put something nice
in their mouths to eat and they put a stick in your eye.
(They sip their tea in silence)

HENNIE   I want Ragie!

MEVROU   You must wait. She's taking a break.

HENNIE   I want Rosa!

MEVROU   You know she's not here.
(Mama and Josef exchange a look)

MAMA   Mmhh! That news about Mr Mandela made the Master
mad!

JOSEF   The pressure is biting these white people now. It's going
up.

MAMA   They don't understand. Mr Mandela is the one who can
help them.

JOSEF   Êê!

MAMA   They must release him!

JOSEF   Ke nnete!

MAMA   Things won't come right until they make him free.

MEVROU   Ragel! Ragel!

MAMA   Coming Madam!

JOSEF   Aiee! They'll take food out of your own mouth and eat it.

MAMA   But they can't eat our dreams!

Mama and Josef clink mugs. Ululation and sounds of the toyi toyi in distance. All go.

SCENE 5
January 1990. First day of school year. News poster headlines:
'EMPTY PLACES IN WHITE SCHOOLS'
'LEEG PLEKKE IN WIT SKOLE'

The stage divides into Mama and Rosa's house and the van Niekerks' house. Mama and Rosa's house is much smaller and more compact. The two scenes run alongside each other and interweave.

CAST *(chanting o/s)* Maandaga ... Labobedi ... Laboraro ... Labone ... Vrydaga ... Saterdaga ... Sondaga ?

Rosa, age 6, enters in a neat black school tunic, white short-sleeved shirt, short white socks and shiny black shoes. Under her breath, she chants the words of the skipping game 'All the Days of the Week': 'Maandaga ... Labobedi ... etc. She is excited as she checks the contents of her little school bag and plays with her doll with the broken leg. Hennie, age 6, enters dishevelled – in a khaki short-sleeved shirt, short khaki pants and one brown sock, followed by Mevrou carrying his shoes. She helps Hennie with his other sock and shoes.

HENNIE   They hurt me Ma!
MEVROU   You're a big boy now. You said you wanted them ... to be like Pa.
HENNIE *(pulling off his shoes)* I can't run with them!
MEVROU *(combing his hair)* You can be just as stubborn as your Pa, can't you?
HENNIE   Ag nee, Ma! Ragie always lets me do it myself!
MEVROU   Well, she's not here now. She lets you get away with murder!
HENNIE   Is Rosa going to school? Is that why Ragie isn't here?

Mevrou avoids answering and goes. Hennie mopes for a little, fiddles with his buttons and pulls off his socks.
Mama enters her house. She looks proudly at Rosa and sits down to fix Rosa's hair.

MAMA   Your Papa would have been so proud of you. His little girl going to school! *(Rosa grins)* He always said: 'This child is going to be very clever!'

ROSA   How did he know, Mama?

MAMA   He always said you had bright-bright eyes. He said you were going to read all the books he wanted to read himself!

ROSA   What if I do something wrong Mama? Will my teacher hit me?

MAMA   No! She will like you.

ROSA   But Hennie told me, Mama! Teachers have big belts like his Pa! *(Rosa realises what she has said – is confused)*

MAMA   Sshush! You will be the best learner in the class!

ROSA   Mama ... what's a pikkenien?

MAMA *(startled)* It's not a nice word Rosa. Come on, we'll be late.

ROSA   What is it, Mama?

MAMA *(pause)* White people sometimes call black children pikkeniens.

ROSA   That's what Hennie's Pa said, didn't he, Mama? What's savage, Mama?

MAMA *(fumbles and drops the comb)* Mmhh Rosa! See what I've done. We must hurry. *(she gets up and Rosa picks up the comb, anxious not to upset Mama)*

Mevrou returns and looks exasperated with Hennie who is twiddling his toes. She inspects him.

ROSA *(looking at her shoes)* Does Hennie have shiny shoes like me, Mama?

MAMA *(smiles)* He does ... but he wants to go barefoot.

ROSA *(giggles)* He likes the sand under his toes, doesn't he, Mama?

MAMA   Pack your bag, my child. You'll always remember your first day at school.

Rosa is excited as she sets off to school with Mama.
Mevrou leads Hennie to school. They embrace, wave and go their separate ways.

CAST *(chanting o/s)* Maandaga ... Labobedi ... Laboraro ... Labone ... Vrydaga ... Saterdaga ... Sondaga ?

SCENE 6

Same morning. Entrance to Poleng Primary School in the township. The Principal enters. Rosa is looking bewildered.

PRINCIPAL I'm sorry, Mma.
MAMA   My child is ready for school, Rra.
PRINCIPAL There's nothing I can do.
MAMA   But she's very, very clever.
PRINCIPAL I have eighty children already in the first class, Mma. I can't take any more.
MAMA   Mmmhh!
PRINCIPAL There's no more space in the classroom, Mma. You must bring your child next year.
MAMA   She must wait one whole year?
PRINCIPAL I'm sorry Mma. It's the white government. They don't send enough money.
MAMA   Mmmhh! Mmmhh!
PRINCIPAL When they release Mr Mandela, we hope things will be better.
MAMA *(moves forward)* Please, Rra, can't you just squeeze her in?
PRINCIPAL *(blocks her way)* It's not possible, Mma. But I promise you ... she will have a place next year.

The Principal goes.

ROSA   Does Hennie have to wait a year, Mama?
MAMA   No, my darling ... There are not so many children in his school.
ROSA   Why can't you take me to his school, Mama?
MAMA   Oranje School? That school, Rosa ... it's only ... for white children.
ROSA   Why Mama? Why?

Rosa is disconsolate. She keeps looking back at the school as Mama leads her away.

SCENE 7

11th February 1990. The stage is divided. Outside in the street and inside the van Niekerks' sitting-room. Outside, the Paper Boy enters and puts up the posters:

'MANDELA FREE: MORE BLOOD TO FLOW?'
'MANDELA VRY: MEER BLOED SAL VLOOI?'

PAPER BOY Aiee! I don't believe this! Mandela is free! Mandela is free! Out of jail! Free at last!

The Paper Boy sings and dances a joyful version of the toyi toyi, e.g. Tshona Malanga. The Cast creates an ecstatic crowd, e.g. in silhouette toyi-toying and singing about the downfall of apartheid. Aiee! Mandela is free! Mandela is free! Out of jail! Free at last!

Paper Boy goes. Excited cheering. Broadcast footage/sound of cheering as crowd greet Nelson Mandela on The Parade, Cape Town. The van Niekerks enter. They sit and watch the television. Meneer is tense. Mevrou is apprehensive. Hennie is curious. Mama is polishing but secretly dances and cheers behind their backs.

MANDELA'S VOICE *(repeating extract from his trial speech)* I have fought against white domination and I have fought against black domination. I have cherished the ideal of a free and democratic society in which all persons live in harmony and –
(Meneer shuts off the sound)
MENEER   As Mandela nou uit die tronk kom is dit die laaste straw! 'n waar Boer sal hom moer ... *(he indicates slitting a throat)*
MEVROU   Moenie praat so nie, Willem! Ons Boere is wettig.
HENNIE   Hoekom Pa?
MEVROU   Your Pa doesn't really mean it. We are lawful people.
MENEER *(to his wife)* Skat! Kom met my!

Meneer insists Mevrou come with him. They go.

MAMA *(to audience)* That day Madiba walked free from his jail, I made a new dream for my Rosa.

Mama remembers Hennie is still there. She spontaneously hugs him and takes him out.

SCENE 8
Time passing. A series of vignettes. Inside Poleng Primary School. 1991 ... A school bell rings. Rosa and Selo, age 7, enter the class, marching proudly and singing.

ROSA/SELO with **CAST** *(o/s)*:
We are marching in the light of God,
We are marching in the light of God
We are marching
We are marching
We are marching in the light of God.

Rosa and Selo sit close to each other on the floor. They are learning to count. Friendly rivalry.

ROSA/SELO Nngwê, pêdi, tharô, nnê, thlano!
ROSA *(hand up, grinning!)* Thatharo!
(Selo makes a face)
CAST *(o/s)* Maandaga ... Labobedi ... Laboraro ... Labone ... Vrydaga ... Saterdaga ... Sondaga ?

1992 ... Rosa and Selo, age 8, wriggle as they share a seat.

ROSA/SELO A ... B ... C ... D ... E ... F ...
ROSA G ...
SELO *(at same time)* J ... *(Rosa looks at him)* G ...
ROSA/SELO H ... I ... J!
CAST *(o/s)* Maandaga ... Labobedi ... Laboraro ... Labone ... Vrydaga ... Saterdaga ... Sondaga ?

1993: Rosa and Selo, age 9, are uncomfortably tight on a higher seat that they share. Selo strains his eyes to see the board. They chant their tables.

ROSA/SELO 7 x 1 ... 7. 7 x 2 ... 14. 7 x 3 ...
ROSA 21.
SELO *(at same time)* 28 ... *(Rosa looks at him pointedly)* 21
ROSA/SELO 7 x 4 ... 28. 7 x 5 ... 35. 7 x 6 ...
ROSA 42.
SELO *(at same time)* 41 ... Tch! 42 *(fed up that Rosa is right again!)*
CAST *(o/s)* Maandaga ... Labobedi ... Laboraro ... Labone ... Vrydaga ... Saterdaga ... Sondaga ?

1994: Rosa and Selo, age 10, stand facing each other. They are preparing for an inter-school quiz. Selo now wears glasses.

ROSA What's the longest river in Africa?

SELO   The Nile. What's the biggest country? *(Rosa looks stumped)* Ha! You lose a point. Sudan.

ROSA   How do you know?

SELO   I heard it on the radio.

ROSA   I'm going to ask Mrs Tshadi.

SELO   Not now Rosa. We won't be ready if we don't practise.

ROSA   OK. But no more geography.

SELO   OK. History. Who landed in the Cape 1652?

ROSA   Aiee Selo! Why that one? Jan van Riebeeck. Who was the first President of Botswana?

SELO *(proudly)* Sir Seretse Khama! ... Which South African Prime Minister was stabbed to death? *(acts out scene melodramatically)*

ROSA   They'll never ask that!

SELO   Why not?

ROSA   They don't like to remember such things.

SELO   Answer the question!

ROSA   OK, clever. Hendrik Verwoerd. If you can ask that – so ... who will be our first democratic president?

SELO *(laughs)* Oh Rosa! History is about what happened. Not what's going to happen.

ROSA *(also laughing)* Then history is going to happen like day follows night!

Cheers and ululation rise. Selo goes. Rosa listens to the rising sound.

SCENE 9

2nd May, 1994: Nelson Mandela's Inauguration Day as President. The stage is divided. Outside Poleng Primary School, a large banner of Nelson Mandela. Inside the van Niekerks' house, chairs in front of the television. The two scenes are simultaneous and interweave. Selo enters outside Poleng Primary School with celebration flags of the new South Africa. Crowd sounds from the Inauguration ceremony with a praise singer making his oration in Xhosa. Rosa and Selo wave the flags and reflect the excitement.

ROSA   Did all these people vote for Mr Mandela?

SELO   Of course! Even my grandmother.

ROSA   But she can't walk!

SELO   She said I must push her in a wheelbarrow to the voting station! *(mimics his grandmother sitting on the wheelbarrow)* 'Before I die, I am going to give Mr Mandela a big cross ... and put it in that box ... and make him our President!'

Rosa laughs. Cheers and ululation in background.
Inside the van Niekerks' house, Mevrou enters with Hennie, age 10, clasping his rugby ball. They sit watching the ceremony. Hennie is engaged by the excitement and Mevrou watches with a mixture of interest and concern. Mama enters with her duster. She cheers silently behind them. Hennie sees and grins. They share a secret moment. Meneer enters. He is drinking a bottle of lager. He glowers at Mama, who returns to her dusting, then sits with his wife and son. Mama secretly cheers the praise singer again. Meneer switches off the television with the remote.

HENNIE   Ag nee Pa!
MENEER *(signals to Hennie to go out)* Go and do something useful.
HENNIE   I was just watching, Pa.
MENEER   To see them rubbing our noses in the dirt?
MEVROU   Don't Willem –
MENEER *(to Hennie)* We're not wasting the whole day! On the field! Ten minutes!

Meneer goes. Mevrou turns on the television again. Mama and Hennie smile. Meneer returns.

MENEER *(irritably, to his wife)* Kom skat! *(gestures to Hennie to hurry)*

Mevrou goes. Hennie mischievously samples his father's beer.

MAMA   Master Hennie!
(Hennie hands over the bottle. Mama smells it and pulls a face)
HENNIE *(awkwardly)* Are you happy today, Ragie?
MAMA   Very happy, Master Hennie. We're all very happy.
HENNIE   That must be nice for you, Ragie ... and Rosa, hey?

Mama unexpectedly hugs him. Hennie is embarrassed but laughs. They go.
The broadcast fades and Selo takes over with his own praise song. Rosa joins in, mimicking the adult pomp and ceremony. They laugh and go.

SCENE 10

Same day. The stage becomes a field. Rugby practice. Meneer enters with Jannie and Hennie.

MENEER   Kom! Kom! *(he signals to the boys to scrum down against him)* I want you to stop me!
(The two boys struggle against his weight. Hennie loses his balance and his father crashes over him as Jannie escapes with the ball)
HENNIE   Einaa!
MENEER *(picking himself up)* Kom! Kom! Stop whining like a bloody sissy! Come, I want to see you passing. Let's go! *(Hennie pushes himself up. Jannie passes the ball)* Keep it moving! This is not a game of netball. Speed it up! ... The ball is not a bloody baby! Donder en bliksem, man! Gooi die bal! *(Hennie misses a catch)* Use your eyes! Your eyes! *(Hennie misses again. Jannie grins)* What's wrong with you today?
HENNIE   Sorry Pa.
MENEER   Concentrate, boy. You must concentrate more.
HENNIE   Ja, Pa.
MENEER   OK, let me see you tackle now. OK. Give Jannie the ball. You have to get it off him. Face him head on! *(Hennie faces Jannie)* Let's go ... ! *(Jannie moves like a weasel)* Grab him, man! Hou hom vas! *(a struggle. Hennie gets the ball, is tripped, crashes)* Kom! Kom! *(Hennie, angry, tackles Jannie again. The struggle intensifies. Meneer signals Jannie to throw the ball to him and taunts Hennie)* Kom! Tackle me! Give me your best!
(Hennie rushes at his father but is 'piggy in the middle'. We feel his frustration as Jannie enjoys his advantage. Finally Hennie lunges at Jannie. They scramble together on the ground, legs and bodies intertwined)
MENEER   OK goed, that's enough for today ... I said that's enough! *(Meneer pulls them apart. They get up and dust themselves down. Hennie looks resentfully at Jannie)*
MENEER *(to Jannie)* You did well, boy. You're younger than Hennie, nè?
JANNIE *(catching his breath)* Ja Meneer.
HENNIE   You were on *his* side, Pa! You were two –
MENEER   Your friend Jannie here has got the right attitude. He's small but he's a fighter.

JANNIE *(very pleased with himself)* Dankie Meneer!
  (Meneer ruffles Jannie's hair)
MENEER *(to Hennie)* Maybe he'll even get Full Colours before you.
JANNIE *(grins at Hennie)* I've got to go. I'll tell my Pa what you said
  Meneer! Baai Hennie! Totsiens Meneer!
HENNIE *(unenthusiastic)* Baai Jannie.
MENEER *(calls after Jannie)* Come next week! I'll give you more
  practice, hey!
JANNIE   Dankie Meneer! Baai Hennie!

Jannie runs off, cocky. Hennie rounds on his father.

HENNIE   It wasn't fair, Pa! You made it two against one!
  (Meneer sighs, preparing to have a heart-to-heart with his son)
MENEER *(lowered voice)* Sometimes it's ten against one. Like in our
  country ... You should know by now that life isn't fair ... You need to
  know that. People let you down. Make promises. Don't deliver. But
  you have to keep going.
HENNIE   Jannie will tell all his friends he nearly beat me.
MENEER   But you saved your face in the end, nè?
HENNIE   He's in the year below me.
MENEER   If I didn't push you so hard, you wouldn't learn, son.
HENNIE *(fights back tears)* Learn what?
MENEER   Discipline ... Leadership ... Focus ... *(pause)* When
  you're a man, how will your workers learn discipline if you don't
  have it? *(scrutinises Hennie)* This is a hard country to live in, son,
  but the Lord sent us here. It's God's will. Our forefathers spilt blood
  for us to live here. They wouldn't have survived if they had been soft.
  We have to survive here too ... *(puts his hand on Hennie's shoulder.
  Hennie slowly looks up at his father)* Shake on it, son?

Hennie relents. Meneer takes his hand then hugs him. They go.

SCENE 11
*A few weeks later. A chilly mid-winter evening. Mama and Rosa's
house. A radio is playing. Rosa enters with a bowl of water for Mama's
feet. Mama enters from work, tired. Rosa massages Mama's feet, then
absorbs herself in a book, wrapped in a blanket to keep warm. Mama
is looking for the right moment to interrupt Rosa's reading.*

RADIO ANNOUNCER'S VOICE The Commander of a Self-Defence Unit in Soweto called today for President Mandela and his new government to recognise the need for education and counselling for youth. Taolo Dikobe told a meeting of community leaders that township youth have become accustomed to violence and that everyday violence has destroyed social life.

COMMANDER'S VOICE During our stuggle against apartheid, the youth lost respect for their teachers and schools ... *(fade from here although voice could continue very low)* We must rebuild the culture of learning because youth don't see that education is the way out of poverty and unemployment. That's why they go to drugs. President Mandela must give us money to tackle the problems in our schools.

MAMA   You should have seen Hennie today, Rosa! He came home head to foot in red dust – with this big smile on his face. He scored three times!

ROSA   Mmm.

MAMA   His Ma was so pleased. She didn't even scold him when he sat straight down on the sofa! But I had to hoover straight away! *(Rosa continues reading)* Rosa? Hennie's Ma asked me about you today.

ROSA   Mama?

MAMA   She asked how you are doing at school.

ROSA   What did you say?

MAMA   I told her what your teacher said. I was so proud! *(Rosa looks embarrassed)* She asked me what time you finish school. I told her twelve o'clock. Then she asked if you can help her after school.

ROSA   I hope you told her no way, Mama!

MAMA   She's going to assist Hennie's Pa with his business ?

ROSA   You told her no, didn't you, Mama? She can ask someone else!

MAMA   She knows you Rosa. She –

ROSA   They chased me away.

MAMA   It wasn't Hennie's mother. It was –

ROSA   His Pa won't like me there.

MAMA   He won't even notice you. You'll see.

ROSA   No, Mama!

MAMA   You'll just be a kleinmeid to him now.

ROSA   Mama, I'll feel bad. Hennie will be there.

MAMA   Hennie was your friend.

ROSA   That's just it, Mama! You talk-talk-talk about Hennie all the time. Maybe you like him more than me!

MAMA   How can that be? You! My own child.

ROSA   You spend more time with him than me!

MAMA   When you were a baby, I had no choice. I had to feed you, my dear.

ROSA   He talks with you when he gets back from school, doesn't he, Mama? He comes to you and tells you, 'I scored three times today, Ragie!' You smile at him and give him chocolate cake. His favourite. You bake it for him. Every day he gets something special, Mama!

MAMA   Oh, Rosa! If you come after school to Hennie's house, we'll spend more time together ... *(pause)* It's only until the end of the year.

ROSA   I don't follow you, Mama.

MAMA   OK. I have to tell you now. We need the money, Rosa. We need every cent we can get. In the New Year I want you to go to Hennie's school –

ROSA *(outburst, disbelief)* Hennie's school, Mama?

MAMA   Yes, Hennie's school! They are not going to keep their Oranje School just for their Hennies. It's going to be for my Rosa too. I've been saving ?

ROSA   I don't want to go there, Mama!

MAMA   What are you saying? All the time you complain! Too many children in your class! Ten – twenty, thirty – children must share one book! The board is so far away you can't see! Your teacher can't even mark your work because she's so busy. You won't complain about these things in Hennie's school.

ROSA   Only white children go there.

MAMA *(laughs)* President Mandela is going to make Oranje School open the doors, my darling. Don't you remember how you asked me to take you there when you were six?

ROSA *(putting her hands over her ears)* I don't like to remember it, Mama.

(Mama draws Rosa close)

MAMA   I struggled to find words to satisfy you then ... But you are not a little child any more. If your Papa was alive, it would be his dream. You have to understand these things.

(Rosa breaks away)

ROSA *(crying)* Leave me, Mama. I don't want to go to Hennie's house and be a kleinmeid for them!

MAMA   So ... what do you want to be when you grow up? Do you want to spend your whole life doing what I do? This? *(indicates her servant's uniform)*

ROSA   I don't want to go to Hennie's school.

MAMA   You don't know what you're talking about, my daughter.

Mama goes. She hums 'Ntate roma nna'.

ROSA   They won't want me there anyway!

SCENE 12
Next day. Early afternoon. A sharp vignette of Scene 1 in winter 1994. Rosa is outside Oranje School on her way to her first afternoon's work as a kleinmeid in the van Niekerks' house. She has her school bag and a plastic bag with her kleinmeid's uniform. Hennie and Jannie enter, playing rugby. Jannie falls. He spots Rosa. He whips himself up, making his hand into a mock pistol.

JANNIE   Pioouu! Pioouu! Hey, got her, man! *(Rosa is startled and her bag spills open)* D'you see that, Hennie! Jiss man!

HENNIE *(glances uneasily at Rosa)* Kom Jannie.

Jannie and Hennie go. Shaken, Rosa picks up uniform that has fallen out of her bag. The Paper Boy enters and puts up posters:
'WHITE SCHOOLS MUST OPEN DOOR' – PRESIDENT MANDELA'
'WIT SKOLE MOET HULLE DEURE OOPMAAK – PRESIDENT MANDELA'

PAPER BOY *Die Star! Die Stem!* White schools must open doors ... *(sees Rosa)* Dumela Sis! *(Rosa silently acknowledges him and goes)* Aiee! White schools must open doors says President Mandela. White schools must open doors! *Die Star! Die Stem!*

Paper Boy goes. The Cast off-stage sing work song (e.g. Shosholoza) as Rosa puts on a maid's uniform.

SCENE 13

Same afternoon. The stage is divided. Outside the van Niekerks' house and inside the sitting-room. Outside, Rosa picks up a broom. She slowly sweeps the stoep. Mevrou enters.

MEVROU   Don't waste time, Rosa. I want you inside as soon as you've finished. I need a hundred and one hands today! It's a big day for Master Hennie.
(Mevrou goes. Rosa pushes the broom to and fro, creating a sharp rhythm)

ROSA *(mimicking)* Don't waste time Rosa! Don't waste time! It's a big day for Master Hennie! *(she drops the broom and starts a clapping game with an imaginary partner)* Don't – waste – time! Don't – waste – time!
(Hennie runs in with his rugby ball and trips over the broom. Rosa is startled)

HENNIE   What are you doing here?

ROSA   Your Ma wanted me.

HENNIE   Ma didn't tell me! Ragie didn't either! No one tells me anything! *(Rosa looks away, embarrassed. Hennie suddenly laughs)* My enemies trip me up in rugby but not brooms! *(Rosa can't help a giggle)* Hey, do you remember when we tied a rope between the paw-paw trees ...? We were only little, man! We forgot to undo it. My Pa didn't see it until it was too late ... Jiss! He was mad, hey! *(Rosa laughs with him)* We used to play down in the donga, hey ... ? You can't see it any more, can you? *(Rosa shakes her head)* Pa made us a swimming pool. He said the hole was already there – so why not use it?

ROSA *(quietly)* It was nice down there.

HENNIE   Ag, it's better having a swimming pool, especially after rugby, man!
(Rosa giggles at his gesture of smelly armpits, then returns to sweeping)

HENNIE *(hesitant)* I – It – it was you today, wasn't it ... ? Outside my playground at school, ja? ... I wondered what you were doing there.

ROSA *(stops sweeping)* Who was that boy with you?

HENNIE   Ag, he's just a kid ... he's younger than me ... He's a domkop ... don't mind him!

Mevrou enters the house and looks out of the window at the children.

MEVROU *(irritably)* Hennie! *(to Rosa)* You should have finished by now, Rosa! You've a job waiting inside ... *(Rosa goes)* Where were you, Hennie? I was calling all over.

HENNIE   Ag Ma, you know I've been practising.

MEVROU   Go and get ready or you'll be late.
(Hennie goes. Mama enters the sitting room with Hennie's boots and a cloth) I want you to roast the lamb nicely, Ragel. It's Master Hennie's favourite.

MAMA   Oh yes, Madam.

MEVROU   He'll always remember his first big match.

MAMA   It's true, Madam. Even when he's an old-old man, he will think about this day.

Rosa enters the sitting room. Mama indicates that Rosa must clean Hennie's boots.

MEVROU   You know, he's worked so hard to get into the team. Practising every day after school. Every spare moment! He really deserves a reward.

MAMA   He really does, Madam!

MEVROU   But, if they lose, Ragel ... ! It's going to be so hard to cheer him up!

MAMA   Don't worry Madam. Master Hennie will help them win.

MEVROU   Ja, good to think positive, hey? *(to Rosa)* How are you getting on with those boots, Rosa?

ROSA   OK, M ... *(can't bring herself to say 'Madam')*

MEVROU   You need to hurry up. The Master will be here soon.
(Rosa keeps her head down and rubs furiously. Meneer arrives)

MENEER   Hullo skat. Waar is Hennie?

MEVROU   Hennie! Jou Pa is hierso! Kom nou!

MENEER   You should have reminded him of the time.

MEVROU   Don't make him panic now, Willem. He's been trying to stay calm. You'll be in time.

Hennie arrives in his rugby outfit, barefoot.

HENNIE   Ready Pa! Just got to get my boots. *(Hennie takes the boots hurriedly from Rosa. His father takes them from him)*

MENEER   These boots aren't polished properly! Look at this one! Why did you leave it to the girl?
HENNIE   I was busy, Pa.
MENEER   They wouldn't pass this in the army, I can tell you that!
HENNIE   I'll do them in the car, Pa ... *(to Rosa)* Give me the cloth! *(Hennie takes the cloth from Rosa. They avoid looking at each other)*
MEVROU   Let me look at you, my boy! *(examines Hennie proudly)* Finish polishing the boots – and you'll be fine.
MENEER   Come on, son.
HENNIE   I'll do my best, Ma.
MAMA   Good luck, Master Hennie.
HENNIE   Thanks, Ragie.

Meneer and Hennie go.

MEVROU   You've cleaned shoes before, haven't you Rosa? *(Rosa nods, head down)* Ragel, you can show her how to get a better shine, hey?
MAMA   Yes, Madam.
MEVROU   Don't you like being here with your mother, Rosa? *(Rosa is silent)*
MAMA   Rosa!
ROSA *(softly)* I like being with my mother.
MEVROU   But you must also learn from her. There are many things she can teach you.
ROSA *(mumbles)* Ja, M ...
MEVROU   It's good when a mother can spend so much time with her child. I wish I could see as much of Hennie ... But when he's not in school, he's out playing his rugby.
MAMA   Mmhh! Master Hennie! He'll soon be captain!
(The tension breaks and Mevrou laughs. Rosa remains downcast)
MEVROU   I'm not cross with you, Rosa. I'm just saying these things to help you. You understand? *(Rosa nods, without smiling)* OK, goed! Now I've work to do in the study ... Those tiles in the bathroom, Rosa, they need a good scrub. Your mother will show you which brush to use.
MAMA   Yes, Madam.

Mevrou goes.

ROSA *(under her breath, mimicking)* 'Ragel!' 'Ragie!'
MAMA *(angrily)* Sshh! What's wrong with you?
ROSA   I hate it, Mama. 'Madam!' 'Master!' Even 'Master
    Hennie!' Are you their slave, Mama?
    (Mama grabs Rosa and pulls her close)
MAMA   Mmmhh! I'll tell you something Rosa. I was like you –
    ten years – when our mother died. She paid for our school fees. Our
    father's money was only enough for food and rent. He sat at the
    table all night. He wouldn't look at us, his children ... We knew what
    was in his head ... We went to sleep. In the morning, he was still
    there ... like a ghost! We knew. I never went to school again ... *(Rosa
    looks guiltily at Mama)* A friend of Mma's took me to this laundry
    owned by these white people. They were looking for someone to help
    with the washing. Later they moved me to the ironing boards.
    (choked voice) I ironed ... and ironed ... and ironed.
ROSA *(hugs Mama)* I am trying, Mama!
MAMA   The work is not too hard, is it?
ROSA   It's not that, Mama.
MAMA   I'll show you what you need to clean the tiles. It won't
    be forever.

Mama and Rosa go.

SCENE 14
*A few weeks later. Outside Poleng Primary School. Rosa and Selo
enter.*

CAST *(o/s)* Maandaga ... Labobedi ... Laboraro ... Labone ... Vrydaga ...
    Saterdaga ... Sondaga ?
ROSA   They have the best facilities Selo.
SELO   Facilities aren't everything, Rosa. Mrs Tshadi says if you
    are determined, you can do anything.
ROSA   So what do you want to be when you grow up?
SELO *(pause, suspecting a trap)* Engineer.
ROSA   Can Mrs Tshadi make you an engineer?
SELO   Of course not! It's up to me.
ROSA   How many engineers do you know from Poleng? *(Selo is
    silent)* White children in Oranje School become engineers. Their

teachers help them because they've got books, everything they need! Even their playground is bigger than our whole school.

SELO   You think they want to share it with us? I don't want those white kids pushing me around ... *(Rosa is now silent)* Tell me something. Do you want to be in a school without your friends?

ROSA   But if we go together, we'll have each other.

SELO *(laughs)* Are you a boy? Do you play rugby? *(Rosa looks frustrated)* Me, I've never played rugby in all my life. Tchaa! It is brutal! Do you want me to end up dead in that playground?
(Selo keels over and Rosa rushes to him)

ROSA   No! ... Selo!

SELO   Got you worried there!

ROSA   Be serious Selo. Mr Mandela says the country needs us to get a good education.

SELO   OK, I won't let their rugby put me off. I'm not a chicken!

ROSA   So will you talk to your parents?

SELO   I'll speak to them.

ROSA   It will be fine if there are two of us.

Rosa and Selo turn away from each other. Each talks to self, facing audience.

ROSA   He thinks I really want to go to the white school.

SELO   I only said yes because she pressured me. I don't want to leave my friends.

CAST *(o/s)* Maandaga ... Labobedi ... Laboraro ...

Rosa and Selo face each other.

SELO   My father says we must 'wait and see.'

ROSA *(alarmed)* Wait and see what?

SELO   He heard white people talking at work ... They are going to make trouble.

ROSA   Trouble?

SELO   Uh-huh ... But he says the new government will send more money to our school here in the township.

ROSA   Come on Selo! We have nothing like Oranje here. They have laboratories for science, a whole library of books ...

Selo shrugs and turns his back on her. Rosa looks hurt, turns away. Each faces the audience.

SELO   The way Rosa was talking about that Oranje School!
ROSA   I only told him what Mama said ...
SELO   Maybe it's true what the others say.
ROSA   Mama wants the best for me.
SELO   Her mother wants a daughter who wears a white child's uniform so she can show her off.

Rosa and Selo face each other.

ROSA *(rising desperation)* Don't your parents want the best for you?
SELO   You know what, Rosa! You'll soon be talking like a white.

Rosa looks upset. Selo is about to walk off but instead he entices Rosa into a township song and dance. Selo goes. Rosa watches him, becoming downhearted again.

SCENE 15
Late November 1994, near the end of the school year. Mama and Rosa's house. Rosa is busy with housework when Mama enters.

MAMA   What do you think, my darling? *(Rosa remains silent)* ... So smart! ... I looked at all the dresses in *Uniewinkels*.
ROSA   *Uniewinkels*?
MAMA   I found one for Oranje School. I was turning the dress this way and that way to learn the pattern.
ROSA *(embarrassed giggle)* Mama!
MAMA   The lady said, *(Mama mimics crisp high-pitched voice of white sales lady)* 'What size are you looking for? I'll find it for you.' I told her: 'The size is in my head!' Mmmhh! She didn't like that! Then I said: 'Thank you, my dear' and walked out of the shop. She was shocked!
ROSA   Mama ... you know you say we should be patient.
MAMA   Yes?
ROSA   Why can't we wait? Just one term, Mama.
MAMA   If we wait, when that time comes, there will be something else we must wait for –
ROSA   No, Mama!
MAMA   – and something else and something else.
ROSA   You know Selo, Mama. He's a very clever boy. His parents are thinking about it.

MAMA   You can't be sure.

ROSA   At least there'd be two of us then, Mama ... *(Mama shakes her head)* It's dangerous, Mama! They say the white children's parents are going to make trouble ...

MAMA   Some people always want to see what others do. Someone has to go first.

ROSA   I'm scared Mama.

MAMA   It will be all right. You'll see.

Rosa reluctantly takes the dress from Mama. As they go we are flooded with voices singing 'Die Stem'...

SCENE 16

Open Day at Oranje Primary School – Laerskool Oranje. The Oranje Principal is on the platform in the hall leading the singing. Meneer (dressed head to toe in khaki with a bush hat) joins the audience and sings with fervour.

PRINCIPAL   Dames en Here ... Kinders ... Welkom! Welcome to Open Day at Oranje School. I'd like, first of all, to give a big welcome to all the new children who will join us at the beginning of the new year. Some of you have older brothers and sisters here. Ja? Moenie bang word nie! You'll soon get to know where everything is ... our fine classrooms, our swimming pool, the netball field for the girls, the rugby field for the boys and, of course, a nice playground for everyone. Here at Oranje School we are like a family. Our mottos are simple ?

MENEER   Mevrou Botha, you are telling us what we already know! Tell us what we've come to hear about! *(strides to the platform)* Tell us what you are going to do when those black township kids try to come here!

PRINCIPAL   Excuse me Meneer van Niekerk. This is not a conversation I want to have in front of the children. If you'd like to make an appointment –

MENEER   No, no, no! This concerns our children. It concerns all of us. We want to hear, right here and now. What are you going to do?

PRINCIPAL   *(hesitates)* All of us here know that President Mandela and his government have changed the law. I will have to admit every child who comes.

MENEER   So you want to let the black kids in?
PRINCIPAL I don't make the laws.
MENEER   So, you'll let them in.
PRINCIPAL Look, our school is far away from the township and I don't think –
MENEER   Answer the question!
PRINCIPAL If you would let me finish Meneer ... I was going to say that I don't believe the township parents will want to bring their kids all this way.
MENEER   But if they come, you'll let them in!
PRINCIPAL My hands are tied.
MENEER   But ours aren't! If you won't stop them, we will. *(to audience)* This is our school. For our children!

The Principal signals to bring the meeting to a halt. Lights off.

ACT TWO
Prologue ...
January 1995. The beginning of the new school year. Sprightly voice of a male announcer on the radio.

ANNOUNCER'S VOICE Ja, it's back to school today for young South Africans across the country ... and indeed, for some, it's a very first day! Our next item is to wish all of you 'Alles van die beste!' and remember, as they say in Old England, 'Chin up, old boy! Chin up!'
CAST *(loud whispers o/s)* Whitey! Coconut! Whitey! Coconut! Whitey! Coconut!

SCENE 17
A hot mid-summer morning. The street outside the playground of Oranje School. Mama, smartly dressed, enters with Rosa in her new Oranje uniform. Mama sings 'Ntate roma nna'. Paper Boy enters and puts up posters:
'WHITE PARENTS PROTEST!'
'GEEN SWART KINDERS IN ONS SKOOL NIE!'

PAPER BOY *Die Star! Die Stem!* White parents protest! White parents protest!

MAMA *(to Paper Boy, buying a paper)* Re a lêboga ... Do you know that President Mandela wants every child to be in school, my son?
PAPER BOY Êê, Mme!
MAMA When will your mother send you to school?
PAPER BOY My mother is dead, Mme. There's no money for school. *(Mama shakes her head and indicates he should keep the change)* Ke a lêboga Mme ... *(gives Rosa a thumbs-up) No Star! Die Stem!*

Paper Boy goes. The Cast off-stage chant 'NO BLACKS HERE! GEEN SWARTES HIER!' Rosa wants to turn back but Mama gently but firmly steers her on. Chants continue.

ROSA Let them keep their school, Mama!
MAMA That's what they want us to do.
ROSA It's not just these white people, Mama!
MAMA You must stand up straight and tall –
ROSA That boy who called me 'Whitey'! He was from my school! And those others – you heard them, Mama!
MAMA Do you think they are clever when they call those names? ... and all these people ... are they clever? *(Rosa shakes her head)* Do they know you? Inside you, my daughter? *(Mama puts her arm around her)* Some people like to pull others down. If you let those people get inside your head, they will make you fall! *(Rosa nods but her eyes tell another story)* Don't let anyone take away who you are, my child ... They will want you when they know you.

Chanting intensifies. Camera lights flash. Mama and Rosa watch as the Oranje Principal enters, pursued by Meneer and a Reporter with a microphone. Meneer appears too engrossed in arguing to take in who Mama and Rosa are.

PRINCIPAL No comment! No comment!
MENEER Let this one in and your troubles begin!
PRINCIPAL I have to let her in.
MENEER We'll take our children away.
PRINCIPAL It's the law.
MENEER. You'll destroy us – our community.
PRINCIPAL If I don't let this girl in, the government will close the school!
MENEER Stand up to them!

PRINCIPAL You don't understand Meneer van Niekerk! I'm telling you. We have no choice. Everyone is watching us ... *(to Reporter)* No comment!

REPORTER Just a brief statement, Mevrou!

PRINCIPAL *(ignoring Reporter, signals brusquely to Mama and Rosa)* Kom! This way.

REPORTER *(to Mama)* Ma'am, one word please!
(Mama ignores him. She hurries with Rosa behind the Principal)

MENEER *(moving to block Mama and Rosa)* Skande!
(Meneer looks properly at them for the first time. He is shocked and reluctantly moves aside. Something has been disturbed. The Principal leads Mama and Rosa away)

REPORTER Praat met my Meneer! Praat met my!

Meneer van Niekerk marches off, pursued by the Reporter. Chanting fades.

SCENE 18

A little later. Principal's Office at Oranje School. The Principal sits behind her desk with Mama and Rosa standing. The 'Invisible' Worker brings Mama a chair. She is grateful. He unobtrusively gets to work with a screwdriver. However, we sense his keen interest and concern. His face is a barometer of the interview.

MAMA   I want to enrol my daughter, Mevrou. She's ready to start Standard Three.

PRINCIPAL *(abrupt, looking at papers)* What school does she attend?

MAMA   Poleng Primary, Mevrou.

PRINCIPAL It's not good for children when you move them here and there.

MAMA   There are eighty children in her class, Mevrou! There's place for my child only in the morning.

PRINCIPAL So your daughter has only been attending half-day?

MAMA   Ja, Mevrou –

PRINCIPAL Then she can't be up to our level for Standard Three!

MAMA   Mevrou –

PRINCIPAL If the child can do only Standard One work ...

MAMA   Mevrou –

PRINCIPAL   ... she must go back to Standard One here!
MAMA   Mevrou –
PRINCIPAL She won't like it ...
MAMA   She's a good pupil, Mevrou! She gets top marks.
PRINCIPAL I can tell you definitely that top marks in Poleng are not the same as top marks in Oranje! We have very high standards.
MAMA   That's why I want her to come to your school, Mevrou.
PRINCIPAL Your mother claims you are a good pupil. Is it true?
ROSA *(whispers)* Ja, Mevrou.
PRINCIPAL Speak up, girl.
ROSA   Ja, Mevrou.
(The Principal picks up a book of Aesop's Fables and selects a page)
PRINCIPAL Here, read this!
(Rosa begins to read, her voice soft at first but gaining in confidence as she is drawn into the story. The Principal's face reflects surprise. The 'Invisible' Worker stops his work to listen, sharing Mama's apprehension and pride)
ROSA   'The Eagle And The Tortoise ... A tortoise was not satisfied with his life. He wanted to stop being a Tortoise. 'I'm tired of crawling,' he grumbled. 'I want to be able to soar through the air.' So he spoke to the Eagle. 'You are not built for flying,' warned the Eagle. 'I've watched how the birds do it,' said the Tortoise. 'I can wave my flippers in the air. Just get me up there and I'll show you. I'll bring you lots of pearls from the sea if you do.' The Eagle was tempted. So he carried the Tortoise up into the sky, higher and higher. 'Now then,' cried the Eagle, 'let's see you fly!' But the moment the Tortoise was by himself, he fell like a stone. When he struck the ground, he was smashed into a thousand little pieces.'
(Rosa hesitates, looking at the words of the moral. Mama looks concerned)
PRINCIPAL Continue. Read the words underneath.
ROSA *(reluctantly)* 'Be satisfied with what and where you are. The higher you fly the harder you may fall.'
PRINCIPAL Do you understand the meaning of this story? *(Rosa senses a trap and looks at Mama)* I'm asking you, not your mother ... *(Rosa barely nods)* Speak up!
ROSA   I understand it, Mevrou.

PRINCIPAL   Hmm! If you can read so well, I don't know why your mother is complaining about your school ... Tell me, don't you want to stay in the same school as your friends?
(Rosa looks at the floor)

MAMA   Mevrou –
(The Principal silences Mama)

PRINCIPAL   Has your mother told you how hard it is to come to a school where you don't know anyone? *(Rosa remains silent. Principal turns to Mama)* Look, I understand how you want the best for your child. But in the child's interest, I strongly advise you against changing her school right now. She's at the top of her class. Even if there are some problems in her school, she's doing well. Why disrupt all that?
(Mama wipes her hand across her face. Moments of doubt, a struggle. Rosa sees Mama wavering)

ROSA *(tentatively)* Mevrou ... I can learn lots of things here they don't teach in my school.

PRINCIPAL   Like what?

ROSA   Science, Mevrou. There's only one science book for all of us in my class ... Please Mevrou ... I want to come to Oranje School.
(Mama holds back tears as Principal scrutinises Rosa)

PRINCIPAL   If you want to come, then I can't stop you. But it's not going to be easy.

ROSA *(very quietly)* Ja, Mevrou.

The Principal goes. Mama smiles with relief at the 'Invisible' Worker and at Rosa. She signals Rosa to stand tall and goes. The 'Invisible' Worker gives Rosa a 'thumbs up' and goes.

ROSA *(to audience)* They will want me when they know me. They will want me when they know me. They will want me when they know me. Won't they?

SCENE 19
A little later. A classroom. The 'Invisible' Worker sweeps the corridor behind it. He remains on stage throughout the scene, observing. Sounds of children outside. Rosa stands alone in the classroom, trying not to show her nervousness. Jannie enters. He sees Rosa and deliberately pushes her from behind, then swaggers to his desk. Rosa

sits at another desk. Hennie and Marie enter the corridor, running. Marie stops at the classroom door.

MARIE   Baai Hennie!
HENNIE *(from corridor)* Baai!

Marie sees Rosa and exchanges looks with Jannie who stops her sitting at his desk. Marie hesitates, then takes the empty seat next to Rosa. Marie makes a show of sorting her books, pencils, pens etc. She flashes Rosa a tight smile. All three sit as if listening to instructions. Rosa sits with her pen poised, uncertain.

MARIE   Did you understand what Juffrou told us to do? What are you going to write about?
ROSA   I'm still thinking.
MARIE   We always have to write about the holidays when we come back. Didn't you do anything?
ROSA   I did.
MARIE   We went to Margate ... we went to the beach every day. *(shows Rosa a photo)* This is a picture of me in my two piece! *(Rosa looks at it without commenting and Marie flashes it to Jannie)* Where did you go?
ROSA   Just around.
        (Rosa covers her book so Marie can't see. Marie flashes her photo to Jannie. She and Jannie begin writing. Rosa to herself) My Holidays... *(self-mocking, agitated)* Every day I went to Hennie van Niekerk's house. I was their kleinmeid. I cleaned the bathroom. I dusted the bedrooms. I made the beds. I polished Hennie's rugby boots ...

The bell rings. Marie hurries to collect the books. Rosa holds on to hers. Marie exaggerates surprise and concern. Hennie enters the corridor.

MARIE   You'll have to explain to Juffrou. Maybe she'll let you do it for homework. Do you know where everything is? The girls' loos?
ROSA   No.
MARIE   I'll show you. They're near the playground.

Hennie sees Rosa and stops outside the classroom door. Rosa sees him. Everyone freezes. Rosa and Hennie each talk to self, facing the audience.

HENNIE	She didn't tell me she was coming here!
ROSA	His face – when he saw it was me!
HENNIE	Ragie didn't say a word!
ROSA	His cheeks –
HENNIE	Coming to our house everyday, keeping it a secret.
ROSA	White like a sheet!
HENNIE	Man, I don't want my friends to know!
ROSA	Does he really think I'll say something?
HENNIE	I can't say anything to her now.
ROSA	What does he think I'll say?
HENNIE	I'll have to tell her when I see her – at home.
ROSA	Tell his friends that we used to play nice games together?
HENNIE	I'll warn her!
ROSA	Tell them how his Pa caught us one day and thrashed him?
HENNIE	What if she doesn't listen?
ROSA	Tell them that I've been his kleinmeid ?
HENNIE	I'll get Ma to tell Ragie to tell Rosa.
ROSA	... cleaning his dirty boots? What does Hennie think I am?

Scene unfreezes. Hennie glances uneasily at Rosa, and goes. Marie looks from Hennie to Rosa.

MARIE   Do you know Hennie van Niekerk? *(Rosa ignores the question)* He's one of our best rugby players ... *(Rosa gives nothing away and Marie turns irritable)* Come on! We're going to miss playtime!

Jannie blocks the doorway. He looks down the corridor in the direction of the 'Invisible' Worker but ignores him.

JANNIE   Jou! Kom hierso! *(Rosa backs. Jannie advances. He smirks at Marie who becomes nervously excited)* I've got a message for you ... I'm talking to you! Ja, you!

ROSA	I have a name.
JANNIE	Jiss! This black says she has a name.
ROSA	My name is Rosa Mogale.

JANNIE *(to Marie)* What did she say?

MARIE	Rose something!

JANNIE   Anyone seen a rose this colour? *(Marie giggles)* Do you think we can pick her? Who said you could come to our school? *(Rosa is silent. Marie tries to look solicitous, playing the go-between)*

MARIE   What was wrong with your school? Didn't you have good teachers?

ROSA   My teachers were fine!

JANNIE   So why did you come then? *(closing in on Rosa)* Who was that native girl with you this morning, hey? *(Rosa tries to push past Jannie. He grabs her wrist and twists her arm, pushing her down. He grins at Marie who looks a little nervous)*

MARIE   Ag, Jannie! Mevrou Botha will –

JANNIE *(mimicking)* 'Mevrou Botha will –!' My Pa says she just gives in to the blacks. No guts. Typical woman!

ROSA *(struggling to free herself)* Aah!

JANNIE   They think they can just push in here and take over!

Hennie reappears at the classroom door. He observes, unseen and tense, but reluctant to get involved. He catches the eye of the 'Invisible' Worker.

ROSA *(crying, struggling)* I want to go to the playground! Let me go!

JANNIE   It's our playground ... for the games that we like to play ... *(to Marie)* She can't join us unless she passes our test, nè? Clean my boots! Lick them clean, hey! *(pushes his boot near her face and starts singing to the tune of 'Bobbejaan Klim die Berg')* Bobbejaan lick my boots! Da-da-da-Dah! Da-da-da-Dah! *(signals to Marie to join in)* Bobbejaan lick my boots! Da-da-da-Dah! Da-da-da-Dah!

MARIE   Da-da-da-Dah! Da-da-da-Dah!

Hennie can't watch any longer and rushes in and pulls Jannie away from Rosa. The 'Invisible' Worker looks relieved.

HENNIE   Leave Rosa alone!

Hennie helps Rosa up. She is shaking. She rubs her twisted arm. Jannie looks scornful.

MARIE *(embarrassed)* Ag, Hennie, we were only playing!

JANNIE *(to Marie)* Just because he's in Standard Four, he thinks he can boss us around!

MARIE   Hennie knows her name!
JANNIE   He's gone mad!

Hennie moves threateningly towards Jannie. Jannie and Marie edge towards the door.

MARIE   If he tells Mevrou Botha –
JANNIE   We didn't do anything. We were only singing.
MARIE   We were teaching her a school song.
JANNIE   If Mevrou Botha has a go at me, I'll tell my Pa.
MARIE   Was he outside today?
JANNIE   He was going to be ... but he had to go to work.
MARIE   Same as my Pa. He might come tomorrow.

Jannie and Marie run off along the corridor. Jannie turns back.

JANNIE   That girl is asking for trouble if she reports us.

Jannie goes. Hennie looks as if he might give chase but returns to the classroom.

HENNIE   You didn't say you were coming to my school! *(Rosa is silent)* Ragie didn't say a word either. Why didn't you tell me ...? That was one helluva secret!
ROSA   Mama said to keep quiet. Some people are too angry.
HENNIE   Ja ... I know ... Pa ... *(struggling for words, awkward)* Did you see my Pa outside? *(Rosa nods)* I heard them shouting at someone ... I didn't know it was you. That's why ... I got a shock when I saw you just now. I wasn't expecting you ... *(Hennie half expects Rosa to attack him because of his Pa. When she doesn't, he relaxes a little)* You had guts, hey?
ROSA   It was Mama's idea.
HENNIE   Walking past all those people ... screaming, shouting at you –
ROSA   She said someone has to go first.
HENNIE   Ragie said that ... ? Jiss!

Rosa stares at Hennie to check his meaning. When he smiles, she allows herself a fleeting smile.

HENNIE *(checks his watch)* Come. I'll show you the playground, ja? *(Rosa nods. Hennie leads the way out to the playground. The 'Invisible' Worker watches. Sounds of children playing)*

HENNIE   It's just there.
BOY'S VOICE   Ons wag vir jou, Hennie! Where the hek have you
   been, man?
HENNIE   Hek, I've got to go! You OK now?
ROSA   I'm fine.

*Hennie goes. Rosa rubs her arm and begins to hum Mama's song
'Ntate roma nna'. She enters the playground on her own. The
'Invisible' Worker watches from a distance.*

ACT THREE
Prologue ...
*October 2000. Music to suggest time passing (e.g. Mbira). A young
man enters carrying newspapers. He wears a T-shirt with 2000 on
the front and back. It is Selo. He is quiet and depressed, in striking
contrast to the previous Paper Boy. He hangs up two posters:*
'THE STRUGGLE GOES ON WARNS MANDELA'
'DIE STRYD MOET VOORTGAAN WAARSKU MANDELA'

SELO *(without spirit) Die Star! Die Stem!* Cheap papers here.

SCENE 20
*Oranje High School – Hoërskool Oranje. The stage is divided – outside
the school, a corridor inside, and the hall where there are seats and a
lectern set up for the Annual Prize-Giving. Mama and Rosa enter
outside. Mama is smartly dressed and Rosa, age 16, wears the high
school uniform. They are both shocked to see Selo.*

MAMA   Selo? Is it you? *(Selo looks awkward)* Aren't you in
   school, my child?
SELO   My father lost his job.
MAMA *(upset)* Mmhhh!
SELO   When he gets another one, I'll go back to school, Mme.

*Mama takes a paper and indicates Selo should keep the change. He
nods and goes.*

ROSA   Selo ?
SELO *(avoids looking at Rosa) Die Star! Die Stem!*

ROSA *(follows him)* Selo! ... Selo!

Meneer and Mevrou enter with Hennie, age 16. They are all smartly dressed – Hennie in school uniform and Meneer in a suit (not khaki). They pass Selo. Meneer waves Selo away. Rosa and Hennie exchange glances. Rosa signals secretly that she wants to speak urgently to him.

MEVROU *(smiles self-consciously)* Oh Ragie! So you are here too?

MAMA   Yes, M –

MEVROU   And Rosa! My, how you are growing up! *(to Mama)* Are you hoping your daughter is going to get a prize? *(awkward laugh)* Even the Governing Body doesn't know yet who the winners are! Isn't that so, Willem?

MENEER   Ja. It's tradition.

MEVROU *(proudly)* You know that the Master – Willem – is the Chair of the Governing Body, don't you, Ragie? He'll be handing out the prizes.

HENNIE   Ma, excuse me ... I've got to get something from my classroom. I'll join you in the hall.
(Meneer looks at his watch and indicates to Mevrou that they should go inside)

MENEER   Don't be late son! ... Kom skat! Ons moet binne gaan. I need time to prepare ... *(takes out his notes. They go)*

ROSA   There's something I must check, Mama. I'll see you inside there.

MAMA *(pulls Rosa and Hennie together)* I'll be very happy if both of you get prizes.

HENNIE *(laughs)* Thank you, Ragie! But I don't think it will be me! Rosa is the clever one!
(Rosa makes a face)

MAMA   Mmhh, Hennie!
(Mama kisses Rosa and pats Hennie affectionately. She goes. Rosa pulls Hennie aside. They are alone)

ROSA   You looked right through me today.

HENNIE   When? Where?

ROSA   You don't even know! In the playground, you looked straight at me, as if I wasn't there!

HENNIE   Was I talking with my friends? Maybe my mind was just miles away! Hek, Rosa, I'm sorry! *(Rosa says nothing)* Anyway,

I thought we agreed. We said we'd keep our friendship to ourselves for now. Didn't we?

ROSA It suits you, nè? I'm like a yoyo. You can pick me up ... play with me ... swing me around ... throw me away ... until you want to play again.

HENNIE Ag, Rosa, it's not like –

ROSA It's time we were honest ... *(Hennie is now silent)* It's not just your friends, is it, Hennie? Everyone else tonight, they'll have a nice time with their friends, their family ... but what about me and you? ... I mean, what would your parents say?

HENNIE Don't bring my parents into this.

ROSA Of course, they're in it. Wake up, Hennie! We couldn't even say hello just now! What would your Ma say if she knew? *(mimics Mevrou)* 'Isn't that nice, Willem! Our Hennie is sixteen and look how he's got himself such a nice girlfriend!'

HENNIE It's not the right time for talking about this, Rosa. They're waiting for us.

ROSA It's never the right time, is it Hennie?

HENNIE Look, Pa is making the speech tonight. We can't go in late. You know my Pa.

ROSA Yes, I know him. He's the one who gave me nightmares. That day he called me a 'pikkenien' ... a 'half-naked savage'.

HENNIE Sometimes he says things when he's in a bad mood.

ROSA A 'bad mood'! That's all you think it is! *(Hennie sighs)* I didn't know you're so racist.

HENNIE I'm not racist!

ROSA You think these words are like – like empty cans! What do you think a five year-old child feels like being stuffed inside them?

HENNIE I also remember Pa shouting that day. It was scary, man. I was frightened too.

ROSA He didn't chase you away!

HENNIE Have you forgotten Pa's belt? The one hanging by his bed?

ROSA You took me to see it!

HENNIE You wanted to!

ROSA You made me creep all the way through your house into your parent's room. *(they both giggle)*

During the following sequence, Meneer enters the hall and checks the lectern. Mevrou shows the 'Invisible' Worker where to place a display of flowers. The 'Invisible' Worker goes. Mevrou checks the flowers and confers with her husband, looking worried about the time. She goes out, looking for Hennie.

TANNOY VOICE Please proceed to the hall and take your seats. Prize-giving is about to begin. Everyone to the hall please.

HENNIE *(looks at his watch)* Hek!

ROSA   I don't feel like going in there, Hennie. You go!

HENNIE   You have to come, Rosa. Your mother is also waiting ... *(more gently)* What's up?

ROSA   I don't know! Just now I saw this boy from my old school. Selo was a bright – bright boy. He was out there selling papers! You should have seen how he looked at me, Hennie.

HENNIE   How?

ROSA   I feel so bad. He doesn't want to know me any more ... and you also don't want to know me!

HENNIE   That's not –

ROSA   Your Pa didn't even look at me just now ... and your Ma makes that false smile. She thinks I'm getting above myself. I can tell! Do you think your Ma is sitting down nicely next to Mama, eh?

HENNIE   I don't know. Let's go and we'll see –

Hennie tries to take Rosa's arm but Rosa blocks him. They freeze. Inside, Mevrou directs Mama into the hall and shows her where to sit.

MEVROU *(anxious)* Did you see Hennie, Ragie?

MAMA *(quietly)* No Madam.

MEVROU   And where's your Rosa?

Mama shakes her head. She is also worried. Jannie enters. Meneer takes him aside.

MENEER *(low, urgent)* Where is Hennie?

JANNIE   I haven't seen him, Meneer.

MEVROU *(tense whisper)* You looked in his classroom, ja?

JANNIE   I did Mevrou. Sorry Meneer. I'm sure he'll come soon.

Jannie and Mevrou sit down, away from Mama. Mevrou tries to hide her agitation. Meneer's eyes veer between the door and his watch.

ROSA   Things are right under your nose and you don't see them. Mama is just a servant to you, nè?

HENNIE   No.

ROSA   Then why do you call her 'Ragie'?

HENNIE   That's her name.

ROSA   No. That's what you call her. It's rude, very rude.

HENNIE   Why?

ROSA   A child doesn't call an adult by their first name. You're in Africa and you don't know that! *(Hennie looks uncomfortable, frustrated)* You've no respect.

HENNIE   But I've always called your Ma 'Ragie'. It's what I was told.

ROSA   That's just it. You got it from your parents. Disrespect! Master Hennie.

HENNIE   Ragi – I mean your Ma – she can call me Hennie. I wouldn't mind.

ROSA   But she has to wait for you to say it. Because you – a boy my age – are the boss over my mother. How do you think that feels?

HENNIE   I – I haven't thought about it.

ROSA   You take my mother and you don't think about it.

HENNIE   I didn't take her. She came to work for us.

ROSA   She looked after you so she could feed me. You had your Ma and mine!

(Hennie tries to calm her)

HENNIE   I'm sorry, Rosa ... but it wasn't really my fault.

ROSA   Does it matter? You had my mother.

They freeze. Inside the hall, Meneer puts up his hand for attention. The 'Invisible' Worker slips in at the back with his broom, unnoticed, to listen.

MENEER   I don't think we should delay any more for latecomers. Dames en Here, Prinsipaal, Onderwysers, Leerlinge. I am very pleased to be asked to do the honours tonight. The Annual Prize-Giving is an important occasion where we come together to celebrate outstanding achievement. Only the Principal and teachers know who the prize-winners are until I open these ... *(holds up a batch of envelopes)*

Meneer freezes. Outside Hennie and Rosa unfreeze. Rosa softens.

ROSA   How can we ever be real friends, Hennie? It can't work
with us.

HENNIE   Rosa, please … I'm sorry. I'm sorry how it is. I don't
want it this way. Look, we have to go inside now. I'll meet you
tomorrow after school … at the donga, OK?

*Hennie mischievously grabs her hair band and runs off. Rosa follows.
Inside the hall:*

MENEER   The prize goes to Jan Beyers. *(Mevrou and Mama clap.
Jannie goes to receive his certificate)* Keep it up Jan Beyers – a fine
young sportsman! *(Jannie grins. Meneer claps)* … The next is
another very important sports prize. It's for Full Colours for rugby
attained at the age of sixteen. As you all know, this is a real
achievement … and this year it goes to … *(opens envelope)* Oh my …
this is rather embarrassing! I assure you, I had nothing to do with
this … it goes to my son, Hennie van Niekerk.
*(Mevrou and Mama clap but both look upset that Hennie is
missing. Meneer puts on a brave show)*
I apologise Ladies and Gentlemen because we don't seem to have my
son here at the moment. We'll continue. We come now to a very
prestigious prize. It's the Hertzog Prize for all-round academic
achievement. Previous winners of this award have all gone on to
obtain scholarships for university. This year the prize goes to …
(opens envelope – an awkward silence) Rosa Mogale.

*Mama gasps and claps with everyone but is very distressed that Rosa
is not there. Mevrou looks tense.*

MENEER   Does anyone know where she is?

*Murmurs rise but stop abruptly as Hennie and Rosa enter. They are
caught like rabbits in the headlights. Rosa hurries to sit next to Mama.*

MENEER   As you can see, Ladies and Gentlemen, we could also do
with some prizes for the old-fashioned virtue of punctuality. Hennie
van Niekerk, would you like to collect your prize for Full Colours?
*(Hennie looks mortified. He shakes hands with his father, collects
his prize and sits down. Meneer remains sombre)*

MENEER   Rosa Mogale – the Hertzog Prize goes to you ... *(Rosa looks at Mama in disbelief)* I only hope you live up to its high expectations. *(Mama pushes Rosa forward and he gives her the certificate)*
ROSA *(respectfully)* Dankie Meneer.
(Awkard silence. Rosa turns to go away. At the last moment, Meneer puts out his hand)
MENEER   Rosa.

Meneer shakes her hand. A bridge has been crossed. Mama restrains tears. Mevrou looks embarrassed but pleased. A brief congratulatory moment. Everyone goes.

SCENE 21
Next day. A hot summer's afternoon. A dry riverbed in the veld. Sound of cicadas. Hennie and Rosa enter. They wear school uniform but look casual and are at ease with each other. They play a game of throwing pebbles at a target before resting.

HENNIE   Nice, hey? ... Quiet.
ROSA   So ... last night ... what did your parents say?
HENNIE   I told them I had an urgent call of nature!
ROSA   Did they believe you?
HENNIE   Pass! Pa was totally silent. Maybe a dormant volcano, hey! This morning I heard him tell Ma she must talk to your mother.
ROSA   Mama knows nothing! It's nothing to do with her!
HENNIE   Did she ask you anything last night?
ROSA *(nods)* I said I wasn't feeling well before the ceremony. Then she asked: 'And Hennie?' I said I didn't know. Now your parents are going to pressure Mama!
HENNIE   What do you want me to do?
ROSA   All this ... pretending, Hennie! Look how we pretend. Lying to our parents and in school we just about say hello. Why? Because if people see us together, they'll start gossiping. It's OK for all the others to have girlfriends, boyfriends ... because they don't mix up the colours, do they? Let's finish this, Hennie. You find yourself a white girl. I'll stay with my black friends.
HENNIE   Don't be crazy, Rosa. We can ignore them.

ROSA   So why do we come to this place here? Why don't we
meet in the playground?

HENNIE   We want to be alone. That's natural.

ROSA   Be honest, Hennie! You don't want your white friends to
see you!

HENNIE   Your black friends wouldn't be too happy with me
either.

ROSA   What do you know? I've been a 'Whitey' to some people
since I first came to your school! I don't let it bother me! Mama
taught me ... Your Ma hasn't taught you anything.

HENNIE   That's not fair!

ROSA *(over-riding)* Fair? No, it's not fair. Lots of things are not fair!
(both are dejected, silent) Look Hennie, I don't want to fight with
you but let's face it. Your Pa is going to find out. He'll order you to
stop seeing me.

HENNIE   Pa is just like his Pa, my Oupa. He's like a rock.

ROSA   Even rocks crack. Look ... *(points to the pebbles)* Where
did these come from?

HENNIE   Pa is scared of change. He thinks we'll lose our way.

ROSA   So what will you do? That's what I want to know, Hennie.
How do you think I'll feel – when your Pa goes mad – if you drop me
then? Tell me now, Hennie! Tell me ... *(Hennie looks miserable)* So
you'll do what he says ... *(fighting tears)* I'd rather go now, myself.

HENNIE   Rosa, wait –

ROSA   For what? So your Pa can strike like lightning between us?
All these nice words from your mouth ... they'll disappear in the smoke.

HENNIE   Wait –

ROSA   Look, it's over between us.

HENNIE   You won't let me finish! I've made up my mind. I'm
going to tell Ma and Pa that we're friends.

ROSA *(stares for a moment)* Now you're mad! You want to tell them?

HENNIE   Ja. Before someone else does.

ROSA   It won't make any difference. They'll still go crazy.

HENNIE   It doesn't matter. You're right. I've been a coward ... In
rugby Pa always taught me I must be harder than my toughest
opponents ... *(mimics Pa)* 'Face them head on!' ... Now I've got to
face him head on.

ROSA *(genuinely worried)* Your Pa is a lot bigger than you.

HENNIE   What can he do to me?

ROSA   I don't want your Pa to hurt you.

HENNIE   I'll tell him when Ma is there too.

ROSA   But your Ma never stood up to him.

HENNIE   You don't know everything about my Ma. I'll tell them both ... *(imagines he is facing his parents)* 'You brought me up to be honest. I've something to tell you ... *(deep breath)* You brought me up to obey the law. The law says we are all equal. When you were brought up, South Africa was a different place. You still want to live in that old place. I want to be in the new place.'
(Rosa impulsively takes his hand)

ROSA   That's what I like best about you Hennie! When you are straightforward! But –

Hennie puts his arms around her. Rosa lets him. A first kiss. Jannie and Marie emerge in the background. Hennie and Rosa don't see them. They hug and smile nervously at each other.

ROSA   Jeez, Hennie. What now?

JANNIE *(stepping forward)* D'you see that? Well, well, well ... *(Rosa and Hennie swing around)* It's our own Hennie van Niekerk.

MARIE   Captain of the A team. Mr Full Colours!

JANNIE   Hey, Hennie! Piouu! Piouu! *(mocking trigger action, laughing)* We've caught some love-birds, ja?

HENNIE   Shut up, Jannie.

MARIE   He always made out he wasn't interested in girls! Just married to his rugby, hey!

JANNIE   Clever ou!

ROSA   Let's go, Hennie.

JANNIE *(mimics)* 'Let's go Hennie!' You take your orders from a black now, Hennie? Sies man!
(Hennie clenches his fists)

ROSA   Don't listen to him Hennie!

HENNIE   If you're looking for a fight, Jannie, kom!

ROSA   No Hennie! They're sick in the head! Ignore them! I had to learn that long ago.

HENNIE *(shaking off her arm)* They're insulting both of us.

JANNIE *(laughs)* That's right, Hennie. Take no notice of her. Sure, I'll fight you!

(Hennie and Jannie face each other, ready to tackle)

ROSA   I'm not staying to watch, Hennie. If you fight him, it's
finished between us! He's stupid and you want to act like him! Fists
instead of brains! Just like your Pa.

*Rosa starts to walk away. Jannie eggs Hennie on. Suddenly Hennie
drops his fists. He gestures scornfully at Jannie, turns his back on him
to run after Rosa.*

JANNIE   D'you see that? Hennie's turned chicken! *(squawks
loudly like a chicken)*

HENNIE   Rosa, wait!

MARIE   Wait till the others hear this!

JANNIE   Jirr! We'll tell them everything, man!

They run off, laughing. Hennie catches up with Rosa.

HENNIE   Please, Rosa ... He got me so mad. I became stupid like
them ... *(Rosa looks at Hennie but remains drained and silent)*
When you said 'You're just like your Pa', it hit me ... Pa used to
coach us together – me and Jannie. It was a fight every time. Pa
used to push me and push me until I beat Jannie. He only praised
me when I won ... *(Rosa remains tense)* I'm sorry.

ROSA   I meant it Hennie. It would have been finished
between us.

HENNIE   But now?

ROSA   I don't know ... I'm afraid for you ... Your Pa, Jannie,
all of them. They want you to be like them. They won't let you be
anything else.

HENNIE   But it's up to me, isn't it?

ROSA   Ja, but can you stand up to them, Hennie? Not with
your fists! You have to use your head and your heart ... like Mama
says.

HENNIE   Your mother ... do you think she guessed last night
about ...? *(signals the two of them)*

ROSA   Maybe ... Mama still thinks of you like her child.

HENNIE   What would she say? If she knew for sure.

ROSA *(pause)* She'd worry for us.

HENNIE   Would she want us to – to –

ROSA   Stop this? I don't think so.

HENNIE   What if Ma and Pa tell her to make you?

ROSA   We're not doing anything wrong! Look, if I'm going to be your girlfriend, Hennie, we can't worry about what everyone else thinks! When Mama wanted me to come to your school, I was terrified. But she said I must be myself. 'They will want you when they know you.'

HENNIE   Your Ma is someone special, hey?

ROSA   She made me face my fears and – step by step – I managed.

HENNIE   Step by step ... I like that.

ROSA   Do you remember my first day? You saved me from Jannie ... You took me to the playground. Then your friends called and you ran off. I had to step into that playground on my own. There was a girl on the other side. I thought she'd smiled at me.

HENNIE   And?

ROSA   She was fine. But even if she had turned her back, I had crossed the playground ... and I knew I could do it again.

Mama begins singing: 'Ntate roma nna' off stage.

HENNIE *(frowns)* I should have walked across the playground with you! Shouldn't I?

ROSA   We each have our own steps to take.

HENNIE   Even when we hold hands?

ROSA   Even when we hold hands.

The Cast enter singing.

The End

Beverley Naidoo

Beverley was born in Johannesburg. As a student she joined the resistance to apartheid, leading to detention without trial and exile in England in 1965. Her award-winning fiction includes *Journey to Jo'burg* (banned in South Africa until 1991), *Chain of Fire, No Turning Back, The Other Side of Truth* (Carnegie Medal 2000), *Web of Lies* and a short story collection *Out of Bounds*.

Her PhD explored teenagers' responses to literature and racism and she has received honorary doctorates from the University of Southampton and the Open University. *The Playground* is her first stage play and was a Time Out Critis' Choice 2004. She is on the web at **www.beverleynaidoo.com**

GLOSSARY

A = Afrikaans T = Tswana

alles van die beste (A)	all the best
as Mandela nou uit die tronk kom is dit die laaste... (A)	if Mandela now comes out of jail it will be the last...
baai (A)	bye (casual)
basimane (T)	boys
bobbejaan klim die berg (A)	baboon climbs the mountain
bokkie (A)	term of affection, literally 'kid', 'little buck'
Die Stem (A)	The Voice
daar's niks stukkend nie (A)	there's nothing broken
dames en here (A)	ladies and gentlemen
dankie (A)	thank you
domkop (A)	derogatory term, literally 'dumb head'
donder en bliksem (A)	thunder and lightning
dumela (T)	good morning/afternoon
êê (T)	yes
een – twee – drie (A)	one – two – three
eina (A)	ow!
goed (A)	good
gooi die bal (A)	throw the ball
hoekom...? (A)	why...?
hou hom vas (A)	hold him tightly
ja (A)	yes
jou Pa is hierso (A)	your Pa is here

juffrou (A)	miss, young lady teacher
jy (A)	you
kan jy dit glo? (A)	can you believe it?
ke a lêboga Mme (T)	thank you mother
ke nnete (T)	it's true
kinders (A)	children
kleinmeid (A)	little maid
kom hierso (A)	come here
kom met my (A)	come with me
kom nou (A)	come now
leerlinge (A)	learners, pupils
maak gou (A)	hurry up
Maandag (A) Labobedi (T) etc	Monday, Tuesday etc
Maburu (T)	Boers, white people
meneer (A)	mister
mevrou (A)	mistress
mme (T)	mother, also as term of respect
moenie bang word nie (A)	don't be scared
moenie praat so nie (A)	don't talk like that
mooi (A)	nice, pretty
'n waar Boer sal hom moer (A)	a true Boer will kill him
nè (A)	is it not? yes?
nee (A)	no
niks (A)	nothing
nngwê, pêdi, tharô, nnê, thlano (T)	one, two, three, four, five
o rata ho kgomotswa ke Mme (T)	he want's a woman's touch
onderwysers (A)	teachers
ons Boere is wettig (A)	we Boers are lawful
ons moet binne gaan (A)	we must go inside
ons wag vir jou (A)	we're waiting for you
ou (A)	guy, old pal
pikkenien (A)	derogatory term for a small black child
praat met my (A)	talk with me
prinsipaal (A)	principal
re a lêboga (T)	thank you
rra (T)	term of respect, literally 'father'
sies (A)	for shame!
skat (A)	dear, darling
thatharo (T)	six
tla kwane (T)	come
totsiens (A)	good-bye
waar is...? (A)	where is...?
wat makeer? (A)	what's happening?

Playwright's Note

I based the play on my observations of the interaction between real people in Durban. I believe there is much to be admired in our evolving democracy, but that true reconciliation between our different cultural denominations requires a deeper and more honest process than what has been forthcoming thus far. People of all races, particularly those in power, present a false image in the media and reflect their true fears and prejudices in their living rooms. I wanted to expose this facade and explore South Africa's increasing shift from a pure race-based struggle to a class-based struggle.

To House is about the connections and conflicts between four characters who live in a sectional titles scheme. Sibusiso and Kajol are a young couple who face an unexpected conflict due to the ill-treatment of Kajol's mother by her extended family. Matters are complicated by Sibusiso's increasing desire for independence and the manipulative intentions of Kajol's machiavellian uncle, Deena. The parallel story of Jason and Sanjay's convenient association with each other revolves around their attempt to destroy Sibusiso's increasing stronghold over the sectional titles scheme and the law department in which Sibusiso and Sanjay work.

In essence, the play acknowledges the continuing divisions between the races in South Africa, whilst exploring an increasing shift towards a class-based conflict. The play is also about the various manifestations of power and the instinct of territoriality but it's not without hope as some characters begin to connect on a deeper level.

The PANSA Playreading Festival is South Africa's foremost play-writing contest, held annually since 2002. I entered *To House* in the 2003 contest, where it was selected as a finalist. I then staged it in Durban, my hometown, at the Catalina Theatre, where it was well-received by the audience and critics. It was particularly gratifying to receive insightful feedback from drama honours students from our local university on opening night. This year's PANSA Playreading festival is the biggest yet, due to massive funding from the National Lottery and increased media support. My new play, *Duped*, a satire on contemporary South Africa, has just been selected as a finalist.

Ashwin Singh

TO HOUSE

Ashwin Singh

First performed at the Catalina Theatre, Durban in 2005, directed by
Ashwin Singh. Designed by Shantal Singh and Ashwin Singh.

CHARACTERS

JASON – a White former businessman, early 40s   Michael Gritten
SIBUSISO – a Black law lecturer, late 20s   Teboho Hlahane
SANJAY – an Indian law lecturer, early 30s   Koobeshen Naidoo
KAJOL – Sibusiso's live-in girlfriend,
    an Indian marketing officer mid-20s   Jayloshini Naidoo
DEENA – Kajol's uncle, a successful entrepreneur,
    early 50s   Afzal Khan
NIMROD – Voice only – Gardener

Setting
Oaklands, a sectional titles scheme, in a middle-class post-Apartheid
suburb. The action takes place in two lounges (which are almost
identical in terms of furniture and styling) and the park opposite the
sectional titles scheme. One set should be used to represent the two
lounges with the coffee table being removed and replaced for the
relevant scenes. The lounge setting will occupy the bulk of the stage.
The common furniture includes a recliner, a two-seater couch, a
sidetable and a drinks table. The park design, which consists of a park
bench and a fir tree, occupies the far right stage.

SCENE 1
*The lounge-room in Jason's cottage. The lounge-room contains a
two-seater couch, a recliner, a coffee table, a side table and a small
drinks table.*

Lights come up on Jason standing next to the recliner. Jason covers the recliner. He is interrupted by a cellphone ring after one minute. Jason answers the telephone.

JASON   Hello. Yes. She can't come? But the chair is waiting for her. Who is this? She said she would come at eleven. *(pause. Sarcastically)* Oh, that's great. *(pause)* No, I won't be here tomorrow. Tell her to phone me on Monday. *(he hangs up)* Fucking bitch. *(Jason walks across stage uneasily, then picks up the phone and dials Joe)* Joe. It's Jason here. Well thanks. Listen, it's a beautiful day. Why don't we go for a stroll on the beach after lunch? Sanjay is coming for lunch. What do you mean, again? He makes delicious food. That's why I need a stroll after that. Oh. Ja. So you're going there. Well, another time then. We must talk man. You know, we live in the same complex, but we hardly seem to chat these days. No, sure. I realise you're busy. Alright then. Take care.

Jason ends the call and looks concerned. He begins pacing again, looking impatiently at his watch. He walks to the window, looks out and notices a gardener called Nimrod. Nimrod will remain off-stage during his conversation with Jason.

JASON   Hey umfaan. Hey Nimrod! You saw Justus today? Mildred told me someone hit him yesterday evening. Did you see him this morning?
NIMROD   Ja.
JASON   Is he OK?
NIMROD   No. His hand is hurt. I think it's broken, maybe.
JASON   Did he go to the doctor?
NIMROD   Ai. I think he's resting. Maybe he'll go later.
JASON   Tell him he must go to the doctor. Tell him, er ... Tell him, if he hasn't got money, he must come see me on Monday. I'll take him to the doctor.
NIMROD   Alright baas.
JASON   Did he tell you who hit him?
NIMROD   No. He said he was Indian. But I don't know if he knows him. Maybe ... maybe he's scared.

JASON   He must tell me who. I don't care if he's Indian. Whatever. I'll sort him out. Nobody assaults my boy.

NIMROD   Ja baas.

Jason is about to close the window but pauses and notices something.

JASON   What's this Khumalo? More furniture? Hey, that looks exactly like my recliner. You fucking copycat. Hey Nimrod. Did you see how boss Khumalo is trying to copy boss Jason's lounge.

NIMROD   Ja baas. Because your house is too beautiful. That's why he's copying you.

JASON   Thanks Nimrod. Hey. Be careful you don't cut your boss's petunias. You nearly cut it now. Ja. *(Jason goes to the recliner and removes the covers. He sits on it and speaks to the audience)* Enjoy your new seat of power, Mr Khumalo. I'll have my final say before I hand over chairmanship of the body corporate. Oaklands will be the way it was again.

Blackout.

SCENE 2

The park opposite Oaklands. Lights come up on Sanjay sitting on the park bench. Sanjay is sitting alone on the park bench, looking around uneasily. He is thinking, uncomfortably, about something. He notices something on the grass, looks around carefully, picks it up and hurriedly puts it in his pocket. He stares ahead, pensively, for a few seconds. Then he takes out his cell phone and dials his mother. His facial expression indicates disappointment as he has received her answering-machine.

SANJAY   Hello Ma. I guess you left early for your meeting. I woke up early today, and I finished prepare lunch. I made your favourite. Anyway, I wanted to ask you to find out about the er, takeaway thing, before you came over. I need to move on that. Er, Jenkins phoned me this morning. He said he overheard Prof. say that they're bringing in a professor from Ghana, to lecture criminal law next year. It must be Sibu's influence. I'm worried about my job, Ma. *(short pause. Then Sanjay speaks at a hurried pace)* Anyway Ma, please ask Beena if her husband can confirm that he's selling his property. It's the ideal location for the takeaway. And find out how much he wants. Thanks, Ma. See you later.

He ends the call, puts his phone away and lights a cigarette. After a few seconds Kajol enters. She notices Sanjay and stops.

KAJOL   Hi Sanjay. *(Sanjay stands up enthusiastically)*

SANJAY   Hello Kajol. How are you?

KAJOL   Fine. How are you?

SANJAY   Well, thanks. Did you work today?

KAJOL   Yes. I had a presentation at the Thekweni Centre.

SANJAY   How did it go?

KAJOL   Very well. How was your trip?

SANJAY   Very productive. I have some interesting information for my article with Sibu. Actually, I was about to come see him now.

KAJOL   Oh, no, don't come right now. He'll be in the middle of his Saturday morning African music ritual. He doesn't like to be disturbed.

SANJAY   Oh.

KAJOL   Ja, but come over in about an hour. I know your article is important.

SANJAY   It is.

KAJOL   Sibu was telling me that your department is going to be doing some exciting projects next year.

SANJAY *(awkward)* Oh, er ja. We have to write this article first though. I haven't been published this year. Got to get published you know. Or else.

KAJOL   I guess academic life has more pressures than people realize, hey?

SANJAY   It does. *(softly)* For some of us. Er, how's your Ma?

KAJOL   Er, not well. My brother ... *(fades off)* You know, he's irresponsible sometimes.

SANJAY *(concerned)* Is there anything I can do?

KAJOL   No, it's OK. I'll sort it out. Thanks Sanjay. Well, I'll see you later.

SANJAY   Er, you'll be at yoga class on Thursday?

KAJOL   I might not make it this week, Sanjay. I have a meeting and I don't know how long it's going to last.

SANJAY *(disappointed)* Oh, that's a pity. The Swami is coming this
week.
KAJOL Oh, that's disappointing.
SANJAY Well, he's down for a couple of weeks. Maybe, you and I
can take him out for lunch?
KAJOL Er, ja, maybe. I'll let you know. OK then. *(she turns to
go, then stops and turns back)* Welcome back, Sanjay. Thursday
evenings weren't the same without you.

Sanjay smiles.

Blackout.

SCENE 3
*The lounge-room in Sibusiso's cottage. Lights come up on Sibusiso
doing a little jig. Sibusiso, after some dancing and shadow-boxing sits
on his new recliner. His lounge is exactly like Jason's except that he
does not have a coffee table. He stares into space, a contented smile on
his face.*

SIBUSISO Woh! This chair is so good. *(he leans back in the chair,
then picks up his mother's photograph from the side table and looks
at it fondly)* Look at me now, Mama. This is all mine. Just like you
said. I remember, Mama, when Thabo and I were students at the
varsity. We would walk down this street sometimes. And I would say
to him. Thabo, when they make me a lecturer I'm going to get that
blue cottage. And for you. The pink one next to it. *(pause)* I wish you
were here, Mama. I wish you could have put your feet up like this.
After cooking all day for that bastard. *(he kisses the photograph and
leaves it on the side table again. He reclines further and closes his
eyes. Then he moves forward and slowly gets up. He looks at the
chair, then looks at his watch and strolls to the window. He looks
out for a few seconds, then notices Nimrod. Nimrod remains off-
stage as before)* Hey Nimrod. Did you come through Parklands
Road today?
NIMROD Ja, Sibu.
SIBUSISO What are the squatters doing? Is it quiet?
NIMROD No. They are fighting.

SIBUSISO   Fighting?

NIMROD   Ja.

SIBUSISO *(looking at audience)* I must go there later. *(back through the window)* Sharp Nimrod. *(about to close the window, then notices something)* Hey Nimrod. What are you doing? You are cutting the flowers. Be careful.

NIMROD   Sorry, Sibu.

SIBUSISO   Sharp. *(he closes the window and walks back to his chair. Kajol enters in a huff. She looks at him, half-smiling)* So? How did your presentation go?

KAJOL   Very well.

SIBUSISO   So? Did you, hey? Did you get the contract?

KAJOL   Yes. *(Sibusiso is happy. He hugs Kajol affectionately)*

SIBUSISO   Good job. So you are going to get the promotion now?

KAJOL   Er, most probably.

SIBUSISO   We must celebrate. Let's go to ... No. I will make supper. A curry.

KAJOL   Wow. I'll take out my apron just in case.

SIBUSISO   No, I'll do it. Just for you.

KAJOL   Oh, thank you darling. *(she kisses him gently)* What are you going to have for lunch?

SIBUSISO   No, I'm not hungry. *(she lets go of him)* Where are you rushing?

KAJOL   I have to go and make lunch for my Ma.

SIBUSISO   Why?

KAJOL   Because dear brother and his porcelain wife have gone out for the day. And left Ma alone. Without any food. Sheila, their neighbour, said she found her on the floor drooling.

SIBUSISO   Aw, that's bad.

KAJOL   I'm sick of them. Last week that bitch swore at my Ma and threatened to put her in an old age home. Last month they dumped her at Uncle Deena's for a week because her flippin' cousins came to stay. Ma should never have given him the house. It just took him a few months to ... I want to just ...

SIBUSISO   Take it easy, baby. C'mon, this is your day. It will get sorted.

KAJOL   No, it won't. *(she exits to fetch something and returns with a few cans of food. She looks at the recliner)* So you bought a new chair.

SIBUSISO Yes. For me to relax in the evening. Smoke my pipe. *(Kajol frowns)* You don't like it.

KAJOL Can we afford it?

SIBUSISO I can afford it. Eh, look its very well-made. It's genuine leather.

KAJOL In the three months we've lived together Sibu, you've bought a new TV, DVD, countless software, and now a recliner. I've bought nothing.

SIBUSISO Hey, I need these things. We both use them.

KAJOL Never mind. You now have a lounge which is almost identical to Jason's.

SIBUSISO He's got good taste.

KAJOL When are you buying his coffee table?

SIBUSISO Aish Kajol. We said I must decorate the house.

KAJOL Whatever. I have to go. I'll be a little while. I'm going to pick up Aunty Savy and leave her with Ma. See you later. Oh, I forgot to tell you. Kevin may be coming later.

SIBUSISO Again. He just came on Thursday.

KAJOL He wanted some legal advice.

SIBUSISO It's Saturday, Kajol. Is his whole family coming too? His little son as well? So he can shit on my new carpet again? *(Kajol is dismayed)*

KAJOL OK Sibu, I'll tell him not to come.

SIBUSISO No Kajol, you see, you know your cousins are always coming here. Whenever they feel like it. They don't even phone.

KAJOL They like you. Aren't you glad they're not like Uncle Deena?

SIBUSISO Ja, but eh, you see today is for us to celebrate. Just us.

KAJOL I know. I know. I'll tell him.

SIBUSISO Tell him to phone me on Monday.

KAJOL OK. See you later darling.

SIBUSISO Give your mum my regards. Tell her she's in my prayers.

KAJOL Do you want to come with me?

SIBUSISO No, I can't. I want to do some work on my article. And I have to prepare supper. I want my curry to be just right for you.

Blackout.

SCENE 4
Sibusiso's lounge. Lights come up when Sibusiso is standing on-stage.

SIBUSISO   Ai, fuck it. I can't do this shit. *(he grabs his cellphone and dials)* Hello. Bobby. How are you, my man? Sharp. Listen, my friend. I need you to make your special fish curry for me. *(pause).* Just me and Kajol. Ja. The other curry. The one she didn't taste. Ja. *(pause. Irritated)* No, it's not the last supper. *(pause)* I'm going to speak to her. I ... I don't know when. Just make my food. *(pause)*

Doorbell Rings.

SIBUSISO   One hour. OK. Sharp.

Doorbell Rings.

SIBUSISO   Sanjay.
SANJAY   Hello Sibusiso.
SIBUSISO   When did you get back?
SANJAY   Yesterday afternoon.
SIBUSISO   I thought you were coming on Monday.
SANJAY   I finished early. My interviews went very well.
SIBUSISO   Working hard, heh?
SANJAY   Yes. Can I come – ?
SIBUSISO   Yes. Come in. *(they enter the lounge)* What's that? *(he points to the parcel Sanjay is carrying)*
SANJAY   Just some kebabs and roti. *(he hands it to Sibusiso)* For you and Kajol.
SIBUSISO   Thank you, my man. Take a seat. *(Sibusiso exits with the parcel. Sanjay remains standing and looks at the recliner. Sibusiso re-enters)*
SANJAY   You bought a new chair.
SIBUSISO   Yes.
SANJAY   It's just like Jason's. *(pause)* Your lounge is identical to Jason's.
SIBUSISO   Not identical.
SANJAY   Yes, it is. Except for the coffee table.
SIBUSISO   Your friend has got good taste.

SANJAY My friend?

SIBUSISO Yes. *(awkward pause)* Is that your research? *(he points to a large file which Sanjay is carrying)*

SANJAY Yes. Transcripts of the interviews. Prof. van Rensburg's articles. And my analysis. *(he hands the file to Sibusiso but Sibusiso doesn't take it)*

SIBUSISO Sanjay. Eh, I'm not going to write the article with you.

SANJAY *(disturbed)* What? Why not?

SIBUSISO Because I'm writing the article with Prof. Hamilton. And not now. I'm working on an article about the squatters in Parklands Road now. You know that park is pathetic. And nobody is taking care of it. Nobody uses it. They come to our park. The government promised ...

SANJAY *(upset)* I don't care. This was supposed to be my holiday. And I spent it on research in Jo'burg for the department. So that you and I could ...

SIBUSISO Yes. And it's good for the department. But you must write the article yourself. Prof and I ... we are going to take a different angle ...

SANJAY Different angle?

SIBUSISO Yes.

SANJAY What angle?

SIBUSISO We are not going to talk about it now. In the meantime, you write this ...

SANJAY Oh, and you think they're going to publish my article without your name on it?

SIBUSISO You have published other articles.

SANJAY Ja, but suddenly Hamilton has major problems with my articles. Besides, everybody knows that very few Indian academics are getting published in the law journal these days. Sibu, you know Hamilton is watching me. If I don't publish this year ... they're trying to push me out.

SIBUSISO That's nonsense.

SANJAY Is it?

SIBUSISO Listen, Sanjay, I'm very interested in researching white-collar crime. But I don't want to write the article right now. Last week one of the firms I was researching called me and said they want me to do some ethics workshops for their employees.

SANJAY   Ethics workshops?

SIBUSISO   Yes. Quite a few of their employees committed theft and fraud against the company recently. So they want me to help with their new ethics programme. You know most of these companies don't charge their workers because of bad publicity. They just dismiss them.

SANJAY *(envious)* Which company wants to hire you?

SIBUSISO   Eh, *Superview Real Estate.*

SANJAY   That's Jason's former company.

SIBUSISO   Yes.

SANJAY   Anyway, this won't take up much time.

SIBUSISO   If you want to do it right, it will. Anyway, I've also got the new module on human rights law to lecture.

SANJAY   Human rights law? Prof told me I was going to lecture that module.

SIBUSISO   What do you know about human rights?

SANJAY *(angry)* What do I know about human rights? You think because you are Black that only you can teach human rights?

SIBUSISO   No, I think because I am an expert that I can teach human rights. I'm a qualified lawyer. You are not.

SANJAY   You know what I think? I think you wanted to get rid of me for a couple of weeks. That's all you need. So you can curry favour with Professor Hamilton. Suck up to the big White professor. Get rid of the charou. Like they're doing all over campus.

SIBUSISO   You are mad.

SANJAY *(angry)* I am mad! You are playing games with me, Mr Khumalo. I can see right through you. You're all the same. Ntuli tried the same thing before he left for Wits. And now …

SIBUSISO *(angry)* I am not Ntuli. Ntuli went to private school. His father was a doctor. I stayed in Ntuzuma!

SANJAY   Here we go. I don't care. You are a liar.

SIBUSISO   I am a Christian. I don't lie.

SANJAY   So what if you are Christian? I'm a Hindu. You think Hindus are liars?

SIBUSISO *(menacing)* You listen now, little man. You get out of my house. I will see you in Prof's office on Monday. Let's see what he says. *(Sanjay withdraws, then stops and turns back slowly)*

SANJAY *(reconciliatory)* Look Sibu, I ... I don't want to cause trouble in the department. But I ... you know I worked hard on this article.

SIBUSISO   So write it yourself.

SANJAY   Y ... yes. I will – I – we are teachers, Sibu. And researchers. We are supposed to be shaping young minds.

SIBUSISO   That's what I'm trying to do.

SANJAY   So am I. I've worked damn hard without recognition.

SIBUSISO   You've worked hard! I work eighteen hours a day. While you sit in the canteen talking about your favourite food with students, I'm slogging in my office, or my study.

SANJAY   You're saying I'm not committed Sibu?

SIBUSISO   I'm saying ... I'm saying you don't have to give everything because if things don't work out for you, some uncle of yours somewhere, will let you run his shop. *(Sanjay shakes his head sadly)*

SANJAY   You should share your views about Indian uncles with Kajol. The Indians in TV commercials are not my relatives, Mr Khumalo.

Sanjay exits slowly. Sibusiso looks at him awkwardly.

Blackout.

SCENE 5
Jason's lounge. Lights come up on Jason sitting on the couch. He is staring into space, looking miserable. Sanjay enters and quietly creeps up behind Jason, without being noticed. Slowly, he reaches up to Jason's mouth and places a samosa before it. Jason bites it slowly and closes his eyes in ecstasy.

JASON   Hmm. Woh. Hmm. So good. *(Sanjay comes around and hands Jason a roti. Jason takes it slowly and tucks into it)* Hmm. Delicious. *(Sanjay sits down, puts his food parcel on the coffee table and starts eating a roti. The two continue eating for several seconds, looking straight ahead and occasionally expressing low moans. Then Jason gets up and pours some whiskey. He hands Sanjay a glass)*

SANJAY   *Johnny Walker Black.*

JASON   The best food deserves the best drink. Sorry, I drank half of it yesterday. *(they toast and slowly sip the whiskey, smiling in approval. Jason eats some more roti)* This is the best roti and kebab I've ever tasted, Sanjay.

SANJAY   Wait till you taste my new sweetcorn samosas.

JASON   Is it ...? *(he points to the parcel. Sanjay nods)* You spoil me, Sanjay. Look at all this variety. You've outdone yourself today. What's the occasion? Is it a special lunch with your mum?

SANJAY   No, I was just in the mood today. *(pause)*

JASON   Why didn't you come over last night?

SANJAY   I just wanted to finish the last bit of work I had.

JASON   Was Khumalo impressed?

SANJAY   He doesn't want to do it. He's doing another article with the H.O.D.

JASON   What's your article about?

SANJAY   White-collar crime.

JASON *(concerned)* I heard from an old mate from *Superview*, that a Sibusiso Khumalo was doing some research for them. *(short pause)* It's him, isn't it?

SANJAY   Yes. He's doing some ethics workshops. *(Jason turns away for a second and then turns back angrily)*

JASON   That's typical of *Superview*. They hire another Black consultant to do some meaningless presentations, but they have no support for their staff. How did Khumalo worm his way in there?

SANJAY   Sibusiso has his fingers in many pies. He's on a high now. And he's about to make his big move at varsity.

JASON   Well, it's time for our counter-move.

Sanjay's cellphone rings.

SANJAY   Hello Ma. Are you on your way? *(pause. Sanjay is disappointed)* Not coming? What's wrong? *(pause)* Oh. Ja. OK. You rest then. Ma, you must take it easy. All these activities are draining you out. *(pause)* Yes, Ajith brought the file. Why does Aunty Nimi do these things? I don't want her to find me a wife. I don't want a wife. *(pause)* No, I'm not interested in her. No. Alright Ma, you take it easy. I'll see you at Rita's tomorrow. Or maybe if you're feeling better you can join me for supper. Bye bye, Ma.

JASON   Women trouble again, Sanjay?

SANJAY   It's my aunt. She wants another City Hall wedding-and-all jol. To give her something to do. *(Jason chuckles. Short pause)*

JASON   But isn't it time you found a nice Hindu girl Sanjay? Settled down.

SANJAY   No thanks. I prefer being unsettled. Anyway, it's difficult to think about a family if you're not going to be employed for much longer.

JASON   What?

SANJAY   My contract ends this year. I don't think I'm going to get a new one.

JASON   It can't be that bad. You've been there a while now.

SANJAY   I don't know. I've heard rumours. And Jenkins phoned me this morning. He said he overheard the H.O.D say that he's going to get a Prof from Ghana to lecture my course next year.

JASON   Shit. Another Black foreigner. Coming to find the African renaissance.

SANJAY   I know one thing. He won't see the spark I see in my students' eyes when I lecture to them. *(pause)*

JASON   So your Ma can't make it for lunch?

SANJAY   No. I prepared all that food.

JASON   Well, why don't you spend the afternoon here? We can watch the cricket match.

SANJAY *(somewhat reluctantly)* Er, alright. *(pause)* There is something I wanted to talk to you about.

JASON   Oh ja, what's that?

SANJAY   I'll tell you later. Firstly, tell me how the body corporate meeting went last week.

JASON   It was a disaster. I wish you'd have been here to support me.

SANJAY   What happened?

JASON   Well, firstly Derek asked if we could extend the parking lot. I said no. But Khumalo said we should. And then Mr. Anderson announced that he was leaving next month. And Khumalo said that one of his friends, some Themba or Thabo or something was willing to buy his place. And you know what? Our neighbours were delighted. I mean for real, delighted.

SANJAY   Well, you know they're always being PC when he's around.

JASON   No Sanjay. They meant it. Khumalo's got them on a leash. They laugh at every stupid joke he tells. Joe nearly cracked his ribs laughing at some dumb story. And when he speaks about legal matters, they hang on to his every word. I don't know how exactly but he's wormed his way into their lives, in such a short time.

SANJAY   He knows how to play the mob.

JASON *(surprised, perturbed)* What?

SANJAY   I mean, he plays the race card cleverly. And he is a good lawyer. *(tentative)* I'll give him that.

JASON   Yeah, good lawyer. Good lover too.

SANJAY   What?

JASON   I caught a glimpse of his other talents last week.

SANJAY   What do you mean?

JASON   They were doing it on the lawn?

SANJAY *(tentatively)* Are you serious?

JASON   Not really. But they might as well have been. Rolling on the lawn like fucking drunken teenagers. He was shirtless. She's fucking shameless.

SANJAY   You must bring this up at the next body corporate meeting.

JASON   Ja, that's the one where we're electing our new chairman. If we don't stop it, I think it will be an AA candidate. So, are you with me?

SANJAY   Yes.

JASON   Are you sure? No second thoughts anymore?

SANJAY   No. I've had enough. It's time we showed the world who Sibusiso Khumalo really is.

JASON   Good. I knew you'd eventually be convinced. I mean, after all, you brought him here.

SANJAY   I did not bring him here.

JASON   You invited him to your place.

SANJAY   He invited himself. I mean, he seemed OK then. He wanted to have a drink. He found out himself that there was a vacancy here.

JASON   And moved in with his hot Indian chic.

SANJAY   That makes no difference.

JASON   Doesn't it?

SANJAY   No. But, I don't think your plan will work. We need to approach it from a different angle.

JASON   Different angle. What angle?

SANJAY   I have to think about ...

JASON   Listen Sanjay. Based on what I've observed of him, and what you've said about him, this is the best way.

SANJAY   But Jason ...

JASON   Anyway, it doesn't matter. The ball is rolling Sanjay. My little niece has been doing her thing. You know she was reluctant at first, but she spoke to him a couple of weeks ago, and she's quite keen now. Must have seen what an arrogant shit he is.

SANJAY *(tentative)* Ja. What did he say?

JASON   Well, he's agreed to be her supervisor on her commercial law project.

SANJAY   Wouldn't it look strange, Jason? I mean, she's a B. Comm. student. She's doing one law course. He doesn't even teach commercial law.

JASON   No, but she spoke to your H.O.D. He recommended Mr Khumalo. He's such a bright young lecturer. *(Sanjay shakes his head)*

SANJAY   I don't think...

JASON   She told me he flirted with her last week in the canteen. And two lecturers saw it.

SANJAY   Really? He flirted with ...

JASON   Yes. Why are you surprised? You told me he flirts with all the pretty girls.

SANJAY   Ja, but he's normally discreet, you know. And it's usually with the Black girls.

JASON   You don't think he'd prefer some white skin? He can't resist Catherine's sexy arse. You've seen her Sanjay. She's stunning. *(Sanjay pictures her in his mind and nods slowly)*

SANJAY   Yes.

JASON   So he asked her out for a drink next week.

SANJAY *(surprised)* He did?

JASON   Yes. And you and what's that guy's name in your department who doesn't like him? You mentioned him earlier.

SANJAY   Jenkins.

JASON   You'll just happen to be having a drink at *Grazers* as well.

SANJAY   Look, you haven't told your niece that I might be involved, have you?

JASON   No, no. It must all look natural.

SANJAY   Good. And then what?

JASON   In a couple of weeks, she'll invite him over to her house. I will have taken my sister-in-law out for lunch. And then we'll barge in on them in a compromising position. She'll start screaming. She'll break down.

SANJAY   She's not going to go all the way, is she?

JASON   No. Just enough to slap a sexual harassment suit on him.

(Sanjay thinks deeply)

SANJAY   No, it won't work. He won't go to her place.

JASON   Sanjay, he will. Black men fantasise about White women.

SANJAY   Really? I thought it was the other way around.

JASON   Don't talk shit! What's wrong with you? I'm being serious.

SANJAY   Alright. Alright. *(short pause)* Surely, the department won't be able to cover up two disasters by their high profile Black lecturers. Ntuli got away with his drinking problem.

JASON   Khumalo won't. My brother will bring down the department to see justice for his princess. *(pause)* You'll be rid of him. And he'll have to fuck off from here.

SANJAY   Yes.

JASON   We'll have our haven back.

SANJAY   Yes.

JASON   There's just one thing, Sanjay.

SANJAY   What?

JASON   Catherine wants five hundred rand.

SANJAY   What? Listen, listen. Just wait a minute. At first you told me that your niece would do this because she would do anything for you. Then you said that if she didn't go through with it, you threatened to tell her father about her Coloured boyfriend. Now she wants five hundred rand. What next? A thousand rand? And then ...?

JASON   No. She won't want more. She needs five hundred rand only. Come on, Sanjay. We need her.

SANJAY   What does she need the money for?

JASON   I don't know. Look, I've got things under control.

SANJAY   We can't trust her.

JASON *(angry)* Fuck, Sanjay. She's my niece. We can trust her. Look, don't give up on me now. Your evidence will be important. Shit, Sanjay. Remember, this is not Gcbobani from up the road. This guy strutted in here with his Indian chic on his arm. From day one he's been carrying on like he's chief of this tribe. Come on, Sanjay. All we have to do is give him the opportunity to screw himself.

SANJAY   So you're going to give her the money?

JASON *(awkwardly)* I'm a little short on cash. I gave her two hundred rand ... I need ... can you spare some?

SANJAY   We'll give it to her after she does her job.

JASON   She wants it now, Sanjay.

SANJAY   Alright. I'll give it to you tomorrow.

JASON   Thanks, Sanjay. Good man. *(he shakes his hand)* Let's have another drink. And more of your delicious rotis.

Blackout.

SCENE 6

Jason's lounge. Lights come up. Jason is facing the audience. He is holding a glass in his hand, staring out of the window. After a few seconds, Sanjay enters.

SANJAY   Why did you put the TV off? The game is about to start.

JASON   Rained off.

SANJAY *(disappointed)* Oh, shit.

JASON   We would've lost anyway. It's Australia.

SANJAY   I think we could have done it today.

JASON   Yeah, right. *(pause. Sanjay sits down. Both men are silent for a while)*

SANJAY   I think I'll phone my Ma. See if she wants to come over for supper.

JASON   Oh. But ... well, why don't you stay a bit? You can call her later.

SANJAY   You don't have any plans?

JASON *(dejected)* Plans? I saw Derek and Paul packing some fishing gear earlier. They must have gone to Scottburgh. I don't know. Maybe they thought I was going out.

SANJAY *(awkward)* Oh.

JASON   Have another drink. *(Sanjay pours another drink)*

SANJAY   Two singles left.

JASON   I'll get another bottle.

SANJAY   What's your brother up to today? You know, I haven't seen him here for a while.

JASON   He's been very busy with work lately. Got to stay one step ahead of the Black pack. *(he peers through the window)*

SANJAY   What are you looking at?

JASON *(awkward)* Nothing. Look at that. Bloody idiots! They behave like adolescents. Khumalo and his spice girl. *(short pause)* Hey, Sanjay?

SANJAY   Maybe that's what young couples do sometimes, Jason.

JASON   Oh ja. What would you know about it?

SANJAY   More than you … *(he fades off, regretting his statement. Jason looks back through the window. Silence for a few seconds. Then Jason becomes excited)*

JASON   Hey. I don't believe it. They're … they're going to do it on their swing. *(Sanjay stands up, looking agitated)* Yeah. They're going to. Good Heavens! Look at the size of his … *(Sanjay leaps towards Jason but Jason pushes him away)* No. Look away! Look away! You'll hurt your eyes.

SANJAY   How could she be so uncouth? I can't believe it. She wouldn't. Let me see. *(he pushes Jason aside)* What? Where did they go?

JASON   Relax. I was just joking. They're inside.

SANJAY *(irritated)* Why did you do that?

JASON   Relax. I just wanted to see that look on your face.

SANJAY   Oh ja. You did. You like toying with me about Kajol, but I've seen the way you look at her.

JASON   What?

SANJAY   It's not a friendly neighbour's look.

JASON   Well, I'm not the one fucking her everyday.

SANJAY   Why do you have to use that word?

JASON   What word? Fucking? Hey Sanjay. Come on. When last did you have it, bru?

SANJAY   When last did *you* have it? *(Jason is hurt. He sits down slowly. Pause)* How is your wife? *(Jason stares at Sanjay)* No, seriously, Jason. Did you hear from her?

JASON *(bitter)* She's shacked up with her stud. And she's trying to take me to the fucking cleaners. She wants that chair now. She did buy it. But she's ... she's just being fucking petty.

SANJAY   You know, Sibusiso bought that exact same chair.

JASON *(sniggering)* Ja. I saw it arrive. *(pause)*

SANJAY   So Angela's being difficult?

JASON   Fuck. Sanjay, this divorce is going to cost me a shit load.

SANJAY   You shouldn't have gone for accrual.

JASON   She didn't even leave me a legacy. You know, she didn't want to have children. Useless bitch. *(he stands up wildly to get the food parcel, but slips on a saucer on the floor and falls awkwardly on his knee)* Aaah! *(Sanjay offers to help him up)* Don't touch me. Get away.

SANJAY   Your knee ...

JASON   I'm fine. *(he gets up slowly)* Why'd you leave a fucking saucer on the floor?

SANJAY   I didn't. You did. *(Jason feels foolish)*

JASON   Sorry. *(he leaves the food parcel and pours another drink)*

SANJAY   Did you hear from Derek about the job offer he was talking about?

JASON   Ja. The salary is not good enough. But there is something on the cards.

SANJAY *(tentative)* Oh ja. What's that?

JASON   I met this guy about a year ago. Got him a good deal on some property. A couple of months ago he told me he's thinking about expanding – starting another factory, and I could manage it for him. Well, last week he phoned me and said he was going ahead. And I should get ready.

SANJAY *(somewhat concerned)* Oh, good. What factory is it?

JASON   A fabric factory.

SANJAY   Hmm. Who's the guy?

JASON   Just a guy, Sanjay. A successful entrepreneur. You won't know him.

SANJAY *(softly)* Well, good luck.

JASON   Yeah, I need some luck. Forty-two and jobless. *(he raises his glass)* To better times.

SANJAY   To better times. *(he raises his glass)* For both of us. *(short pause)* Try this mince samosa.

JASON   Shit. Sanjay these samosas are fantastic.

SANJAY   It's my mother's special recipe.

JASON   You know, last week I felt for some samosas. So I went down to *Bobby's*. Hey. Very disappointing. Oily. And too crisp. Can't compare to yours.

SANJAY   Bobby is an amateur. Someone who just inherited his father's business. He's lucky he's got so many customers. *(pause. He becomes excited)* You know Jason, there's something I really want to do. I was thinking about it in Jo'burg as well. I mean, I know you've got this factory thing, but nothing is certain, right? This is a good business proposition.

JASON   Business proposition?

SANJAY   Yes. You remember, we spoke about the takeaway a couple of months ago?

JASON *(tentatively)* Ja.

SANJAY   You said you had saved a reasonable amount. You could put that in. And you've got your retrenchment package too. And I will put in the money I've saved. And we could start a takeaway specializing in Indian food right here.

JASON *(hesitant)* J-ja.

SANJAY   I mean, just the people here at Oaklands will come every other day. And the others. They love Indian food.

JASON   Hmm.

SANJAY   Yes. This is Durban. And the closest place they've got is *Bobby's*. In the CBD. I know someone who wants to sell his tearoom just a couple of miles from here. I'm telling you Jason. We should go for it.

JASON   Ja, but Sanjay I've got to see how much my divorce is going to cost. And partnership. Well... you have to be certain before you commit yourself to a partnership. I don't even know anything about your business acumen. *(Sanjay is rueful)*

SANJAY   Well, it's just something to think about.

JASON   We need another ...

SANJAY   What are you going to do with your money?

JASON   I told you. My divorce ...

SANJAY   Your wife is not going to get everything. You'll still have a reasonable amount left. I mean, c'mon Jason, do you really want to work for someone else? In this climate? You might have a chance to start your own business. Right here in Oakhills.

JASON   Running a takeaway?

SANJAY   Well, the takeaway can ...

JASON   I don't want to do the takeaway. It'll be your show anyway. What will I do? Collect a cheque at the end of the month.

SANJAY   It's not just about money, Jason. It's about making a place where people come to experience something different. A really amazing Durban meal. And we'll set up some nice tables. If people want to relax and chat. The Oakhill's social meeting place.

JASON   The Oakhill's social meeting place? *(short pause)* It's your thing. You can do it yourself, Sanjay. You don't need me. But I have to say. You teach at varsity. And you want to be a shopkeeper?

SANJAY *(irritated)* Not a shopkeeper. A real businessman. With expertise in Indian cuisine.

JASON   Well, you certainly are the expert on Indian food. *(he eats another samosa)* I need a drink. Let's get another bottle. I'll order one. Sorry, I can't get another *Johnny Walker*.

SANJAY   Order a *Bells*. I'll sort it out.

JASON   Thanks, Sanjay. *(Sanjay opens the food parcel and takes out a chilli bite)*

SANJAY   Chilli bite?

JASON   Hmm. *(Sanjay gives one to Jason)* Woh. Hot!

SANJAY   Too pungent?

JASON *(elated)* Fucking electrifying! Hmm. That's so good. Sanjay, you are a master chef.

Blackout.

SCENE 7

Sibusiso's lounge. Lights come up. Sibusiso and Kajol are seated on the couch. Sibusiso is feeding Kajol kebabs.

KAJOL   Hmm. Wow. Hmm. This is delicious Sibu.

SIBUSISO   Thank you.

KAJOL   I had no idea you could make such tasty kebabs. And roti.

SIBUSISO   I have to confess something. I didn't make the roti. They're from *Bobby's*.

KAJOL   That's OK. It's hard to make roti. I'll teach you some day.

SIBUSISO   OK.

KAJOL   I know the kebabs are not Bobby's. He doesn't make kebabs like this.

SIBUSISO   This is just for starters. When we have supper later you will taste my special fish curry.

KAJOL   Hmm. You used tamarind?

SIBUSISO   Eh, ja, yes.

KAJOL   When did you learn all this?

SIBUSISO   Eh, well, while watching you.

KAJOL   You never watch me. You just sit and wait for the table to be laid.

SIBUSISO   Aw. I have helped you. Anyway the truth is when I was with Bobby sometimes he taught me how to make curry. Mutton curry. Chicken curry. Fish too. And kebabs.

KAJOL   Well, you definitely did something different with the kebabs. It's more potent.

SIBUSISO   Oh, sorry.

KAJOL   No, I like it. You know, it's a lot like the kebabs we had at your department's law ball last month. Yes, the one's Sanjay made.

SIBUSISO   He didn't make that. His mother did.

KAJOL   No, he did. He's a very good cook.

SIBUSISO   How do you know?

KAJOL   He always gives me something nice after our yoga classes.

SIBUSISO   Oh. I think he wants to give you something more than curry.

KAJOL   What?

SIBUSISO   He's after you, that one.

KAJOL   Don't be ridiculous. He's just a sweet guy.

SIBUSISO   Ha!

KAJOL   He's nice to talk to. He makes me laugh.

SIBUSISO   You don't know him. He's a snake!

KAJOL   No. He ... Look, maybe he's tense with you because of work. I think he's intimidated by you. Because, I mean, he's been there longer than you, a few years. You are there for a year and you've sort of overtaken him in the department.

SIBUSISO   He's very envious. And I think I should be careful of him.

KAJOL   What do you mean?

SIBUSISO   Nothing. Don't worry. Eat some more.

Kajol's cellphone rings.

KAJOL   Hello. Hi Nirej. Fine. *(pause. She looks at Sibusiso)* Er,
not today Nirej. Maybe next week sometime. OK. Take care. Bye.
(ends call) Nirej wanted to come over. *(Sibusiso shakes his head)*
SIBUSISO *(irritated)* And you told him next week.
KAJOL   Yes.
SIBUSISO   Let me tell you something, Kajol. I don't like Nirej. All
he does is drink and talk about horse racing. Hey. Don't these
people have things to do on weekends?
KAJOL   They like visiting people.
SIBUSISO   Well, you have a big family. They must visit other people.
KAJOL   Sibu, it's not like my entire family comes here. A lot of
them think it's disgusting for me to be living in sin with a Black
man. At least some of my cousins approve.
SIBUSISO   Why does that matter so much to you?
KAJOL   Because all my life people like Uncle Deena told me
never to go near the big, bad Black man. *(short pause)* At least my
cousins are supportive. And my Ma.
SIBUSISO   And if they weren't? Would it make a difference?
KAJOL   No, I mean … I would still have moved in with you. But
I'm glad they approve. It's good to have family support. I mean, I'm
sure you wish your sisters didn't move to Jo'burg. *(quieter)* And things
were OK with your brother. *(Sibusiso looks away, awkwardly)* I
mean, look at today, with my Ma. If my cousins had not rallied around
me, I don't think my brother would have been so pacified.
SIBUSISO   Well I'm happy that things are sorted with your mother.
KAJOL   Sibu. I told you they're not sorted. This weekend is
sorted. Monday it will …
SIBUSISO   It will get better. I'm going to pray for her. *(Kajol smiles
and touches his hand)* Let's have some wine. *(he stands up and
pours some wine. Kajol sits on the recliner)* No more about your
mother now. Just be selfish today. It's your day. Next week you'll be
Senior Marketing Officer. No more orders from Devan. And more
money too.
KAJOL   Well, I should get the promotion.
SIBUSISO   You must get the promotion. This is the thing with
Indian firms. They make false promises. I know. I worked for an

Indian firm when I was serving my articles. But they have to promote you. What else do you have to do?

KAJOL   Yes, I have earned my promotion.

SIBUSISO   So they better do it. Or they will hear from me. As a lawyer. *(he toasts to Kajol)* To you. Beautiful, intelligent and talented Kajol.

They sip, then Kajol kisses him. He does a short dance with Kajol, strolling towards the window. He tosses her back and then nearly drops her as he waves to somebody through the window.

KAJOL   Oops. Who's that?

SIBUSISO   It's Simons. I think he wants to talk to me.

KAJOL   Why does he peer through the window? We have a door. Is he hoping to see something?

SIBUSISO   Let me see what he wants. *(he exits. Kajol has some wine. He re-enters after a few seconds)* He wanted some legal advice.

KAJOL *(irritated)* What did you tell him?

SIBUSISO   I told him to see me on Monday. In my office.

KAJOL   These Whiteys think they can get freebies whenever they want.

SIBUSISO   I'm not giving him a freebie. It's good business.

KAJOL   Remember what he used to call us when we first moved here?

SIBUSISO   I forgot.

KAJOL   Spicy nuts. And then they all joined in.

SIBUSISO   Not all of them.

KAJOL   Most of them.

SIBUSISO   Well, it's different now. They respect me. They know now who Sibusiso Khumalo is.

KAJOL   Do they respect you, or are they just trying to get whatever they can from you?

SIBUSISO   Look Kajol, I know how to handle white people. I work with them every day. These people here are not the Durban North kind. They just want a nice, safe place to live.

KAJOL   Some of them still make me uncomfortable. Especially Jason. I don't like the way he stares at me.

SIBUSISO They all stare at you. You are beautiful.

KAJOL He doesn't stare at me like that. I ... I don't like him.

SIBUSISO He's alright. I think, maybe, a lot of things have gone wrong for him.

KAJOL *(goes to the window to draw the curtains)* Well, before we get another Peeping Tom, I think we should shut ... *(she peers through the window, having noticed something)* Look at Sanjay. Shit. He's taking food to Jason again. Why does he do that?

SIBUSISO Isn't he always giving food to everyone? He should start a takeaway.

KAJOL I don't think Sanjay has many friends.

SIBUSISO Don't feel sorry for him.

KAJOL I'm not feeling sorry for him. I'm just saying that, besides his mother, I don't think he's close to anyone. I don't know. He just seems lonely.

SIBUSISO It's the same at work. He doesn't really get along with anyone. Well, except maybe Jenkins. He always brings him samosas.

KAJOL And you think he's just trying to curry favour.

SIBUSISO Of course. Jenkins is a glutton.

KAJOL You really don't like Sanjay, do you?

SIBUSISO No, I'm not saying that. But you don't know Sanjay. You don't know how he operates.

KAJOL Well, I don't want to talk about Sanjay. I don't want to talk about any of our neighbours. *(Kajol draws the curtains)*

SIBUSISO Do you really dislike them, Kajol? You know you should tell me if you are not comfortable living here.

KAJOL No, I'm not saying that. Look, I want to be with you. I like our home. That's what matters. *(Kajol holds Sibusiso's hand. He smiles uneasily)*

SIBUSISO More kebabs?

KAJOL No. I think it's time for some dessert. *(she massages his shoulders)* You're so tense.

SIBUSISO No. I'm alright.

KAJOL I'll make you better. *(starts unbuttoning his shirt)*

Blackout.

SCENE 8

Sibusiso's lounge. Lights come up on Kajol sitting on the couch. She is sitting alone, looking very worried. Sibusiso enters with a bottle of wine.

SIBUSISO *Chateau le Blanc*, Madame. *(pause)* What's wrong?

KAJOL My brother phoned me. The higher council on domestic affairs just made a decision.

SIBUSISO What?

KAJOL My brother, Uncle Deena and Uncle Ramesh. They're going to circulate my mother. Like a fucking yoyo. One month at a time. At each place.

SIBUSISO Shit.

KAJOL She can't be sent from place to place. This is what her life means now. *(pause)* I should have seen this. This is what happened to my friend Rekha's mother. You read about it in the papers every week. This is what Indians are becoming.

SIBUSISO I'm sorry.

KAJOL I didn't think my brother would be this cruel. He used to be reasonable.

SIBUSISO What does your Ma say?

KAJOL What can she say? She's an old woman. My brother is the legal owner of the house. And Uncle Deena is the family's great patriarch.

SIBUSISO And your cousins?

KAJOL *(despondent)* They'll help out. I mean, with money. But they won't keep her at their houses. She's not their mother. *(pause)* You know, I always took care of her. Especially after my father died. I was the perfect daughter. Cook. Clean. Go to work. Always smile. Never mind she's not fair-skinned. And my brother was the perfect son. Went off to business school. Toured India. And had his city hall wedding. *(pause)* I just got tired. I needed a break.

SIBUSISO *(touching her hand)* This is not your fault. *(pause)* Maybe ... maybe if they can't take care of her, they can put her in a Home for old age people. There are some good Homes. Maybe that'll be the right thing to do.

KAJOL No, that will be the white thing to do.

SIBUSISO What?

KAJOL   That's what white people do. Dump their parents in Homes. And then pop in for tea with some *Woolworths'* goodies once a week. No, they won't do that. That would be outrageous. No. Circulation amongst the family. That's the new trend. They probably would have done this anyway, but they made the decision today because I went over there. Let's show the little girl who has the power. *(she pours some wine and gulps it down. He sits down on his recliner. They sit silently for a while, then she becomes quite emotional)* Sibu. I was thinking before ... I wanted to ... Now, I have to. You know I've always been very close to my mother. But lately I've been focused on work, and our relationship.

SIBUSISO   You had to work hard. To get the promotion. Otherwise you would just take orders.

KAJOL   It's just a job, Sibu. Yes, I like it. But my mother ...

SIBUSISO   What do you want to do?

KAJOL   I want ... I want to bring my mother here. To live with us, for a while.

SIBUSISO   What?

KAJOL   For a while. Until I figure out what to do. I mean, we have another bedroom. She'll ...

SIBUSISO   Who's going to take care of her?

KAJOL   Me. And Beauty, when I'm not here. Sibu, I work flexi hours. And with the promotion, there'll be less work for more money.

SIBUSISO   It's not going to work.

KAJOL   You won't have to do anything. I mean, you don't do anything here anyway.

SIBUSISO   What?

KAJOL   I do everything for you.

SIBUSISO   Hey, I can take care of myself. *(awkward pause)* You think your mother is going to live with a Black man?

KAJOL   What do you mean? She's fine with you.

SIBUSISO   Ja, fine with me. Because she's a polite lady. And I'm a lawyer. And I give her family free advice. But I can see in her eyes. She doesn't ... she won't want to live here.

KAJOL   She doesn't have a choice. The alternative will finish her off.

SIBUSISO   How do you know for sure?

KAJOL   You don't want her here, Sibu?

SIBUSISO   No. Look Kajol, I like the peace and quiet here.

KAJOL   Peace and quiet?

SIBUSISO   Yes, I like this place to be ... Look next month I will probably become Body Corporate Chairman. And I want this place to be ... to be for young people. Professionals. There are many things I want to do in this complex.

KAJOL   Sibu. You of all people should understand. You are fighting for the squatters' rights to housing, just up the road. And this is my ...

SIBUSISO   That is different.

KAJOL   How? Look, Sibu you said your mother was pushed around before she died.

SIBUSISO   My mother was always pushed around. She was a domestic worker.

KAJOL   So help me with my mother. Let's show them their money means nothing.

SIBUSISO   Kajol. I will help you. Financially, I mean. We can find a place for your mother.

KAJOL   She's diabetic. She has angina. You want her to live by herself?

SIBUSISO   No, you will ... I'm saying, you can see her every day.

KAJOL   What? Pop in for tea? She needs ...

SIBUSISO   I don't know what else to do! I'm tired of this shit. Tired of hearing about family! She's not moving here. Now let's ... let's have a drink. And then we'll eat supper. My fish curry.

Kajol is silent for a few seconds, looking depressed.

She exits and Sibusiso looks at the audience in deep concern.

Blackout.

SCENE 9

Jason's lounge. Lights come up on Sanjay sitting on the couch. Sanjay is sitting alone pensively. He forces down his drink and cringes in discomfort. Jason has gone to see who is at the door. The Bell's whiskey is two-thirds full. (In this scene Sanjay drinks very little but Jason continues to drink fairly rapidly. He does not fall into a

drunken stupour but becomes quite boisterous and aggressive.)
Sanjay looks anxiously at his watch a couple of times. He takes out his
cellphone and makes a call. Nobody answers.

SANJAY *(irritated)* C'mon. Where are you Ma? *(he puts his phone off. Jason enters, quite agitated)*

JASON They came to talk to me about the squatters in Parklands Road. Two old bats. From the church. They want me to pray with them for those arseholes. *(sits down and shakes his head in disgust, pours himself a drink and is about to pour one for Sanjay)*

SANJAY No Jason. No more for me.

JASON Come on, Sanjay. I thought you charous could put it away. *(Sanjay looks at him uncomfortably and Jason sees this)* Well, there's no hurry. *(Jason eats a samosa)*

SANJAY There's more rotis in the other bag in the kitchen. For your supper.

JASON Oh, cheers Sanjay. I was going to make lobster thermidor. But the kebabs will do. *(Jason laughs. Sanjay smiles)* You know, this once a week is no good. I should hire you as my personal chef. Three to four times a week. I'll pay you – what –? Five hundred rand a month. Let's face it. There's not going to be a woman here for a while. Unless, when Kajol leaves Khumalo she moves in with me. Hmm? She's Indian. She'll be a good cook. *(Sanjay is irritated. Jason starts gulping down his drink but Sanjay grabs his arm)*

SANJAY I think you should cool it. *(Jason yanks his arm free)*

JASON Fuck you. I'm fine. *(he smiles at Sanjay)* Don't be a nag. *(Sanjay withdraws)*

SANJAY I think I should be getting ... *(Jason grabs his arm)*

JASON You know what would be perfect now Sanjay? Some mangoes. Wouldn't you like some of my lovely mangoes?

SANJAY Er, not really.

JASON You know I planted all those mango trees. I wish ... I wish that I could climb that tree and grab one of my delicious mangoes. But I can't, can I? Because when they attacked my home, they slashed my leg. *(awkward pause)* I was taking care of Oaklands again. While everybody was out partying on a Friday night. And I was trying to protect her. Ungrateful bitch!

SANJAY   I'm sorry, Jason.

JASON *(sarcastic)* Yeah, sorry. Sorry your leg was fucked mate. But hey, you're alive. They didn't kill you. Thank God. You read about it every day in the papers. Another brutal murder. But you're alive. And they didn't rape your wife. Shit, they didn't take all your belongings either. Now, if the SAPS masterminds caught them, they'll be punished by our powerful justice system. What do you say criminal law lecturer? They won't run out of the back of a police van, hey?

SANJAY   Look Jason, the criminal justice system ...

JASON   Fuck the criminal justice system. You know what I want to do now, Sanjay? Sometimes I ... *(he hits his palm hard)* You know I used to live in Redwood for twelve years.

SANJAY   Ja, you told me.

JASON   It was a united community there, hey. We're still finding that here. But we will, we will. Redwood was beautiful for many years. And then it started deteriorating. We had shit sometimes before that. But me and my brother, and a couple of neighbours used to fuck them up. I remember this, what ... Thaban or Thabang, fucking drug dealer, he tried to push us around. Shit. We fucked him up good. Broke his jaw. Cracked his ribs. He and his impis. *(Jason pours another drink)* But we couldn't stop those bastards after that. The crime just got out of control. *(short pause)* You must have done that too, Sanjay. I know you used to fuck them up in your townships.

SANJAY   No. I didn't. Well, that one time. I was provoked. My cousins fucked these up one time. They were laughing at the Hindi music we were playing. Mocking us. You know they always do that.

JASON   Well, your Lotus music is quite funny sometimes.
(Sanjay snaps at him)

SANJAY   I thought you said you enjoyed some Indian music.

JASON   Well, ja. Some of it. Er, so what did your cousins do?

SANJAY   I told you they fucked them up. The cops joined in too. Shit. It was a blood bath.

JASON   You sound scared. You couldn't do it?

SANJAY *(defensive)* I fucked this ou up one time. He was coming on to my sister. I told him to lay off. But he was giving me style.

JASON *(somewhat mockingly)* So you gave him a couple of slaps.

SANJAY   Ha. I gave him a lot more than that.

JASON Hmm. Are you saying there actually is a dangerous side to you Sanjay?

SANJAY I don't like the way some Black men think they can just get Indian women. It's disgusting. *(short pause. Jason gulps down his drink)* You know. Yesterday, I just came back and there was ... there was an incident. I went to the ... nah. Never mind.

JASON No, c'mon. Tell me Sanjay. What happened?

SANJAY I went to the kiosk in the park. In the evening. To buy cigarettes. And one of them was there. Pissed out of his mind. He was messing around with this young Indian couple. Swearing at the girl. Pushing her boyfriend around. The guy was timid. *(Jason starts becoming suspicious and has a disturbed look on his face)* I tried to intervene, but he took a swing at me. Hey. I landed him with a right hook. He fell awkwardly on his hand. Shit. Then he grabbed my legs and pulled me down. Fuck. And then he started biting my neck. Like a fucking vampire. *(he shows Jason a bite on his neck)* Shit. I didn't want to hurt him. I hardly ... I hardly touched him. Next thing I know he's running away and screaming. Shit. The worst I did was pull his dreadlocks.

JASON *(horrified)* Dreadlocks. Justus. You bastard. That was you! *(he lunges wildly at Sanjay. Sanjay pushes him off and gets up)*

SANJAY *(shocked)* What? What are you doing?

JASON Justus was my boy, you arsehole! You broke his arm, you prick! *(he gets up and awkwardly pursues Sanjay because of his limp)*

SANJAY Your boy? I didn't ...

JASON I should have known it was some coolie bastard!

SANJAY Jason, I ... I didn't know he was your boy. I ... I thought ... your boy is Philemon.

JASON I fired Philemon last month. Justus was my sister's boy. For ten years. I brought him here when she emigrated last month. And you fucking ...

SANJAY But he was drunk.

JASON Justus never drinks. I know him for ten years. Not one problem.

SANJAY I was trying to protect the girl. I ... I'm sorry.

JASON You're a macho man now. Hey? You come here. *(he grabs Sanjay, but Sanjay pushes him off and hurls him to the floor)*

SANJAY   I said I was sorry! *(Jason lies motionless. Sanjay walks away but then returns and offers Jason his hand)*

JASON   Fuck off, you coolie! *(Sanjay kicks Jason wildly)*

SANJAY   Don't call me a coolie, you crippled fuck! *(Sanjay walks away and then stops. He stares at the audience for several seconds, deep in thought. Then he walks back slowly to Jason)* Look, I'm sorry Jason. I ... I didn't know he was your boy. I was trying to protect the girl. Maybe he was ... let's just move on.

JASON   Get out.

SANJAY   What? *(Jason slowly sits up)*

JASON   You heard me. Get out of my house! *(Sanjay hesitates, then turns around and walks away briskly. Then he stops, turns around and walks back to Jason)*

SANJAY   I want my rotis back. *(Jason gets up and flings the parcel at him)*

JASON   Fuck off!

Sanjay exits.

Blackout

SCENE 10
Sibusiso's lounge. Lights come up on Sibusiso standing.
The doorbell rings. He answers the door, and Deena, Kajol's uncle storms in.

DEENA   Hey it's me! Where's my favourite niece? It's Uncle Deena.

SIBUSISO   What do you want?

DEENA *(examining the furniture)* Look at this. Very nice.

SIBUSISO   Alright, you saw the jondol. Now get out.

DEENA   Hmm, very western. What is it you teach again? Is it customary or corporate law?

SIBUSISO   Just get ... *(Kajol enters, looking despondent)*

KAJOL   What are you doing here, Uncle Deena?

DEENA   Hey, I wanted to see you, my girl. Find the muti. Just joking. You know me Kajol. I'm a joker. *(Sibusiso exits)*

KAJOL   Uncle Deena. What do you want?

DEENA   I wanted to see you. See how you are.

KAJOL And inspect my living conditions. Hey? Living in sin. With a Black man.

DEENA No, no. That's not the case. *(Sibusiso returns with a spear)*

KAJOL Anyway, I don't want to see ... Sibu!

SIBUSISO This is a traditional weapon. Traditionally used by Zulus against their enemy.

DEENA Hey, hold on. I'm not Xhosa. *(he giggles to himself)*

KAJOL Sibu. What are you doing?

SIBUSISO I'm giving him his Zulu image. What? You want me to dance now? *(Sibusiso does a few awkward Zulu dancing steps)* No, sorry Uncle Deena. I can't dance. *(Deena starts dancing)*

DEENA Come on. I'll show you how to dance to the Banghra beat. *(he grabs Kajol's hand and she tries to wrestle free. Sibusiso pushes Uncle Deena onto the couch and stands over him)*

SIBUSISO She doesn't dance. I don't dance. Let me tell you what I do. I phone the police, and they arrest you for trespassing. I send the labour inspector to investigate your factory, to see how you are treating your Black workers. I represent your Black workers at a CCMA hearing. You see, you shit. I'm a lawyer!

KAJOL Sibu! *(Sibusiso turns away and throws down the spear)* Just tell me what's on your mind, or get out. *(Uncle Deena becomes serious)*

DEENA You know, I didn't disapprove of your relationship because he's Black. *(Sibusiso laughs sarcastically)* No, it's true. I mean, it's not a bad match – you both have dark skin. But I wanted you to marry Rajesh. You know that. He's a wonderful guy. And he's a doctor. I always wanted you to marry a doctor. You know that.

KAJOL Please, Uncle Deena. You didn't come here to tell me that.

DEENA No. *(pause)* I need to talk to you. About our family. Alone please.

KAJOL Just speak!

SIBUSISO I want to hear this. *(Deena is displeased. He stands up slowly)*

DEENA Your brother did a bad thing with your Ma today. I know you were upset. That's why you called your cousins over.

KAJOL So you came to ask why I didn't phone you.

DEENA No, no. I know why you didn't phone me. I haven't been doing my duty lately. I've been working hard. Too hard.

SIBUSISO   Making lots of money.

DEENA   Yes. Lots of money. So I too can buy this nice lounge suite.

SIBUSISO   Oh, please man.

DEENA   Anyway, I'm taking charge of the family again. I've been going to the temple again. I go for satsang. I want ... I mean, Kajol, look everywhere, everywhere you see that Indian families are breaking up. People are abandoning their culture.

SIBUSISO   What's that supposed to –

DEENA   Let me finish. I'm saying I don't want this to happen to our family. That's why I'm taking charge. I want our Sunday get togethers again. And for us to remember each other's birthdays. To go to temple together. And go on family trips. You remember ...

KAJOL   Uncle Deena.

DEENA   Yes.

KAJOL   You say this every few months. We don't need you to take charge of the family. I don't want anyone in charge of the family.

DEENA   Why? You got a problem with me? Or you don't respect me? That's it. You think I'm a –

KAJOL   I'm not going to –

DEENA   You go to your Ma's place, and make wild accusations. You say the men in this family are useless. They do nothing. Your brother and I came up with a good plan. Let us all take care of your Ma. Now, on my way here he phones me and says you swore him on the phone. *(angry)* Who do you think you are?

SIBUSISO   Hey, be careful how you ...

DEENA   You don't know shit!

SIBUSISO   You listen. Who do you think you are speaking to? This is my house!

DEENA   Oh, my house. *(to Kajol)* You hear that?

KAJOL   I think you should leave Uncle Deena.

DEENA   And what you gonna do about your mother, my sister? You think everything will sort itself out?

KAJOL   No. It won't.

DEENA   You think your cousins will help you? It's just big talk.

KAJOL   No. I will sort it out. My mother has always been closest to me. I'm her only daughter. She'll be happy with what I decide.

DEENA   What you gonna do?

KAJOL   I will find her a place.

DEENA   Where? Some jondol in Phoenix?

KAJOL   Just get out now, you pompous shit!

DEENA   You'd better look for a place for yourself as well.

KAJOL   What?

SIBUSISO   Alright, enough now. *(approaches Deena menacingly)* You leave now or I'll remove you.

DEENA   Oh, the big Black man is going to hit an old defenceless man.

SIBUSISO   That's right.

KAJOL   What do you mean Uncle Deena?

SIBUSISO   He's talking rubbish again, babe.

DEENA   It's not rubbish. It's important.

KAJOL   What is it?

DEENA   I didn't want to say anything. It's not my place.

KAJOL   Say it!

DEENA   Yes, I will. You need to know the truth.

SIBUSISO   Whose truth? *(Deena sits down again, and looks as if he's carrying a heavy burden on his shoulders)*

DEENA   Last week, I went to *Bobby's* to buy a takeaway. You know, the Wednesday kebab and roti special. You know, Aunty Charmaine doesn't make nice kebabs. *(Kajol is irritated so Deena quickens the pace of his story)* Anyway, your man had visited Bobby a few days before. You know his big friend Bobby, his drinking partner. But I know Bobby too. From a long time. And Bobby told me what he said to him. He said ...

KAJOL   What? *(meanwhile, Sibusiso is feeling very awkward)*

DEENA   He said that he is planning, he didn't know when, but soon, to ask you to leave here. He wants to live ...

SIBUSISO   That's bullshit! I'm going to ... *(he grabs Deena's collar. Kajol tries to separate them)*

DEENA   You touch me and I'll charge you with assault. They'll lock you up and throw away the key, Black man! *(Sibusiso lets go. Kajol snaps at Deena)*

KAJOL   It's bullshit.

DEENA   It's not bullshit. I can prove it.

KAJOL   Why didn't Bobby ...?

DEENA   He didn't want to interfere. He didn't disapprove of your relationship. In fact he thought the two of you will be happy together. But he was worried about what Sibusiso said. He couldn't tell you. But he thought he should tell me.

SIBUSISO   Kajol. He's making this ... they're making this up. To break us up. Because I'm Black.

DEENA   He talked about being crowded. He said a man and a woman, should not live together. Women don't understand how men are.

SIBUSISO   Is that me Kajol?

DEENA   Bobby is his friend. Why will he lie? I will phone Bobby. You can speak to him. *(he takes out his cellphone and starts dialling)*

KAJOL *(in deep thought, disturbed)* You didn't want my mother to live here ...

DEENA   He doesn't believe in family, Kajol. He doesn't believe in our culture.

KAJOL   Shut up!

SIBUSISO   He is lying Kajol. You know when Bobby gets drunk he talks nonsense.

KAJOL   You drink with him. Are you saying you were talking nonsense?

DEENA   Hello, Bobby. It's Deena. I told Kajol. About what Sibusiso said. Just take it easy. Listen, she needed to know. Just calm down. Speak to her yourself. *(he motions to Kajol)*

KAJOL   Is it true, Sibu? *(Sibusiso is perturbed. He puts his hand on his mouth and looks away. Kajol takes the phone from Deena)* Bobby.

SIBUSISO   Cut it.

KAJOL   Never mind. *(she gives the phone back to Deena)*

SIBUSISO   I ... I wasn't going to tell you to leave. I was ... I was going to ask you. Ask you if you agreed that maybe we should live in separate places. But still see each other. Because I care about you, Kajol. *(Kajol shakes her head despondently)* I mean, this house. I always wanted a place like this. To be my little place. So I put my feet up. And shadow-box, naked. And work in my study. Finally, I can work at home. And sometimes I will call Thabo over. And get pissed. And not explain to anyone. *(pause)*

KAJOL   Now you can do ...

SIBUSISO   I lived in Ntuzuma Kajol. I ...

KAJOL   Oh please, don't give me that.

SIBUSISO   Don't give you that. No, I must give you that. Because you lived in Clare Estate, Kajol. You were not rich, no. But you had your own room. I lived with my mother and father. My brother and two sisters. And my aunt, with her two sons. In a shithole in Ntuzuma. And every time I wanted to shit I had to follow the queue. So when I came to varsity, I stayed in Varsity Drive. Renting one small room with Thabo. And Mr. Naidoo charged us one thousand Rand a month for that shithole. And his two sons would stare at us. So I moved to the varsity residence. The toilets don't work. The thugs come and take over your room. Eat your food. You can't even read. There's so much shit. I ... I wanted some peace here. I didn't want your cousins to come every other day. I wanted to ...

KAJOL   Why did you ask me to move in with you?

SIBUSISO   Because I care about you. I thought maybe we could ... And you were having financial difficulties then. You said your brother was asking you to contribute too much money to the household.

KAJOL   Oh, I see. The Black knight saving his little princess. I made financial contributions here. I'm not a fucking free loader.

SIBUSISO   I'm not saying that. I want you Kajol. My beautiful Kajol. I tried to see if we could live like a couple. But it's me. I wanted ...

KAJOL   A live-in maid. Someone to cook your food. Iron your clothes. Warm your bed.

SIBUSISO   No.

KAJOL   But now I'll be promoted. And you can make your own fish curry. *(she begins walking out)*

SIBUSISO   Kajol.

DEENA *(puts his hand on her)* Come with me. We'll bring your Ma too. Full-time. Serious. Aunty Charmaine will take care of you. Hey, we'll take a trip to Cape Town. Just like we did when you were in college.

KAJOL   Go home to your pathetic life, Uncle Deena.

SIBUSISO   Where are you going, Kajol?

KAJOL   For a walk. And then I'll start looking for a place for my Ma and I.

DEENA   Five thousand Rand a month won't get you much.

KAJOL   It'll be enough. We don't plan to move next door to you. *(Deena lowers his eyes)* I loved you Sibu. *(she exits. For a short while both men are silent, then Deena speaks)*

DEENA   So you got what you wanted. *(Sibusiso grabs him and shoves him hard against the couch. Deena is in pain)*

SIBUSISO   You got what you wanted, you bastard!

DEENA *(gasping)* You can't hit me. You can't.

SIBUSISO   I will snap your neck, old man. You came here to destroy our relationship. I was going to tell her properly. Like a gentleman. Consult with her. You don't understand that, hey? You take whatever you want. And then chuck it away, when you feel – *(he places his elbow against Deena's neck)*

DEENA   Assault is a striking off offence.

SIBUSISO   You're right. I won't assault you. You look like you've been assaulted enough, you sick, old man. *(he lets go of him)* Get out of my home. *(Deena begins to exit slowly, clutching his stomach. He pauses and composes himself)*

DEENA   She'll never come back to you.

Blackout.

SCENE 11

Jason's lounge. Lights come up on Jason standing alone. Jason phones Sanjay.

JASON *(tentatively)* Hello Sanjay. Er, you left, er, some chilli bites behind.

Doorbell rings.

JASON   Maybe you can ... do you want ...?

Doorbell rings

JASON   Coming. Can you pick it up later? *(pause)* Oh. Er, alright. Thanks. *(Jason goes to the doorway and Deena enters)*

DEENA   Hello Jason.

JASON *(concerned)* Deena. What are you doing here?
DEENA   We need to talk.
JASON   You shouldn't be here.
DEENA   Relax. Nobody saw me come here. And what if they did? You're a businessman. I'm a businessman. Well? Can I come in?
JASON   I'm not in the mood to talk now.
DEENA   Are you alone?
JASON   Yes. But I ...
DEENA   Don't you think you should show more respect to your future boss? *(Jason reluctantly lets Deena in. Deena looks at the lounge and laughs)* Who copied who?
JASON   What?
DEENA   It must have been the darkie. Trying to keep up with the wit ous.
JASON   What can I do for you, Deena?
DEENA   What's wrong my man?
JASON   Nothing. Just ... nothing. It's a kak day.
DEENA   Let go of her, Jason.
JASON   What can I do for you Deena?
DEENA   What, no tea? Biscuits? If this was an Indian house they would have come with a tray of biscuits, samosas and some masala tea too. You don't even offer me water.
JASON   I'm not Indian.
DEENA   No, you're not. Well, may I sit on your lovely recliner?
JASON *(irritably)* Er, y-yes. Sit. *(Deena reclines and puts his legs on the ottoman. pause)*
DEENA   It's a nice place you have here. Very homely.
JASON   Thank you. Er, how's business?
DEENA   Very good. The new factory will be fully equipped by next week. We'll be ready to go in the next month.
JASON   Oh, good. That's good news.
DEENA   Ja. You know the other day I caught up with an old family friend – Selvin Naidoo. He also got retrenched recently. You know, he's also a good candidate to manage my factory.
JASON   What? What are you saying Deena?
DEENA   I'm just saying I obviously didn't know he was available until I bumped into him. He's very experienced. Well organized. And he's a family friend.

JASON   Are you playing games with me? Hey? You told me I
was the perfect candidate. Just last week, on the phone, you said
that again.

DEENA   Yes, I still give you the edge over him. I'm just saying –
maybe I need to put you on probation for a while.

JASON   Probation? I'm a good businessman. You forget that
great deal I got you on your property a year ago. I have twenty years
experience.

DEENA   Selvin has more. Plus degrees in management. You just
have a B.Comm. degree.

JASON   You want me to sell myself to you, Deena? All over
again? Is that what you want?

DEENA   Look, I'm a businessman. I'm not a charity for
retrenched whites.

JASON   So, is this an Indian thing now? You want to help your
Indian brother?

DEENA   Good business knows no colour.

JASON   So what's the problem? You want me to stroke your
ego? Tell you what a great entrepreneur you are. Even though you
were a victim of Apartheid. I'm not going to suck up to you.

DEENA   Hey, you watch your mouth. I know you need me. Your
savings are going quickly. Your retrenchment package can't be
much. How many people want to employ a forty-two year old
retrenched white man?

JASON   So that's what you came for? You came all the way here.
To my home. To tell me how hopeless my situation is.

DEENA   I came to see my niece.

JASON   What? You went to Sibusiso Khumalo's house?

DEENA   Yes. And I've made more progress than you.

JASON   What do you mean?

DEENA   I got my niece to leave him. I showed her what he's
really like.

JASON   What? How?

DEENA   That doesn't matter. The point is that you told me a
month ago that your niece was sorted out and you were going ahead.
But you've done nothing.

JASON   You don't need me now. You got what you wanted. She
left him.

DEENA   Ja, but he's poisoned her mind against me. Filthy Black man. He treated me like shit. He assaulted me.

JASON   He assaulted you?

DEENA   Look, you want him to leave this place. And to lose his power. I want the same. So, when are you going to do it?

JASON   In a few weeks.

DEENA   Bullshit! You are just playing games. You don't know what you are doing. Your niece is probably taking you for a ride.

JASON *(angry)* Listen, old man. This is a delicate situation. It can't happen just like that.

DEENA   You are weak. You probably don't have the balls to do it. I'm giving you one week. To start making things happen. Otherwise, I'll be contacting Selvin.

JASON   So, this is why you're really here. To give me an ultimatum. Tell me, Deena. Is this how you do business? Is this how you made your money? Get your managers to do all your dirty work.

DEENA   Let me say it simply Jason. If you don't do something in the next week, then you don't deserve to be manager of my factory. *(Jason laughs sarcastically)*

JASON   Get out. I don't need you.

DEENA   It's easy for you to say that now. But when I'm gone and you think about it, you'll know that you need me. Much more than I need you. *(he begins to exit)* I'll call you next week. Or maybe you can e-mail me. Give me a detailed report on your progress. Let's see if you can write like a manager. *(Deena exits)*

JASON   Fuck!

Blackout.

SCENE 12

The park opposite Oaklands. Lights come up on Sanjay sitting on the park bench. Sanjay is sitting alone on a park bench. He is smoking a cigarette, deep in thought. After a few seconds Kajol enters. She notices Sanjay and hesitates. Then she approaches the bench.

KAJOL   Hello Sanjay.

SANJAY   Kajol. *(she sits down next to him. Sanjay is a little awkward)* How are you? *(Kajol doesn't answer)* You look ... Have you been crying?

KAJOL   Can I have a cigarette?

SANJAY   You smoke?

KAJOL   Sometimes. *(Sanjay gives her a cigarette and lights it)*

SANJAY   What's wrong?

KAJOL   I don't want to talk about it. *(short pause)*

SANJAY   Is it Sibu? *(Kajol does not respond for a few seconds)*

KAJOL   It's Sibu. It's a lot of things. *(awkward silence for a while as they continue smoking)* Sanjay, you remember you told me that your Ma was moving out of your sister's place? Because your sister was getting married. Did she find a new place?

SANJAY   Ja. She moved in a couple of weeks ago. With one of the ladies from her inter-faith group. They got their own little flat. I told her, you know, why don't you move in with me. But my mother likes her independence. That's why she said, let my sister and her husband have their own life.

KAJOL   Ja. That's ... *(she fades off)*

SANJAY   Already she's been inviting her circle around. Cooking for them. Her inter-faith group, you know.

KAJOL   Your Ma is very active, hey.

SANJAY   Ja. She's full of energy.

KAJOL   How old did you say she is?

SANJAY   Sixty-eight.

KAJOL   My Ma is sixty-five. But ... you know she's quite sickly. She needs to ... I've been thinking, you know, she needs to spend time with people like your Ma.

SANJAY *(excited)* Well, why don't you bring her to the inter-faith group's meeting. It's on Tuesdays. You know, I join them sometimes as well. I mean, they do some good work. It's a mixed group. All ladies, but different religions, different races. You know, my Ma and I are Hindus. You too. But no one is trying to convert you there or change your views. And they work with kids, abused women. Volunteers, you know.

KAJOL   Ja. I think my Ma ... it'll be good for her.

SANJAY   Ja. Bring her on Tuesday. You know, the four of us ... we can, well, er, maybe we can go for coffee, after the meeting.

KAJOL   Sanjay, do you think my Ma could, just for a little while. A couple of weeks. Do you think she could stay at your Ma's place? Until I find a place for us.

SANJAY   Us?

KAJOL   Yes. I've got to find a nice place. Not some dump. Rent is so heavy. But I ...

SANJAY   So you're moving out of ...

KAJOL   Yes.

SANJAY   What happened Kajol? *(Kajol is silent for a few seconds)*

KAJOL   You know, you never really know someone. Completely. How they think. What they're really feeling. You meet someone you think, well you think he's different. Intelligent. Mature. And you're attracted to them. So you go with the flow. But ... we're just ... we're different, it seems. *(Sanjay is shocked)*

SANJAY   Is it, er ... is it another woman?

KAJOL   What?

SANJAY   I mean, often with men it's another woman.

KAJOL   No. I don't think so. No.

SANJAY   I'm sorry. But, you know ...

KAJOL   I think if you tried to live with someone. And it didn't work out. Then you ... you shouldn't still see them. *(they are silent for a while, both contemplating)*

SANJAY   I'll talk to my Ma.

KAJOL   It'll just be for a few weeks. I'm getting a promotion. I'll be able to afford a nice place then.

SANJAY   Congratulations.

KAJOL   Thanks.

SANJAY   I'm sure my Ma will be happy to do it.

KAJOL   I will pay. For the food and lodging. And I'll cook for ...

SANJAY   Please Kajol. We are Indians, hey. I mean, we must help each other.

KAJOL   Thanks. *(they are silent for a few seconds. Then Sanjay picks up a parcel)*

SANJAY   Have a sweet corn samosa.

KAJOL   You're always carrying nice food with you. *(she takes one)* Hmm. That's great, Sanjay. *(Sanjay smiles)* You put just the right amount of chillies.

SANJAY   Have I?

KAJOL   Yes. It's delicious.

SANJAY   Thanks.

KAJOL   Thank you, Sanjay.

Blackout.

SCENE 13
*Jason's lounge. Lights come up after the recliner is removed with no
one on stage. Jason enters with a file. Sibusiso enters a few seconds
later.*

JASON   What are you doing here? The body corporate meeting?
SIBUSISO   There's still half an hour. I didn't overdo the
preparation. It's mainly honkies. What do you know about good
food and drink?
JASON *(irritated)* What do you want?
SIBUSISO   To expose you.
JASON   What?
SIBUSISO   Your niece and I talked. After I fucked her last night.
I know everything.
JASON *(shocked)* You what?
SIBUSISO   She told me everything.
JASON   She slept with you?
SIBUSISO   Yes.
JASON   Bullshit!
SIBUSISO   Phone her. I'm sure she'll enjoy giving her blackmailing
uncle all the details. How her white skin rubbed against mine. How
she screamed for me not to stop. *(Jason spits at Sibusiso and tries
to grab his collar. Sibusiso grabs his arm and twists it around his
back)* I'm sure the body corporate would love to hear how you
wanted to fuck up its new chairman.
JASON   Go and tell them. They'll never believe you Black man.
(Jason twists out of Sibusiso's grip)
SIBUSISO   You're probably right. But I know what you tried to do.
And you know I fucked your niece. She betrayed you. What kind of
man are you? You blackmailed your own niece. You know what she
told me to tell you? That you can go ahead and tell her father about
the Coloured boyfriend. She's no longer seeing him. She's graduated
to a Black man now.
JASON   I can't believe she slept with a filthy shit like you!
SIBUSISO   Maybe it's my big dick. *(Jason sneers)*
JASON   You attack me. But you sleep with your students, you
disgusting animal!
SIBUSISO   I didn't force her. She's a big girl. She wanted to do it.
JASON   For all I know you're blackmailing her. Threatening to

fail her if she doesn't do what you ask. You'll do anything for some white skin.

SIBUSISO   Actually I prefer black skin. It's much smoother and silkier.

JASON   And what about the brown skin you had? You just used her too?

SIBUSISO   I love Kajol. But she's not with me right now. That's her choice. So I can do what I want.

JASON   You're a ...

SIBUSISO   You are in no position to judge me, you racist pig! If you have guts, why don't you tell the body corporate that you don't want me to live here? Or why don't you come after me in the open? Why are you playing games? You know why? Because you don't have the balls. You're afraid of me.

JASON   I'm not afraid of you.

SIBUSISO   You should be. I know what you really are.

JASON   What? What are you talking about?

SIBUSISO   You're a common thief.

JASON (*tentative, turns away*) Common thief.

SIBUSISO   Yes. I was doing some research with *Superview Real Estate*. They told me how their senior salesman committed cheque fraud for twenty-one thousand Rand

JASON   If I'm a fraudster, why am I not in jail?

SIBUSISO   These firms don't prosecute their employees. Why must they go through the bad publicity? Risk losing clients. And investors. They just fired you. That's humiliation enough.

JASON   Alright, alright, so you know. But you don't know what really happened. I was deceived by a client. I was set up.

SIBUSISO   No, no. It's better if you say you were a victim of corporate manipulation. You worked so hard for them. But they just used you. And they started bringing in token Blacks.

JASON   That's right. Like the assistant manager. Sat on his arse and laughed at me. The one slogging to bring in the money.

SIBUSISO   Ah shame. You brought in so much money you had to steal some.

JASON   Fuck you. They had no right to disclose any information to you.

SIBUSISO   I'm doing research. It's all confidential.

JASON   Yes, so you can't even tell anybody. You'll violate your research ethics.

SIBUSISO   I know that. I don't want to tell anyone. I know. And you know I know.

JASON   Fuck you, Khumalo. You can't judge me. You're a fucking criminal yourself. You manipulate everyone. You're trying to push Sanjay out of the department. You sleep with your students. You play the race card whenever you want something you don't deserve. Without affirmative action you'd be mowing my lawn.

SIBUSISO   Without Apartheid you'd be sweeping my floors.

JASON   Ha! I'm still on my feet.

SIBUSISO   For how long? You know I knew about your fraud for two months. But I didn't judge you then. I even tried to understand. These firms treat their employees like shit. But I know now that you are a stupid White man who has no place in our new world. *(Jason laughs sarcastically)*

JASON   Our new world. And are you the King of this world? The one who wants our lounge suite? And our cars? And who wears our clothes. And steals our jobs.

SIBUSISO   *(sarcastic)* Steals our jobs. In the company from which you stole? I know why you did it Jason. You're used to a certain lifestyle. Your wife shops at *Gateway*. You want these nice things. Taking some money from a big firm is OK. It's the way you were brought up. You were always given everything.

JASON   Don't presume to know me. It's typical of you Blacks to assume that every White person was rich. My father was a mechanic. My mother baked biscuits and sold them to our neighbours. We had …

SIBUSISO   Ah, ah, shame. You were one of the poor Whites. You had an economic system designed to make you rich. But you still failed. Your family must have been pathetic. *(Jason is disgusted. He rushes wildly at Sibusiso who steps aside smartly. Jason trips and falls awkwardly on his knee)*

JASON   Aaah! *(Sibusiso bends and speaks directly in Jason's ear)*

SIBUSISO   I'm going to have to start the body corporate meeting without you. *(Jason tries to get to his feet. Sibusiso looks at him for a couple of seconds and then knees him over. Sibusiso laughs and towers over Jason)* In a few minutes I'll be body corporate chairman. Next month I'll be senior lecturer. Soon I'll be on TV talking about the squatter issue. The world will know Sibusiso Khumalo. And you'll be sitting alone, sipping cheap whiskey and dreaming of the world you lost.

Sibusiso exits. Jason begins crying. Slow fade on Jason crying.

The End.

Ashwin Singh

Ashwin is a lawyer, lecturer and playwright. He is also involved in stand-up comedy and has performed at a variety of South African comedy festivals since 1997. A selection of his poetry has been published in three anthologies by the Poetry Institute of Africa. *To House* is his first dramatic play and was written to expose the complexities and contradictions of an evolving democracy. As a political activist, Singh is inspired to live in a country which experienced a peaceful political transition, but believes that the journey to true reconciliation will be a long and challenging one.

Playwright's Note

Rejoice Burning is based on real lives, people I knew and know but the middle owes a lot to Uys Krige and the end to Robert Frost. The play's theme – the weird separation of the worlds of people who live so closely together (African and European, settler and native) – is the essential South African theme. It is, perhaps, the crucial post-colonial theme worldwide.

Although written for radio, *Rejoice Burning* is entirely stageable. The arena would be divided into areas suggesting Rejoice's room, the Whites' house and Harmony's room. All actors would remain on stage all the time. Instructions for sound effects would become signals for changes of scene and light state. A coffin and fire would be combined to manifest the title image.

We are the irrelevant and minute inhabitants of an obscure planet in an infinite mystery. We are fuelled by the sun. We flicker and die. The bravest and the best, rejoice burning.

James Whyle

REJOICE BURNING

James Whyle

In memory of Rejoice Mpofu

First broadcast on BBC Radio 3 on the eve of World Aids Day, 30th November, 2003, as *A Man Called Rejoice*. With thanks to Producer/Director Claire Grove, who commissioned the play and collaborated in its creation.

CHARACTERS

REJOICE IQUDU is joyful in the face of adversity. He is a man who likes a fine pair of woollen trousers, a pretty girl and a job well done.

First performed by Peter Mashigo

SUSAN WHITE is the face of liberal South Africa, the woman who hires Rejoice to fix the roof and finds herself being drawn into a strange new world.

First performed by Jennifer Steyn

ORCHARD IQUDU is Rejoice's brother. He is the intellectual in the family, a man with a firm grasp on 'short algebras' and the finances of 'The Society'.

First performed by Errol Ndotho

WARREN WHITE is Susan's husband. At first skeptical, it is he who gets to work with Rejoice and witness his death.

First played by Mark Faith

HARMONY BANYADITSE is the wife of Rejoice's rival Mketwa and the secret lover of Rejoice.

First played by Juanita Waterman

CLIFF, friend of Rejoice.

1.

FX: ROOF, DISTANT TRAFFIC.

Rejoice Iqudu is doing some work on a tin roof.

REJOICE *(sings)** Hey baby, hey, hey beautiful girl ... *(hammers)*
   Come along, come to kiss me, before I'm going. Come along, come
   to kiss me, before I'm going. *(hammers)* Won't you kiss me nice,
   nice, before I'm going.

2.

FX FADE ROOF.

*Orchard speaks directly to us, his presentation is light, smiling,
focused. He is concerned with accuracy, but determined to look on the
bright side.*

ORCHARD   I am Orchard Iqudu, brother of Rejoice. I am the last
   born from a family of five. Our father was Joseph Iqudu. Iqudu is an
   antelope. It is an animal. If you come with the skin of that antelope,
   I do not touch it. There is connection to that animal. There is
   respect. It is our ancestor. If you touch that skin, it means danger
   for your kids. You can get a kid without teeth. For life. Because you
   are not respecting it. You can eat the meat, but not the heart. Two –
   don't touch the skin. Whether it is dry or it is wet, never touch the
   skin. That one will affect your kids.
WARREN   It was Susan who found Rejoice. She made a deal with
   him. He got a room out behind the garage. And the arrangement
   was, he had to do one day a week for us. Gardening, painting,
   whatever. *(beat)* Susan's got a way with these guys. She can really
   relate to them.

3.

FX HOUSE. DISTANT RADIO OR TV. SUSAN AND WARREN ARE
FINISHING SUPPER.

SUSAN   I wish you wouldn't talk like that, Warren. *(beat) They*
   not them.

WARREN   They sure as hell aren't the same as us.

SUSAN   Of course they are.

WARREN   That's naïve.

SUSAN   Well, all the things that you say you can't do, like tiling, and getting rid of that hideous old toilet in the spare bathroom ... Rejoice is going to do.

WARREN *(beat)* His name is Rejoice?

SUSAN   Yes, and he has a wife in Zimbabwe called Hardship, and a girlfriend in Joburg called Harmony.

WARREN   How do you know this?

SUSAN   Margaret Jones. He did their floor. If you buy a house that needs tender loving care, Warren, then you actually have to do the tender loving care. You can't just let it rot around your ears.

WARREN   I wonder if he's any good with roofs? There's a horrific leak in the garage.

SUSAN   Well, hello.

WARREN   How on earth do you get a name like Rejoice?

FX: BACK ROOM. SMALL, CRAMPED. A GAS PLATE GOING.

ORCHARD   Eish, Rejoice. Mketwa is a good man. He has authority.

REJOICE *(cold)* Where is that tea?

ORCHARD   It's nearly boiling. You mustn't be impatient. *(beat)* What does it matter?

REJOICE   Orchard, we are Ndebele. Not Zulu. Ndebele.

ORCHARD   But this is Johannesburg. Everything is just mixed.

REJOICE   Even Shaka Zulu could not conquer our ancestors! They escaped him and fought for land in Zimbabwe. We took land there from the Mashona and we made our own place. We must never forget that.

ORCHARD   What I'm saying, it is a simple thing. Mketwa has a car. And because of that it is good for him to be president of the society.

REJOICE   Orchard, that man can never be president.

ORCHARD   He is an important man!

REJOICE   No.

ORCHARD   Why not?

REJOICE   A thing like the society can only be organized when there are responsible persons in charge. You cannot just appoint any dunderhead because he has a motorized vehicle!

ORCHARD   Rejoice, you are not seeing.

REJOICE *(fierce)* Mketwa will cheat you! He will cheat you out of your own box!

FX: FADE BACK ROOM.

ORCHARD   Rejoice and me, we grew up in Zimbabwe, there at Imvula, in the rural areas. There's a school, and there's an orchard, and a dam behind. That name, Imvula, is from the dam. It is almost never dry. We like it because it has a lot of fish. Imvula is a mountainous region. If there's rain, everything is growing. Even in the veldt. Only in the veldt you have to manure. Me and Rejoice, from when we grew up, we knew how to grow things.

FX: GARDEN. DISTANT TRAFFIC, BIRDS, TWO STROKE ENGINE.

SUSAN   Rejoice. *(louder)* Rejoice.

FX: ENGINE DIES.

SUSAN   Sorry, Rejoice. Warren asked me to give you this. In case you need petrol.

REJOICE   Thank you, Susan. In fact I think it is nearly empty.

SUSAN   And he wanted to know if you can start work with him on the garage roof tomorrow.

REJOICE   I can only work in the afternoon. In the morning I am very busy.

SUSAN   Oh. He'll be disappointed.

REJOICE   Unfortunately I have to go to the society.

SUSAN *(beat)* The what?

FX: HOUSE. TAP RUNNING. TEETH BRUSHED.

WARREN   The Society?

SUSAN   Ja.

WARREN   Pass me the mug. Thanks. *(rinses)* On a Sunday morning?

SUSAN   Ja.

WARREN   Can't be a building society. Can it? On a Sunday?

SUSAN   I don't know.

WARREN *(beat)* You look dead sexy in that.

SUSAN   Good. I'll see you later.

FX: DEPARTING FOOTSTEPS. A DOOR SLAM. FADE HOUSE.

FX: BACK ROOM, COOKING.

ORCHARD Eish, careful of the stew, Rejoice.

REJOICE Why must you cook right here by the mirror.

ORCHARD *(laughs)* Because that is where you put the stove. If you put your stove right by the mirror, then that is where I must cook!

REJOICE Did you use all my hair cream?

ORCHARD I never touched it. Your hair is very nice.

REJOICE And the jacket?

ORCHARD Quite beautiful, really.

REJOICE These trousers are pure wool. From Naidoo's second hand in Elof St.

ORCHARD How much?

REJOICE Thirty-five, seventy-five Rand. *(beat)* The shoes. Are they shining enough?

ORCHARD They are shining too much. How do you get them so clean?

REJOICE Spit. *(beat)* You'll keep food for me?

ORCHARD Of course. What you think?

REJOICE *(beat)* It's better if you come.

ORCHARD Rejoice, I have already told them that you have got my vote!

FX: FADE BACK ROOM

ORCHARD I don't know why Rejoice was so worried. Because in fact the society doesn't take only Ndebeles. We have got people from Pretoria. People from Bloemfontein. We don't mind. What we judge is the distance. Because if the distance is too much, the cost can be too much. That is where these short algebras become useful.

FX: HOUSE, SUPPER.

WARREN Rejoice was all dressed up again this morning. Did you see? Dark fifties suit. Wide lapels.

SUSAN I know. Like some … movie character off to meet a girl. *(beat)* Do you know what his surname is?

WARREN Eku … something. *(beat)* Apparently it means some kind of buck.

FX: FADE HOUSE.

ORCHARD   Our father, Joseph Iqudu, was a poor man. He worked as a security guard in a shop. He tried to support us, me and Rejoice and three more brothers, five of us! And so we managed to get a small education.

FX: BACK ROOM. ORCHARD IS TASTING THE STEW. THE DOOR OPENS.

REJOICE *(entering, sings)* Come along, come to kiss me, before I'm going. Won't you kiss me nice, nice ...

FX: REJOICE HUMS, CEASES, SIGHS. ORCHARD PUTS DOWN THE SPOON.

ORCHARD   What happened?
REJOICE   Eish.
ORCHARD   What?
REJOICE   They voted.
ORCHARD   And?
REJOICE   We must share the position. *(outrage)* They have made me and Mketwa joint President of the society! *(sings/hums)* I send a messenger to tell that I want to meet you, at the station ... Won't you kiss me, nice, nice ...
ORCHARD *(suspicious beat)* Why you singing like that, Rejoice? *(beat)* Rejoice?
REJOICE   I was so angry with the voting that I had to make a little detour past Harmony.
ORCHARD   You went there? To Mketwa's place?
REJOICE   She is so soft that one. She is like butter. Like fresh cream straight from the cow. After tasting there, I feel like a man again. If Mketwa wants to share my chair at milking time, then I will share his cream.
ORCHARD   Eish, Rejoice. You are taking too much risks, really.

FX: HOUSE. SUSAN IS WASHING UP.

SUSAN   Anything interesting in the paper?
WARREN   Just the normal stuff. Rape. Mayhem. Minister of Health refuses to admit that HIV causes AIDS.
SUSAN   You know it's killing five hundred people a day.

WARREN Oh please. Did you read the Malan piece in that magazine?

SUSAN Classic denial.

WARREN But you NGO types do make up figures so that you can get funding. You test pregnant women and then you say for every pregnant woman who is positive, there will be five other people in her community who are also positive. It's a wild guess. Besides being a cultural insult.

SUSAN I see the government figures at work. There are at least five hundred people dying a day! And that is a conservative estimate. *(beat)* And it takes up to five years from infection till people start getting sick. The majority of infected people in South African don't even know they're positive. In five years time, three thousand a day will be dying.

WARREN Well ... if you are right about the figures ... I don't know if we should be here. We should be thinking about moving.

FX: ROOF. NAILS HAMMERED INTO CORRUGATED IRON.

REJOICE *(sings)* Come along, come to kiss me, before I'm going. Come along, come to kiss me, before I'm going.

FX: WARREN UP THE LADDER.

WARREN I see you replacing some of those panels.

REJOICE Many of them are rotten, Warren. They are finished. Always, when you working on a roof, you much check the zincs. All those ones that are rusted, you must throw them out. The rust is the first thing that can kill a roof.

WARREN You the expert. I brought you some tea.

REJOICE Thank you.

FX: TEA POURED. PASSING IBIS CALLING.

REJOICE *(laughs)* They are noisy, those ones. *(imitating)* Haaaa ... Haaaa ...

REJOICE They are angry that we are sitting on their roof.

FX: IBISES IN THE DISTANCE. TEA ENJOYED.

WARREN How did you get your name, Rejoice?

REJOICE My father gave it to me.

WARREN It's your proper name? On your passport?

REJOICE   Yes. *(beat)* I first came to Johannesburg in 1992. The comrades were still throwing stones. The Zulus were marching with traditional weapons. In those days guys with balaclavas were getting onto the trains and just killing anyone who happened to be sitting there.

WARREN   They called it the Third Force.

REJOICE   They were hitting them on the head with a panga and leaving them for dead.

WARREN   I know. I saw guys walking around with AKs in the middle of town.

REJOICE   It's true. And so many people thought it was better to have some kind of political name like Mandla. Power. They thought these names like mine are not good. But I was considering the meaning of the word, 'rejoice'. And I decided I like that meaning. I decided I will keep it always. *(beat)* Sitting on a roof with the sun just passing away over Johannesburg ... *(beat)* I know I made the right choice.

FX: FADE ROOF.

ORCHARD   Our father, his first kid wasn't born. He died. Our father wasn't happy. Then he got a second one. It was a lady. She died also. Then came Rejoice. He came in 1956 after two years of trying. When our mother first told him that she was pregnant, my father touched her there by the stomach and he said: 'This guy ... is Rejoice.'

FX: BACK ROOM. REJOICE AND HARMONY CLOSE ON MIKE.

HARMONY Rejoice!

REJOICE   Harmony!

HARMONY Oh Rejoice.

REJOICE *(sings)* Won't you kiss me nice, nice ...

HARMONY Oh Rejoice! Rejoice!

REJOICE   Your skin has the taste of milk with chocolate. When I put my head against you here, you are as warm as a cow that is being milked beneath the hill at Imvula.

HARMONY Oh Rejoice, Rejoice, Rejoice!

REJOICE *(alarmed)* Sh, Harmony! Do you want to wake up the whole of Johannesburg?

HARMONY *(subsiding)* Oh Rejoice. I love you so much.

REJOICE   Sh, my baby. Not so much noise. This is meant to be secret, what we are doing.

HARMONY I love you so much. I want you to buy me a fridge.

REJOICE Sh, my baby. *(beat)* Where do you think I will get money for a fridge?

FX: FADE BACK ROOM.

ORCHARD In fact the name, in our culture, it often associates you, when you are still in the mother's stomach, from how she reacts to other people. You can find that suddenly she comes violently. But you know that she is not a violent person. It is you that are making her violent. From inside her stomach. And then they can give you the name of Violence. *(beat)* My own name, Orchard, is very powerful. It is not just an ordinary name, like white people have.

FX: ROOF AMBIENCE.

REJOICE At Imvula there is an orchard. It sits just there between the village and the school. Every year those trees are fruitful. Beautiful apples and everything like that. And hidden inside that orchard where you go in, there is a ... what-you-call-that-thing. A water storage.

WARREN A dam?

REJOICE No, that small deep one.

WARREN Uh ... a well?

REJOICE That one. That well is so deep. When you drop a stone you have to wait long time before you hear it hit the water. It is very wonderful to the village because the water is much sweeter than the dam. Even during the drought when parts of the dam can become stagnant. But it can be dangerous. One time an old woman drowned in there. We struggled many days to get her body out.

FX: FADE ROOF.

ORCHARD It was in my father's mind when he named me that the orchard was good, but also dangerous. The orchard gives you fruit, but if you fall in the well you will be vanished from this world. *(beat)* Sometimes, when the moon is straight above, I can see things in the water of that well. *(beat)* One time, when I was still a small child, I looked into that water, and I saw Rejoice. But instead of feet, there were just flames.

FX: ROOF AMBIENCE.

WARREN   Where did you learn to fix roofs?

REJOICE   I learnt that side, in Zim. I worked on a farm there. I
learnt every single thing that was known about that farm.

WARREN   Oh ja?

REJOICE   Before I was finished, I was even the manager. I knew
all what was going. Everything, everybody who was employed there,
has to pass by me first. I show him how to milk with the machine.
If this cow doesn't want the machine, I show how to milk it by hand.
(beat) That lady, Mrs Wells, the owner, she came to rely on me in
every way. I did all the different functions. Inseminating, whatever
you want me to do.

WARREN   You do artificial insemination?

REJOICE   It's very easy, that one. Even if you have fifty cows, I will
inseminate them all, right here on your front lawn.

FX: FADE ROOF AMBIENCE.

ORCHARD   It happened to me in 1983 that I didn't have school fees.
My mother was not happy that I was not at school. But she knew I
was a loving-school guy. So she told me, 'No, better go to your
brother. Just to get relaxed.'

FX: COW SHED, COWS.

REJOICE   You must pull gently. And smooth. Always aiming in the
bucket. Like this.

FX: MILK HITTING THE BUCKET.

ORCHARD   It looks quite simple, really.

REJOICE   Here. Take the stool.

ORCHARD   OK.

ORCHARD   Eish. It's very low.

FX: MILK HITTING BUCKET. TENTATIVE.

ORCHARD   Like this?

REJOICE   No. You must lean against the cow! You must be the
friend of the cow.

ORCHARD   OK. Like this.

REJOICE   That's better.

REJOICE   Good!

ORCHARD   How many cows are there on the farm Rejoice?
REJOICE   A hundred and sixty-four. And two bulls. Nice and easy.
Lean into the cow.
ORCHARD   And how much milk does each cow give?
REJOICE *(proud)* The best cow on this farm last year was Butterfield
Dreamer Three. She produced six thousand, eight hundred and
eighty-eight kilograms in one year.
 ORCHARD   Yes, but I am trying to find the total. I am trying to find
out how much milk is produced all the cows in one year.
Mathematically.
REJOICE   Orchard, can't you just think about what you doing?
ORCHARD   I am capable of doing two things at the same time. OK,
so there are one hundred and sixty-four cows.
REJOICE   Anyway, at this time only eighty cows are being milked.
REJOICE   OK eighty. And lets say the average is four hundred
kilograms a year.

FX: MILK BECOMES ERRATIC.

REJOICE   Orchard!
ORCHARD   I can do this in my mind. No paper. No pen.
REJOICE   Orchard, think about what you are doing!
ORCHARD   Four hundred kilograms, times eighty cows ... *(triumph)*
Three thousand, two hundred ...

FX: MOOO. BUCKET FALLING ON CONCRETE.

REJOICE *(alarmed)* Eish! Look what has happened!
ORCHARD   I'm sorry.
REJOICE *(disappointed)* Maybe it is better if you stick with just the
maths, really.

FX: ROOF AMBIENCE. SUSAN UP THE LADDER.

SUSAN   OK. Here are the roof nails and fibre glass strips. And
here's the sealant. I hope it's all right. Warren was in a bit of a hurry
when he gave me the list.
REJOICE   Thank you, Susan. I'm sorry to disturb your work.
SUSAN   No problem. Oh and Rejoice. *(beat)* Harmony was here
to see you. Early on this morning.
REJOICE   Harmony? *(beat)* Where is she now?

SUSAN   I don't know. I told her you weren't here.

REJOICE   Eish!

(Susan ventures into difficult territory)

SUSAN   Rejoice ... you do know about AIDS, don't you?

REJOICE   I know about it, Susan.

SUSAN *(struggles)* I know in your culture, sometimes a man can ... I
don't want to disrespectful or anything but ... Basically I just ...
(bottom line) I know from work how dangerous it is. You've got to
be so careful, Rejoice.

REJOICE   You mustn't worry about me, Susan. I am a strong man.
Ever since I was a small child I have been looking after everyone.
Because I am the oldest brother. So I must be like a father. Always
providing. Looking after Orchard. Sending food and money for
Hardship. Looking after the children.

SUSAN *(beat)* They were saying on the radio that there are terrible
food shortages up there.

REJOICE   Every month I must send mielie-meal. Every month
without fail. Then those thieves at the border are stealing it. And the
war veterans are taking over the farms. They have never been in
war. They are just Mugabe's tsotsis. *(beat)* It is a long time,
sometimes three, sometimes six months, before I see Hardship.

FX: FADE ROOF. ENGINE TICKING OVER.

REJOICE   Have you got everything packed?

ORCHARD   I've got it all. Don't worry yourself.

REJOICE   The clothes for Progress and the baby?

ORCHARD   They are in the bags.

REJOICE   And the shoes? Four pairs. For Naledi, Mandla,
President, and Nicholas.

ORCHARD   I've got them, Rejoice. Don't worry.

REJOICE   And the money for Hardship. Don't even tell them about
it at the border. Better just hide it and take it through and change in
on the black market.

ORCHARD   That is what I will do.

FX: HOOTER.

ORCHARD   Come. Help me load this mielie-meal now. These guys
wanted to leave two hours ago already.

FX: ROOF AMBIENCE.

SUSAN *(impressed)* Five children?
REJOICE   Five!
SUSAN   And how many wives?
REJOICE   This one, Hardship, she is my third wife.
SUSAN   All at once?
REJOICE   No, not all at once. First, the mother of Progress. But unfortunately we were fighting and we were divorced. Then, two, the mother of Naledi. Then divorced again. Now this third one, Hardship, the mother of President and Mandla and Nicholas.
SUSAN   No divorce this time?
REJOICE   No divorce. Not ever again. Hardship is a very beautiful lady. Very good and honest. And dressing nicely. Even like yourself.
SUSAN   Why, thank you, Rejoice.
REJOICE   Every single thing that a man could wish for in a woman, Hardship has got. There is just the problem with the distance. *(beat)* Thank you for the tools, Susan.
SUSAN   That's a pleasure. You just shout if you need anything.

FX: FADE ROOF.

ORCHARD   All I have to do on the farm, where I lived with Rejoice, is to go and collect the cattle for milking. It is taking me thirty minutes. Two o'clock to half past two. Then I go back to sleep. In the morning I take them back at six o'clock. Then my work is finished. I'm paid for that and I don't pay anything myself. Even food, I don't pay anything. And I told that Mrs Wells that I want to go back to school. So, every day, two o'clock, she comes to me. She teach me maths, English. In fact I can't even say I wasn't in a school. I was in a private school with just me and Mrs Wells.

FX: HOUSE AMBIENCE. WARREN PREPARING SUPPER.

SUSAN   I told him I want him to do the bathroom.
WARREN *(astonished)* Rejoice?
SUSAN   Yes.
WARREN   Pass me the tomatoes.
SUSAN   His tiling is excellent. He did a great job for the Joneses.
WARREN   Ja, but plumbing! Plumbing is something else.

SUSAN   Rejoice knows what he's doing. *(beat)* He was going to start on Sunday, but he has to go to the society again.

FX: FADE HOUSE.

ORCHARD   As the society policeman there are many things that I can tell you. For instance: It can get very hot that side. Maybe thirty, thirty-five degrees. Especially in the reserve areas. So you can't keep somebody for two weeks. One day is more than enough to keep somebody. If you arrive there maybe four o'clock in the morning, it means by ten o'clock everybody has seen the corpse. And then we bury that person. Because of the heat. So as to avoid more sickness to other people.

FX: BACK ROOM.

REJOICE   When I think of you, it's like my heart is burning. I am on fire with desire.
HARMONY   Rejoice! *(giggling)* You are a mad person!
REJOICE   It is you that makes me mad. This week I couldn't work because I was thinking of you. The roof nails were dropping from my hand.
HARMONY   Rejoice you are meant to be at the Burial Society Meeting! Mketwa already left ten minutes ago.
REJOICE   I know. I waited until he caught the taxi. What is wrong with the his motor vehicle?
HARMONY   I don't know. He says maybe the carbu ... something. All his money is wasting on that car. That is why he cannot buy me a fridge.
REJOICE   Come, my baby. Let's not talk about motor vehicles now. And fridges. How often do we get these chances.
HARMONY   What if Mketwa comes back?
REJOICE   He won't.
HARMONY   You will be late for the meeting.
REJOICE   Not if we are fast. *(beat)* Harmony is such a beautiful name. I lie in bed and I think of how soft you feel, and your name is like a tune that sings in my head.
HARMONY   Oh Rejoice! I can't help myself when you touch me like that.
REJOICE   I know that, my baby.

HARMONY Oh Rejoice! Rejoice!
REJOICE Come my baby. Just let me come and say hello with you.
HARMONY Oh Rejoice, Rejoice, Rejoice.

FX: ROOF AMBIENCE. PASSING IBIS.

REJOICE The society is simple, really. It's just the box and the transport that we are concerned with. That's all. Doesn't matter if it's Cape Town, doesn't matter if it's Gijaburu. *(beat)* My brother, Orchard, he is the policeman. He is working out all the maths.
WARREN The policeman?
REJOICE *(proud)* He checks everything. The figures, whatever you want. He is making sure that the whole organization is running smoothly. If there is some discrepancy they will go to Orchard. Because of his ability with numbers.

FX: FADE ROOF.

ORCHARD It was when I was being taught by Mrs Wells that I discovered that maths is something which is just in my blood. Especially short algebras. When I went back to school I looked like a teacher. If there's some sections that the students have jumped, the teacher would ask me what is wrong. I would say: 'No, from here, you were supposed to go this side. You must go third floor, second floor, first floor. You must make the whole journey. You cannot just fall to the ground.' You see?

FX. TOWNSHIP STREET.

REJOICE This is the place. Number 3279 Freedom Street.

FX: FOOTSTEPS. KNOCK ON THE DOOR. REJOICE HUMS

FX: DOOR OPENS.

WOMAN Hello?
REJOICE Hello, Mama. Are you Mrs Matabane?
WOMAN *(SeSotho)* Yes.
REJOICE I am Rejoice Iqudu, co-president of the Imvula Burial Society.
WOMAN *(SeSotho)* What you want here?
ORCHARD And I am Orchard Iqudu, the policeman of the Imvula Burial Society.

WOMAN   Eish.

REJOICE   My sister, unfortunately we must investigate some claims concerning your husband.

ORCHARD   You claimed money to bury Mr Matabane in Thaba N'Chu when some of our members saw you burying him right here in Johannesburg. So all these expenses: petrol, five hundred and twelve, seventeen Rand; phone calls sixteen, thirty-nine Rand; meat, four hundred and fifty-one Rand; other refreshments, three hundred andnineteen, eighty-five Rand. All these things you have written down, and claimed, are not good mathematics.

REJOICE   In fact, Mrs Matabane, many of them are just plain lies.

WOMAN *(SeSotho)* Have pity. Have pity. *(begins to cry)*

FX: FADE STREET.

ORCHARD   The thing which is most strange is that finally I failed maths. And the ones I was teaching, they passed. I got a C instead of an A. Even though I was a teacher there. *(long beat)* Maths is something which can just turn you around like this!

FX: HOUSE AMBIENCE.

SUSAN   It's not funny, Warren.

WARREN   Isn't it?

SUSAN   You can't get ground maize in Zimbabwe. You can't get flour. You can't get oil. They're desperate. And the AIDS statistics are probably worse than they are here.

WARREN   Ag statistics!

SUSAN   You think the numbers aren't true?

WARREN   Where are they? All these dying people? Our population has risen by ten per cent since 1996!

SUSAN   They test positive and then they get sent home. The doctors write TB on the death certificate. TB or malaria or pneumonia. *(beat)* There's horrific denial going on in this country and you are part of it.

FX: FADE HOUSE.

ORCHARD   The loss of his job on the farm was not the fault of Rejoice. Mrs Wells left. She took all those people that were working there and went to another farm. But it didn't help. The war veterans

came and it was finished. So everybody have to know where to go.
Rejoice went back to Imvula. I came this side. I came here before
Rejoice did. I was the last born, but I was the first to come to
Johannesburg.

FX: BACK ROOM. TEA PREPARED.

CLIFF   That little one of yours, Nicolas, was so excited with his
new shoes. All day he was just chasing the dog. He said he could run
faster because of the shoes.

REJOICE   It is my great wish that I could also have travelled home
this time.

CLIFF   How was the work here?

REJOICE   Just the one gardening job. Tuesday and Thursday. On
the weekends fixing the bathroom here in the house.

CLIFF   Did you manage to put in the toilet?

REJOICE   There have been some few problems. Nothing that you
can worry about too much. But when you add it with the box in the
garage ...

CLIFF *(astonished)* You have put a coffin in the garage?

REJOICE   Mketwa was paying two hundred rand a month for that
other place. This is for free. And we save some of that storage money
for other purposes.

CLIFF   But Susan and Warren won't like that, Rejoice. They
won't be satisfied, really.

REJOICE *(angry)* What do you know? You haven't even met them!
They don't even know that you have lost your place and you are
staying here!

FX: FADE BACK ROOM.

ORCHARD   The thing which pushed me to come to South Africa is a
girl. We did a mistake. She was a school kid and I was a school kid
and we did a mistake. So because of that, she was expelled from her
home for good and I have to marry her forcibly. But we loved each
other. So there was no problem. My father was already ailing at that
time. I talked to him about the situation. He said: 'Because you are
not working, where will you get the money?' I said: 'Don't worry. I'm
going. I've finished schooling. What I have to do, I have to see for
myself.' And that was when I came this side.

FX: BATHROOM. TOOLS PACKED AWAY.

REJOICE   It's looking good now. Tomorrow I will do the grouting. When does Warren come back?

SUSAN   Next week, Tuesday. You think we're going to be finished by then?

REJOICE   Yes, we'll be finished. Just if this new toilet bowl is still leaking there might be a problem.

FX: GARDEN AMBIENCE. CAR TICKING.

WARREN *(irritated)* Some what?

REJOICE   Silicone. Just the normal one for the bathroom. That is stopping the leaks. Otherwise I must take that bowl out again and put in the new connection. And that is quite a big operation because you have to break away the cement of the floor.

WARREN   You put the bowl too close to the wall, Rejoice. The seat won't stay up.

REJOICE   Just maybe an inch or two. I did a mistake. But I'm very much hoping that silicone will heal everything.

WARREN   Silicon won't keep the seat up! *(beat)* And there's a coffin in the garage! Why is there a coffin in my garage, Rejoice?

REJOICE   I'm sorry, Warren. It's that Mketwa. I explained everything with Susan. *(beat)* Just that bit of silicone. Then I can be finished.

WARREN *(sighs)* Look, I've got a very busy day, but I'll see what I can do.

FX: CAR PULLS OFF.

REJOICE *(shouting)* And some two by fours for the garage ceiling. And some nails. Please Warren.

FX: HOUSE AMBIENCE. SUPPER.

WARREN   I knew that the plumbing would be beyond him.

SUSAN   He'll fix it. Don't worry.

WARREN   And the coffin?

SUSAN   It's just temporary. Just a couple of weeks. He was so worried that you'd be cross about it and I promised him it was fine. Please don't give him a hard time.

FX: FADE HOUSE.

ORCHARD   Me and that girl, we were not financially secure. But thanks to God, Rejoice was working again. He was Inseminating. This was in 1986. So the first time Rejoice was paid, he went to pay damages to the parents of the girl. Not big damages. They charged me just one cow. It was sixty dollars at the time. The price was quite low, really, because the girl wasn't pregnant. I was the first to take a wife in the family. I said to Rejoice: you see this person. She is here to help everybody. And I liked her because she helped my father. Sometimes my father would just ... go over himself. The eyes weren't seeing. The feets were swollen. He couldn't walk. She had to take his clothes. Wash them clean. And give them back to him clean.

FX: HOUSE AMBIENCE.

SUSAN *(beat)* Damages to ... what?
WARREN   To her ... tackle.
SUSAN *(beat)* You mean he ... he *hurt* her?
WARREN   No, no. No, no. It's just what they call it, you know. Breaking the virginity.
SUSAN *(dry)* Them.
WARREN   Yes. They call it damages.

FX: BACK ROOM AMBIENCE. REJOICE AND HARMONY IN BED.

REJOICE   Why do you have to make such a noise. It's like you want to wake the whole city.
HARMONY   I don't care if I wake them up. You make me feel so good. You are so strong and big down there. Just like Mketwa.
REJOICE   Eish. How can you talk about Mketwa at a time like this?
HARMONY   It was him that bought me the fridge.
REJOICE   Only because he sold that rubbish motor vehicle. And sometimes he buys cheap boxes and takes the extra money for himself. The guys are watching him, Harmony. He won't be co-president much longer, I can tell you.
HARMONY   He treats me very nicely, Rejoice. That fridge has even got automatic ice.
REJOICE *(beat)* Where is he?

HARMONY   He won't be back for a long time. He went to see the Sangoma in Pietersburg.

REJOICE   In Pietersburg? What for?

HARMONY   I don't know. *(beat)* I think maybe he was stroked.

REJOICE *(beat)* Serious?

HARMONY   Yes. Just a little bit. The side of his face here. It's not moving.

REJOICE   Vocabulary stroke?

HARMONY   No, he's still talking.

REJOICE   Eish. *(beat)* I must go. Where are those trousers of mine that you mended?

HARMONY   I don't know.

REJOICE   You don't know?

HARMONY   No.

REJOICE   Where are my trousers, Harmony?

HARMONY *(beat)* They are with Mketwa.

REJOICE   Why has he got them?

HARMONY   He found them! I could not tell him they were yours!

REJOICE   They are pure wool, those trousers.

HARMONY   I told him I bought them for him.

REJOICE   They come from Naidoo's Indian second-hand in Elof Street!

HARMONY   What was I meant to do, Rejoice? He found them here in the room!

FX: GARDEN.

WARREN   Rejoice we have to talk about this. I really don't understand why I have to have a coffin in my garage.

REJOICE *(regretful)* It was Mketwa's idea that we have some few boxes.

WARREN   For the burial society?

REJOICE   Yes. Just on stand by. Because the TB is hitting the guys. It is better if we can just buy when the price is right. But storage is where the problem comes. So Mketwa arranged for the storage. He found a shed there in Alexandria township. But now that shed has burnt down. That is why it becomes very necessary to store just this one single coffin here with you.

WARREN   Rejoice, I'm really not too happy about this. I have to be honest with you.

FX: A HAND ON COFFIN.

REJOICE   I have arranged it so it takes up very little space. It is just temporary, really. I can even maybe cover it with some plastics so nobody can notice.

WARREN *(beat)* How long is temporary, Rejoice?

REJOICE   Maybe just one week. Maybe ... two. Just a short time. Serious.

FX: HOUSE.

WARREN *(beat)* I'm sorry but sometimes you have to learn to say 'No'. Sometimes 'No' is the best option.

SUSAN   We're helping him, Warren. For heaven's sake! What harm can it possibly do to you to have a coffin in the garage?

WARREN   Give them an inch and they'll take a mile.

SUSAN   Oh nonsense.

WARREN   We'll end up with a garage full of coffins!

SUSAN   And a house that isn't falling apart at the seams.

FX: BATHROOM. TROWEL ON CEMENT.

REJOICE   This is the first time I have ever fitted a toilet bowl. *(apologetic)* It was just two inches too close.

WARREN   I knew you'd never seal it with silicone.

REJOICE   I'm sorry. I did a mistake. Just a couple of inches. But I've fixed it now. We can even test. Look.

FX: TOILET FLUSH.

REJOICE *(proud)* Nothing. It's dry, dry, like a drought.

FX: FADE BATHROOM.

ORCHARD   Our father, Joseph Iqudu, died a clean man on November 7, 1989. I was working here in Johannesburg by the Belem Shopping Centre. I was cleaning at the *Sizzling Gourmet Grill*. That was my first job in South Africa. They would not allow me to go home for the burial. In fact I had only been working two weeks. Which they said was too soon to take leave. But in 1990 I went home. And I found that everything was done properly by Rejoice, all the ceremonies, and I could go and speak to my father with no problems at all. I was able to communicate with him perfectly.

FX: GARAGE. COFFIN SHIFTED.

REJOICE   I'm sorry for this, really. We can just put it down here.
There is Orchard and some other guys waiting to help. If I can just
ask them to come in.

SUSAN   Of course you can. *(beat)* It's not someone in your
family is it?

REJOICE   No, thank you, Susan. *(beat)* It is Mketwa.

SUSAN   Mketwa died?

REJOICE   Regretfully ... this what happened.

FX: KNUCKLES ON COFFIN.

REJOICE *(continuing)* Mketwa is going home in this very box.

SUSAN *(beat)* What did he die off?

REJOICE *(grave)* First the stroke, then pneumonia.

SUSAN   How old was he?

REJOICE   Maybe ... forty something years.

SUSAN   Pneumonia is curable.

REJOICE   Yes, Susan.

SUSAN   How long was he sick for?

REJOICE   Just a few weeks. *(beat, checking the deal)* Mketwa's
family will replace this coffin. I even spoke to him on the phone
before he died. He promised me that we will get another one, same,
same. *(beat)* So it won't take up any more space than this one.

SUSAN   You want to keep it here? The replacement?

REJOICE   Yes please, Susan. Now I am the sole president of the
society the guys expect me to arrange everything.

SUSAN   Rejoice, that's fine. Of course.

REJOICE   Thank you. I hope Warren will not be getting angry.

SUSAN   Don't you worry about Warren.

FX: FADE GARAGE.

ORCHARD   We are not like European people. When we die, we go to
join our ancestors. We sit down with them and we talk. I, myself,
Orchard Iqudu, will join the assembly of the ancestors. When that
times comes, there will be cows grazing on the green field above
Imvula dam. The trees in the Orchard will be hanging with bright
fruit. There will be children laughing. The men that are left from our

family, the Iqudus, will put the juice from the gall of the ox on their bodies. That gall tastes very bitter to living people. But to dead people, it is like flowers. That is the sweet smell that calls me and Rejoice back to the world. *(beat)* In these things, we are not like European people.

FX: GARAGE. COFFIN SHIFTED.

REJOICE   I will just put this cloth over so you are not worried by the sight of it when you are going to work in the morning.

WARREN   My morning wasn't the same while I couldn't touch wood on a coffin. *(beat)* What did you go up in?

REJOICE   A combi.

WARREN   With Mketwa inside?

REJOICE   No. Mketwa travelled in the trailer. Eish, but the border is terrible these days. The queue is ten kilometres! You have to wait, maybe, for another whole day.

WARREN   Ouch.

REJOICE   But luckily our driver knew what he has to do. He took all our passports and goes straight inside. He told them, 'No, I've got a dead person.' They let us pass.

WARREN   And the funeral? Did it go OK?

REJOICE   It was good. *(regretful beat)* But that Mketwa was just the same as ever. I was looking at the trousers he was wearing.

WARREN   His trousers?

REJOICE   I was just regretting a little bit because he got those trousers from me.

WARREN   Oh.

REJOICE   The only reason he had them was because of a terrible misunderstanding. *(beat)* Then I saw, eish Warren, down here ... Mketwa was stiff like a pole.

WARREN   True?

REJOICE   Harmony says that Mketwa can never change. Even now that he has gone to join the ancestors.

FX: HOUSE.

WARREN *(beat)* What's he like? Orchard?

SUSAN   He's nice.

WARREN   If he's going to be living with us, I sincerely hope so.

SUSAN   Don't worry about it. *(beat)* He's tall and ... I don't know. Serious. I think he's quite bright.

WARREN   Has he got a job?

SUSAN   Yes.

WARREN   There isn't space for two people in that room. *(beat)* You know they're keeping trailers behind the garage now?

SUSAN   They've got nowhere else to keep them. And how else are they going to send food home?

FX: HOUSE. CARPENTRY.

REJOICE   I spoke on the phone. They are all well.

SUSAN   Progress's baby?

REJOICE   He is better now. It was just flu.

SUSAN   Good. And your little one? Nicholas?

REJOICE *(proud)* Susan, he is a warrior. I have got a small brown dog at the house there. Hardship says that Nicholas runs the whole day after the dog. It is his best friend. Hardship had to make him take off his shoes. Otherwise in one month he wears them finished.

SUSAN   Are you going to go up for Christmas?

REJOICE   Yes, I'm going.

SUSAN   I'll give you some things to take. For Hardship and the children.

REJOICE   Thank you, Susan. They would like that, really.

FX: FADE HOUSE.

ORCHARD   The most important thing in our culture is the kids. We don't worry much about grown-ups. We worry about the future of the kids. In our culture, if you can look at it, you say, 'These people are returning back.' People die, but then later they return. And in fact you can see it with your own eyes. Because this person resembles so and so that was dead a long time ago.

FX: HOUSE.

WARREN   People are dying, Susan.

SUSAN   I know.

WARREN   I never believed the figures, but everyone I know knows someone who is dying.

SUSAN   This is just the first wave.

FX: GARDEN, CRICKETS, AGED CAR ENGINE.

WARREN   How many of you going in that car?

REJOICE   I think there are six of us. Maybe seven.

SUSAN   Have you got a good driver? The roads are awful at this time of year.

REJOICE   No, he is a good driver. Very good. Very careful. Not going too fast.

SUSAN   Have you packed the presents for the kids?

REJOICE   They are all there inside. Thank you, Susan.

SUSAN   Here are blankets that the Joneses dropped off for you. And some extra ones from us.

REJOICE   Thank you.

WARREN   You have a great holiday, Rejoice.

SUSAN   And a good Christmas. We'll see you after New Year.

REJOICE   Good bye.

WARREN   Good bye.

SUSAN   Good bye. And drive carefully!

REJOICE   Yes, we will.

FX: DOOR SLAM. CAR PULLS OFF.

FX: HOUSE. FIREWORKS.

WARREN *(waking)* What the hell is that?

SUSAN   Fire works. *(laughs)* It's New Year's Eve.

WARREN   Holy cow. I thought it was the revolution all over again. *(beat)* When did I drop off?

SUSAN   About half an hour ago. Happy New Year.

WARREN   It's been a good one.

SUSAN   I know. It has. *(beat, snuggles)* I'm glad we got the house done.

WARREN   Well, you were right. I couldn't have done it.

SUSAN   Yes. *(beat)* You know Rejoice is moving out.

WARREN   No.

SUSAN   He said you were right. There isn't space for two people in that room. And some people he gardens for have offered him a place.

WARREN   So it's just Orchard now.

SUSAN   Ja. He's going to do one morning a week in the garden.

WARREN *(beat)* And we still get to store the coffins and the trailers.
SUSAN   I suppose so. *(beat)* Come here.
WARREN   Should I get a condom?
SUSAN   No. Come. Come here.

FX: FADE HOUSE.

ORCHARD   It was when the farming got too bad that Rejoice moved
to Johannesburg. This was in 1992. Rejoice is a hard-working man,
and very soon he was getting jobs. So then there was me and
Rejoice, and every month we were sending food and money to the
family at Imvula. To my mother and to Rejoice's children. And, that
side, if you can count every single one, there are twenty-seven
people who are depending on us.

FX: GARAGE. REJOICE LAUGHING. FOOTSTEPS.

SUSAN   Rejoice? Rejoice? Is that you? *(astonished beat)* What
are you doing?
REJOICE *(laughs)* I'm just testing, Susan. Just so I can know for sure
what is happening. You can never know with these people.
SUSAN   Testing what? Why are you lying in there?
REJOICE   Eish. *(fighting tears)* That Mketwa.
SUSAN   Rejoice please ... what's wrong? Why are you lying in the
coffin?
REJOICE   Those bastards. Those dunderheads. They have stolen
everything.
SUSAN   What? Stolen what?
REJOICE   They have taken everything from me. Every last thing.
They have broken everything. Even my feet. Even the simplest thing
no longer works. The water cannot flow positively. They have told
me that I am finished and everything is gone. Those Dunderheads.
SUSAN   Who? I don't understand what you're talking about.
REJOICE   Susan, my feet are burning. I cannot sleep. I lie with my
feet on fire. The whole night I lie awake and the sheets are wet with
my sweat. All through the night it is as if I am walking in fire. Even
if I put my feet in cold water, I am walking in the fire.
SUSAN   Rejoice get out of there, please. Let me help you!
REJOICE   No! All my life I have been saying, 'I must rejoice! It
doesn't matter if the child is too thin. I must rejoice. It doesn't

matter if I cannot go home to see my wife. I must rejoice. It doesn't matter if the cow has no milk. I must rejoice. It doesn't matter that a man who works hard cannot find a job in his own county. I must rejoice. It doesn't matter that the money is stolen at the border. I must rejoice. It doesn't matter that the farms are broken. I must rejoice. It doesn't matter that the war veterans are just murderers. I must rejoice. It doesn't matter that the bags are broken and the mielie-meal is spilt with the milk on the ground. I must rejoice. The cow is dead. I must rejoice. My feet are burning. I must rejoice. I cannot walk. I must rejoice. I must rejoice. I must rejoice.'

SUSAN   Rejoice, come. Please. Let me help you out of there.

REJOICE   Mketwa left this box for me. *(beat)* But it's too short. That guy is always stealing the last laugh. First my trousers, now this! *(laugh/cry)* I will have to take my last journey with my knees bent up. He has forced me to lie in my own box with my knees bent up like a bicycle rider. They want my whole family to be just like a joke.

SUSAN   Rejoice, calm down. You're not making any sense.

REJOICE   I'm sorry. *(beat)* I went to the hospital for testing. They told me that I am positive.

FX: HOUSE AMBIENCE.

WARREN   Positive?

SUSAN   That was the word he used. *(beat)* But Warren ... he um ... I've never heard him talk like that. *(fights tears)* I think it might be dementia. I think ... I think the truth is ... he's got full blown AIDS.

FX: FADE HOUSE.

ORCHARD   Many people do not know why Rejoice got sick. They can find it hard to understand what happened. *(beat)* You see in our area, if you try to make something, people are not happy. From the death of my father, Joseph Iqudu, our neighbours thought our family would be a circus. A circus where people can laugh whenever they like. But they didn't find that. They found that everything is under respect.

FX: HOUSE.

WARREN   I think we should look into it.

SUSAN   And go where? Warren, people from all over Africa flock here because there's work, medicine, food. If you can pay for it there's even anti-retrovirals.

WARREN   In Sweden there are fifty people who are HIV positive and the health department knows exactly who they are. *(silence)* I just ... I think we should start a family. And I think we should do it somewhere else.

FX: HOUSE.

ORCHARD   The time Rejoice got sick, I was also sick. When he moved from Susan and Warren's house, I couldn't visit him at first. When I did visit him, I found that he could not swallow one thing. His feets were swollen. He could not walk. I said, 'Brother, go home. Be nearer to your kids. Talk to your kids. Before you die. Because I can see there's nothing I can do.' *(beat)* It was already too late to tell him what I knew about the neighbours. In fact I was too stressed to tell him that those very same neighbours were making me sick also.

FX: BACK ROOM.

ORCHARD   Perhaps ... I can make you a little tea.
REJOICE   Thank you. It doesn't matter.
ORCHARD   You must drink something.
REJOICE   I had some milk. These other things are hurting my mouth.
ORCHARD   You cannot live if you do not eat and drink.
REJOICE   Yes. *(beat)* It will come to you, my brother.
ORCHARD   What? What are you talking?
REJOICE   When I am dead there will only be you. For all the family at Imvula.
ORCHARD   Rejoice, go home. Go to Imvula. Go and drink the water from the well. That is the sweetest water. And eat the fish from the dam. And, in a short time, you will be getting better. You will see.
REJOICE   No. I must stay here. I must see if I can find a work. Maybe something in a vegetable garden. Something where I don't have to stand.

FX: FADE BACK ROOM.

ORCHARD   Rejoice said to me, 'My brother, I am HIV positive.' But, because of my African beliefs, I already knew that. You see, I had a dream. In this dream, I went back once more and looked into the well in the orchard at Imvula. The moon was very big straight above and the water was like a mirror. But I did not see myself in that mirror. Just like it was when I was a small child, I saw Rejoice. And where his legs ended, was just flames. *(beat)* Because of that dream I went to a Sangoma, a traditional healer. And he told me I was supposed to die also.

FX: HOUSE.

SUSAN   You know what the difference is? Between here and New Zealand and Australia.

WARREN   What?

SUSAN   In those places the original inhabitants have been wiped out. And if there are any left, they're derelict.

WARREN   Half the people are derelict here also. More than half.

SUSAN   There are historical reasons for that.

WARREN   You sound like the government.

SUSAN   Warren, Africans are the government here. The Aborigines aren't the government in Australia.

WARREN   So?

SUSAN   Your idea of some safe European middle-class super-clean haven is bullshit. The twin towers are down. There is no centre of civilisation and democracy. And there's no axis of evil. There's just us. South Africa is as good as it gets.

FX: FADE HOUSE.

ORCHARD   You see with this bewitchment … I have a very good example. Because the Sangoma told me what was happening to Rejoice's dog. *(beat)* The Sangoma doesn't know Imvula. But he knows what is happening there. He told me the dog was sick. *(beat)* When I went to Imvula, it was just like that traditional healer said. The dog was sick. The feets were swollen. It could not even eat. *(beat)* First the dog … then Rejoice.

FX: HOUSE.

WARREN   Is he working?

SUSAN   He can't.

WARREN   So what's he going to do?

SUSAN   I don't know. *(beat)* I think you must take him to Doctor Flismas.

FX: FADE HOUSE.

ORCHARD   When I realized it was getting too serious, I went to the
burial society. I told them, 'Please, can you come and see your
President?' They sent me about four people. Then, including
relatives, I found there were about eleven people gathered there. I
didn't say any word. And Rejoice said –
REJOICE   I am going home.
ORCHARD   He gave the society two days. And they accepted because
he was the President. I said, 'My brother, you can see, I am also sick. I
would have liked to go with you. But I don't think it can be a good idea.'

FX: HOUSE.

SUSAN   When's he leaving?
WARREN   Tomorrow. *(beat)* Flismas says every single symptom
Rejoice has got is treatable. The thrush in his mouth, the chest
thing. It's all treatable. And for something in the region of eight
hundred rand a month we could put him on anti-retrovirals. If we
can find that, we can keep him alive.

FX: FADE HOUSE.

FX: STREET. FOOTSTEPS. CAR DOOR.

REJOICE *(beat)* It will be better at home.
WARREN   You won't get treatment there.
REJOICE   Just to see my kids and my wife.
WARREN   But Rejoice, you can get treated here. Flismas is a great
doctor. I've heard him speaking on the radio about AIDS. Don't
worry about the money. We can make a plan. We'll talk to the
Joneses. We can all chip in.
REJOICE   Thank you, Warren.
WARREN   Think about it.
REJOICE   It is better if I go home.
WARREN   Rejoice ...
REJOICE   Warren, the roof keeps the rain from falling on your
head. Just remember that one thing.
WARREN *(beat)* Yes.
REJOICE   You must paint before the rust is coming. Once the rust
comes you can say that roof is finished. You must know how the

water is flowing in the gutters, all this things. That is what I am telling Orchard.

FX: FADE STREET.

ORCHARD   I listen on the radio. I watch on the TV. 'Be wise, condomize.' I agree with that. Because this AIDS sickness is a dangerous thing. It is like short algebras. You never know which way it will come.

FX: HOUSE.

WARREN   It's not just a relationship. It's a decision to grow a family. Of course, I'll change nappies. What do you take me for? *(beat)* Will you think about it? While I'm gone.
SUSAN   I'll ... I don't know ...
WARREN   I'm going to miss you.
SUSAN   I'll miss you too.
WARREN   Orchard said he'd keep an eye on things here. Keep everything safe.
SUSAN   Yes. *(beat)* Has he heard from Rejoice?
WARREN   No.

FX: FADE HOUSE.

ORCHARD   When a man's brother dies, if the wife has what we call heritage ... you have to inherit that wife. This is not a forced matter. After we have finished with the burial and all the ceremonies, that woman, the widow, must be very quiet. We treat her like the antelope, the Iqudu. It takes at least another three, four months before it becomes possible to normalize the situation. Especially if it's a young female. Then we'll do everything necessary to free her as quickly as possible. We will perform all the ceremonies. And by so freeing her, she can choose. Is she going, or is she staying?

FX GARDEN. CRICKETS. CAR PULL UP. DOOR. FOOTSTEPS.

WARREN   Hello.
SUSAN   Hi.
WARREN   Looking at the moon?
SUSAN   Mm.
WARREN   Isn't it stunning?

SUSAN   Like a silver dollar. *(she takes a breath, can't talk)*
WARREN   Susan, what?
SUSAN   I uh ...
WARREN   What?
SUSAN   Warren, there's two things.
WARREN   Ja?
SUSAN   I'm pregnant.
WARREN   Holy cow.
SUSAN   Yes.
WARREN   When did you find out?
SUSAN   Two weeks ago. I didn't want to tell you on the phone.
WARREN   Of course.
SUSAN   Warren, we're going to have to decide whether ... we're going to stay or ...
WARREN   Yes. *(beat)* What's the second one.
SUSAN   Rejoice is back.
WARREN   No! Where?
SUSAN   He's inside. With Orchard. *(beat)* He says he wants to help you do another coat on the roof.
WARREN   But ...
SUSAN   He heard about some special sealant on the radio. He says it has a fifteen year guarantee. He wants Orchard to help so he can teach him how to do stuff with his hands. He says Orchard doesn't know how to do stuff with his hands.

FX: HOUSE.

REJOICE   Listen to me. I don't want tea. I need something else. Orchard, can't you understand what I am looking for?
ORCHARD No.
REJOICE   I want a house that is clean and dry. I want to know that Hardship is safe. I want to know that Nicholas is warm in his bed. I want to know that there are strong men there that can keep the war veterans away. I want to know that the money is flowing positively.
ORCHARD What are you talking?
REJOICE   You never learnt this things!
ORCHARD What things?
REJOICE   You get lost in the water storage. It's too deep that one. I want you to think about the roof. You must keep the rain off these people Orchard. You must console them.

ORCHARD   Eish, Rejoice.
REJOICE   You must learn ...
ORCHARD   What?
REJOICE   You must take a bucket of water up to the roof. You must check that the money is flowing positively.

FX: GARDEN.

SUSAN   He might be sleeping now. I made a bed up for him in the spare room. I don't know where he should be. Maybe he should be ... in hospital or ...
WARREN   Why isn't he with Hardship?
SUSAN   He said he ... he drank the water from the well and he felt better.
WARREN   From the well?
SUSAN   I think so. He jumbles things up.
WARREN   What do you want me to do?
SUSAN   I don't know. Just ... just go in and see him. Talk to him. He so wants to see you.
WARREN   Have you spoken to Orchard?
SUSAN   Yes. *(beat)* Orchard can't look after him in that tiny room. You know that. *(beat)* He thinks the same as you. He thinks he should be back with Hardship.
WARREN *(beat)* OK.

FX: FOOTSTEPS, DOOR.

SUSAN   Warren?
WARREN   Ja?
SUSAN   Be gentle.
WARREN   Yes.

FX: FADE GARDEN.

ORCHARD   I think that if you are approved HIV positive, you must try to be out of things like beer, cigarettes. Anything which can destroy your blood. I wish each and every one, every six months, must go and check for AIDS. Just like that. But I think if you are a happy guy with happy people, you can live longer. I would like each and every one to bear that in mind. Because once you think of that HIV/AIDS, you are likely to be stroked. The stroke comes first. If it's a vocabulary stroke, you will die the same time. Heart attack.

FX: GARDEN, DOOR, FOOTSTEPS.

SUSAN   So?
WARREN   He um ...
SUSAN   Do you think we should take him to hospital?
WARREN   Rejoice is dead.

FX: FADE GARDEN.

ORCHARD   Rejoice was buried at Imvula on the 28th of March, 2003.
There were many people there. There were even fifteen from the
Society which travelled from Johannesburg. The journey was good
and there was no problem with the heat. *(beat)* Those children,
Progress and Joseph and Naledi and President and Mandla and
Nicholas, they come to me. Their mother, Hardship, is now my wife. I
love her very much. But the payment is on my shoulders. I am the
small father. In Zulu they say, *'Ba'ncane.* Little father.' So whatever
they might need, I must provide. It is I, Orchard Iqudu, that must
console them. *(beat)* In September, just after I heard that Harmony
was dead, I went to Imvula for certain ceremonies. We cleansed the
spades that were used to dig Rejoice's grave. We performed each thing
that was necessary for him to take his place among the ancestors. The
next time I go back I will visit his grave. From up there I will look
down at the dam and the village and the school and the orchard. From
far away I will hear the voices of the children. My brother will come to
join me. Me and my brother will sit there on that green hill above the
dam at Imvula, and we will rejoice. We will rejoice.

The End.

James Whyle

James Whyle is an actor, writer, director and producer. He turned from acting to writing in 1994 when it first became possible for the real issues of South Africa to be addressed on South African Television. James was head writer for TV3's acclaimed *Hard Copy*, and has written for TV2'S Emmy nominated *Zero Tolerance*, M-Net's crime drama *Snitch*, the TV1 series *Mzansi*. He continues to write radio drama for the BBC. *Dancing with the Dead* (2002, Radio 4), the leading role was played by Richard E Grant. *A Man Called Rejoice*, was re-broadcast for the third time in May 2004. James is a senior writer and, on occasion, story liner, on the South African daily series, *Isidingo – The Need*.

In 1981 James wrote his first play, *National Madness*, based on his experience in, and escaping from, the SANDF. *National Madness* was performed at the Market and Baxter Theatres in the early 80s and published in *Market Plays 2*, edited by Stephen Grey. (AD. Donker, 1986) His second play, *Hellhound*, was performed at the Market Theatre in 1992. A story, *Sapper Fijn and the Cow* appears in *The Penguin Book of Contemporary South African Short Stories*. (1993)

*Acknowledgement:

Song Rejoice sings is –*Hello My Baby* by J. Shabalala of Ladysmith Black Mambazo from One Shaka Zulu CD, CDGMP40157H.

Made in R.S.A copyright © 1988 GMP.
Marketed and distributed by Gallo Record Company.
Rights to be cleared before use in performance.

Playwright's Note:

'What will you write about now that apartheid has gone?' This was the perennial question posed to theatre-makers after 1994. Yet, South Africa today is a much more interesting place to explore creatively. Rather than the stark polarities of the past, there is much more fascinating room for contradiction, for complexity and for irony in our nascent democratic, non-racial and non-sexist project.

Generally though, writers appear to have shied away from dealing with contemporary issues. Some say that after the force-fed 'protest theatre' diet of the past, audiences no longer want to see such work, that they want theatre to help them escape rather than confront their realities. Others say that it is not yet time to raise awkward questions, and that artists should concentrate on building the rainbow nation. Still others contend that writers are afraid to deal critically with contemporary politics for fear of alienating those in power, those who dispense public largesse to the struggling arts sector.

I've always believed that if we are serious about democracy and about the exercise of our constitutional right to freedom of creative expression, then we must simply practise it. Not to do so, is to risk compromising democracy by leaving it to others to define in their potentially self-serving image. Rather than wait for 'the right time' for issues to be debated or questions to be asked, theatre-makers should provoke thought, stimulate debate, challenge current dogmas and provide the intellectual and emotional spaces for these. And do it in a way that entertains.

Green Man Flashing explores how power affects morality, how power defines what is right and what is wrong. It poses the contra-dictions between patriotic duty and human rights. It juxtaposes the greater collective good to justice for one person. It does this by placing a range of characters in a particular situation and giving them choices. We try to understand why they choose to do what they do and ask ourselves what we would do if we were in a similar situation. These are themes that confront people and artists in South America, Asia, Europe, North America, the Middle East. And here in South Africa. It is here where we live. It is here where we are engaged in the ongoing project to build a more just, more humane, more democratic society.

Mike van Graan

GREEN MAN FLASHING

Mike van Graan

The play was first performed at the National Arts Festival in Grahamstown, July 2004, directed by Clare Stopford.

CHARACTERS

GABBY ANDERSON is a 43 year-old, white woman from a liberal family that used to own a publishing company. She is a former 'student lefty" who studied English, Psychology and Politics at university, and was a member of the National Union of South African Students (NUSAS). She left Cape Town and South Africa in 1980, at the age of 24, to evade constant detention of her partner, Aaron Matshoba, and because of the harassment they faced as a mixed couple. Their path took them through various countries, till they settled in East Germany, where Aaron underwent basic military training, but also studied further in the realm of international law, and soon became one of the leading exiles. Gabby gave birth to a son, Matthew, in East Germany, and much of her time was spent looking after him, although she did some work for Radio Freedom. Gabby, Aaron and Matthew returned to South Africa in 1992.

performed by Jennifer Steyn

AARON MATSHOBA is 45 years old and is one of the major political party's leading troubleshooters. He was part of their negotiating team which brought about the interim constitution, and since then – rather than formally going into government as a politician or bureaucrat – he has chosen to remain active as a "soldier" of the party for whatever its requirements. A former student leader, highly articulate, he is passionately committed to the new South Africa, and to making a success of it. He is principled, loyal, hardworking and firm, yet a sensitive human being. His choice to stay out of government is representative of his committed nature i.e. he believes that not all skilled people should go into government, but should be available to get their hands dirty in "unsexy" work. He has a conscience, but his commitment to the party is paramount.

performed by Vusi Khanyile

ANNA RICHARDS is a 44 year-old lawyer who runs her own legal practice. She is a divorced mother with two daughters aged 19 and 14. She is more of a feminist than Gabby, a strong woman whose experiences have made her a bit cynical about life and love.

performed by Charlotte Butler

LUTHANDO NYAKA is the quintessential party hack. In his early 50s, he is a party hard-liner, not in a political sense (as he is the kind of person who would change his politics depending on what the leadership said), but rather in terms of loyalty, defence of the party, etc. He is dogmatic, defensive, arrogant and not shy to use force or the threat thereof to obtain his ends. He is the ultimate "bad cop" in a "good cop, bad cop" approach to persuasion. This may be because he feels he needs to prove his loyalty and commitment more so than others, because of rumours about his past.

performed by Sechaba Morojele

INSPECTOR THEO ABRAHAMS is a 54 year-old, coloured policeman. During the apartheid era, he served in the security branch of the police force. With the changes in the political system, and after receiving amnesty at the Truth and Reconciliation Commission, rather than take "the retirement package" like many of his colleagues, he requested a transfer to the Violent Crimes Unit. He is basically a sincere, good policeman, who simply wants to do a good job. Under the old regime, he genuinely felt that he was fighting communism, although he was not party to many of the violations of human rights that were exposed at the Truth and Reconciliation Commission. While never one of the security police inner circle, his policing skills and colour were assets in the work of the security police at the time, and so was treated with respect without ever being pressured to do more than he wanted to. Under the new regime, he is happy to serve as a good policeman, intent on serving people rather than ideology or politicians.

performed by Andre Samuels

Setting

The play is set in Cape Town in contemporary South Africa, about six weeks before the second national elections in June 1999.
The play explores themes such as individual human rights versus the greater political good, personal relationships versus political loyalty and moral responsibility for individual choices – universal themes played out against the backdrop of the second South African non-racial, democratic elections.

Style

The play does not that start and end in one locality, within real time. Rather, the style of the play is filmic in that the narrative unfolds through a variety of initially disparate scenes. The play starts towards the end of its story, and the middle part tells how the action and characters bring the story to that end.

The Set

The action takes place in a variety of spaces including a courtroom, the living room area of Gabby's upmarket townhouse, the living room of Anna's suburban home, a hall for the TRC hearings, the video link-up to Australia for Gabby's evidence at the inquest, etc. With the variety of locations, the set is simple in order to move rapidly between scenes. It may be best that the action takes place on a split level stage with the courtroom and TRC hearings happening on the 'upper level', while the primary action in the living rooms takes place on the lower level/s of the stage.

Opening Scene: *Inquest into the death of Luthando Nyaka. Lights come up on Aaron and Anna.*

AARON	I was outside when I heard the shots.
ANNA	Outside?
AARON	Outside her house.
ANNA	What were you doing outside?
AARON	I was taking a call on my cellphone. The reception was better outside.
ANNA	What went through your mind when you heard the shots?

AARON   I thought that *he*, had shot her.

ANNA   What made you think that?

AARON   I didn't know that she had a gun.

ANNA   And did you know that he was armed?

AARON   Yes.

ANNA   Then what did you do?

AARON   After I heard the shots, I ran inside the house, shouting her name.

ANNA   And what did you see?

AARON   Gabby ... Ms Anderson ... was standing there ... shaking. She had a gun in her hand.

ANNA   And where was Mr Nyaka?

AARON   He was lying on the ground. He was bleeding from his chest.

ANNA   And what happened next?

AARON   I asked her what had happened. She couldn't answer. She was in a state of shock.

ANNA   And then?

AARON   Then I checked on Mr Nyaka. He was breathing, but with great difficulty. I knew it was only a matter of time ...

ANNA   Mr Matshoba, was there any indication that Mr Nyaka had tried to harm Ms Anderson in any way?

AARON   Well, he was still clutching his gun when I checked on him.

ANNA   What were you and Mr Nyaka doing at Ms Anderson's home?

AARON   We flew down from Johannesburg that morning to attend a conference. I hadn't seen Ms Anderson in a while. We still had some time before our meeting, and since it was in the area where she lived, we popped in to say, 'Hi'.

ANNA   Why was Mr Nyaka armed?

AARON   It was Mr Nyaka's job to protect senior party officials.

ANNA   Isn't that what the VIP Protection Unit does?

AARON   Only for cabinet ministers and members of parliament. Parties are responsible for the security of their own officials.

ANNA   So Mr Nyaka was accompanying you to protect you?

AARON   Yes.

ANNA   And what happened to have made him draw his gun on Ms Anderson?

AARON   I have no idea. As I indicated, I was outside at the time.

ANNA   And you had no indication from what went on before you went outside, that this would happen?

AARON   None at all.

ANNA   What were your impressions of what took place?

AARON   It appeared that for some reason, he had threatened her. But somehow, she managed to get in first and shoot him.

Scene changes to inside of Gabby's apartment. Gabby is seated, reading a one-page document. Luthando is standing a little away from her, observing her resentfully. When he speaks, he constantly looks back over towards the entrance, aware that Aaron, who is outside speaking on his cellphone, could walk in at any minute. He tries to keep his voice down, but his resentment comes through.

LUTHANDO   You got yourself a good deal, lady. *(pause)* You were lucky to have Comrade Matshoba *(gesturing towards the door)* fighting for you. If it was up to me ... *(shaking his head)* Eish. *(pause)*

GABBY   Please ...

LUTHANDO   Please what? *(pause)* Sign the bloody document, so we can go.

GABBY   I'm not signing anything without my lawyer's advice.

LUTHANDO   This has got nothing to do with lawyers. You get lawyers involved in this and ... Eish! It's all there ... in black and white. What more do you want?

GABBY   I want what is right.

LUTHANDO   I'm telling you, if you weren't white, this thing would be handled differently. If you were a black woman ...

GABBY   Then what ... ?

LUTHANDO   I don't think I'll ever understand women. But I know that I'll never understand white people. We're offering you a deal for the sake of the country. And all you want is your white justice.

Lights fade on Luthando and Gabby. Spotlight comes up on Abrahams. Alternating with Aaron in the following sequence.

ABRAHAMS   I swear to tell the truth. *(spotlight fades on him)*
ANNA *(spotlight comes up on Aaron)* How many shots did you hear?
AARON   There were three shots. *(spotlight fades)*
ABRAHAMS *(spotlight coming up on him)* I swear to tell the truth.
   The whole truth. *(spotlight fades on him)*
ANNA *(spotlight up on Aaron)* You heard three shots?
AARON   That's right.
ANNA   And then you ran into the house, calling her name?
AARON   Yes. *(spotlight fades)*
ABRAHAMS *(coming into light)* I swear to tell the truth. The whole
   truth. And nothing but the truth.

*Lights come up on Luthando and Gabby. Gabby is pointing a gun at
Luthando.*

LUTHANDO *(arrogantly, smirking)* Are you threatening me?

*Throughout this sequence, Luthando steps forward towards Gabby,
and she backtracks even though she has a gun. She's reluctant to use it.*

GABBY   I asked you politely to leave ...
LUTHANDO   Pointing that firearm at me ... you've made it personal,
   lady ... I don't care who you are ... who you are connected to!
GABBY   Get out! Please ... !
LUTHANDO   The last person who pointed a gun at me ... *(walking
   towards her)*
GABBY   Please! Please ... just leave! Go!

*Luthando lunges at Gabby in an attempt to grab her gun. She screams
and a shot goes off. Luthando is hit in the shoulder.*

GABBY *(shocked at what she's done)* Shit! I'm ... I'm sorry.

Aaron rushes in.

AARON   Gabby!

Luthando is standing with his hand clutching his right shoulder.

Gabby is pointing her gun at him. Fast fade.

Lights come up on Abrahams in the witness box at the inquest into Luthando's death.

ANNA   Inspector Abrahams, you were the first on the scene after the shooting at Ms Anderson's townhouse.
ABRAHAMS   That is correct.
ANNA   Could you tell this inquest what you saw?
ABRAHAMS   When I came to the house, Mr Matshabo opened the door for me. Miss Anderson was seated on the sofa. Mr Nyaka was lying on the ground with a newspaper over his face.
ANNA   So Mr Nyaka was dead by the time you got there?
ABRAHAMS   Yes.
ANNA   And how long had he been dead for?
ABRAHAMS   His body was still warm. I believed that he died within half an hour before I got there.
ANNA   We've heard testimony that Mr Nyaka was still holding a gun in his hand?
ABRAHAMS   That is correct.
ANNA   Had any bullets been discharged from his gun?
ABRAHAMS   No. But three rounds from Mrs ... from Miss Anderson's gun had been fired.
ANNA   And they all hit Mr Nyaka?
ABRAHAMS   Yes. One in the right shoulder, and two in the chest.
ANNA   Were they fired from the same range?
ABRAHAMS   More or less, yes. From quite close range. So I suppose it was difficult for her to miss.

Scene changes to Gabby's townhouse. Aaron is seated and reading the Weekend Argus (Saturday) and Luthando is walking around.

LUTHANDO   Only when I got to East London itself, I realised they gave me the wrong gun. When you go into the City Hall, they've got these metal detectors. I put my briefcase through it, and they tell me to open it. In my rush, I forgot. Normally, I keep my gun in a shoulder holster. So I open the plastic bag they wrap the guns in and ... it's not mine! A little Rossi revolver! That's what they gave me, comrade. A woman's gun! You can't stop a dog with that! That's why, whenever I fly now, the first thing I check on arrivals is that they gave me the right gun. *(shaking his head)* South African Airways! First they delayed on the tarmac by forty-five minutes. Then they ran out of J&B on the flight. Then they gave me the wrong gun! *(pause)* And the food, comrade. Even in business class ... You saw for yourself this morning. Fried tomatoes! Mushrooms! It's five years since we took over, and they still serve us white food.

AARON *(dryly, without looking up from the newspaper)* The tomatoes were red. And they were black mushrooms.

LUTHANDO   You know what I mean, comrade.

AARON *(turning the page)* Maybe next time, you should order a special meal ... *Kentucky.*

LUTHANDO   I know it's party policy to support the national carrier, but it's time they also came to the party, comrade. This morning they greet us in English. Then they say they can also help passengers in Afrikaans, German and Arabic. German and Arabic! Since when are these official languages, comrade? And then the captain thanks us for flying SAA ... in Afrikaans. And hopes to see us all back again soon ... in English. When are we going to transform SAA? We have black people in high positions in every part of our national life ...

AARON   Except in the cockpits ...

LUTHANDO   Exactly.

AARON   Some high positions require training ...

LUTHANDO   Comrade, you're treating this like a joke.

AARON   It is funny. Couldn't you feel the difference between a Rossi revolver and ... what is the latest party issue?

LUTHANDO   Vector. 9mm parabellum.

AARON   Couldn't you feel the difference in the shape? The weight?

LUTHANDO   I was in a rush, comrade. I was late ...

AARON *(turns back to the newspaper)* Whatever. I don't want to talk about guns. They make me nervous. *(pause)* It's six weeks before the elections, and what does the *Weekend Argus* have on its front page? 'Stormers star on drunken rampage.' 'Blind man asked to leave restaurant.' 'Woman fined for dog poo.'

LUTHANDO   That's Cape Town, comrade. It's not part of the new South Africa.

AARON   Listen to this. *(reads)* 'A national poll conducted by The Institute for a Democratic South Africa has found thirty-two per cent of the electorate to be undecided. forty-one per cent said they would vote for the ruling party, while twenty-seven per cent indicated that they would vote for one of the opposition parties.'

LUTHANDO   They suck these polls from their thumbs, comrade.

AARON *(continuing to read)* 'More than forty-five per cent listed crime, the economy, unemployment and education as their major areas of concern.'

LUTHANDO *(dismissively)* Concerns.

AARON   'The poll found that only three Cabinet ministers enjoyed an approval rating of more than fifty per cent. They were Ruth Mkhonto, Minister of Welfare and Children's Affairs with fifty-three per cent, Raj Govender, Minister of Water and Forestry with fifty-seven per cent and *(slows down for emphasis)* Minister of Trade and Tourism, Shadrack Khumalo, with sixty-two per cent.'

There is a general pause as they both take in the importance of this.

LUTHANDO *(quietly)* This is an important mission, comrade.

AARON *(resentfully, folds up the newspaper)* I spend my life cleaning up after bastards!

LUTHANDO *(shocked, even outraged)* Comrade ... !

AARON *(sharply)* What?

LUTHANDO   Comrade, I know this must be difficult for you.

AARON   You don't know anything. *(pause)* Have you been dragged out of bed at three in the morning because the Mayor of Jo'burg has written off his car, pissed out of his mind? And the comatose woman in the passenger seat, is not his wife? How many times have you had to devise a strategy to protect some senior party member who's about to be exposed for something or other? Find the spin angles. Develop the party line. Handle the media. *(pause)* The Minister of Damage Control *(grunts dismissively)* ...

LUTHANDO   Everyone has the highest regard for you and your work, comrade.

AARON   This was going to be my first Saturday off for weeks. Instead, I'm on the first flight to Cape Town to clean up another mess.

LUTHANDO   With respect comrade, you didn't have to come.

AARON *(with a hint of irritation)* With respect, Luthando, I had to.

LUTHANDO   You're too emotionally involved, comrade.

AARON   And you're not? You're here because of Khumalo.

LUTHANDO   Comrade Khumalo is key to us getting a two-thirds majority.

AARON   Comrade Khumalo – if the intelligence reports are true – has just messed up pretty badly!

LUTHANDO   We all make mistakes, comrade. And anyway, we don't know if the reports are true.

AARON   You saved Khumalo once before. He's been good to you since.

LUTHANDO   The party values loyalty, comrade.

AARON   This mission requires sensitivity.

LUTHANDO   Like you comrade, I'm here to ensure the best interests of the party.

AARON   But you've never handled situations like this before.

LUTHANDO   I've sorted problems out for the party.

AARON   Maybe you have. But we are not going to solve this issue with strong-arm stuff. This requires reason. Logic. Sympathy.

LUTHANDO *(pause, then, quietly)* So ... what are we going to do?

AARON   Luthando, we have our instructions. It's simple. *(pause as he suddenly thinks of something)* We do have the same instructions, don't we?

LUTHANDO   Yes.

AARON   You're not bullshitting me?

LUTHANDO   Comrade, what the leadership agreed last night, is what we have to do. Get the document signed, and get back to Jo'burg as soon as possible.

AARON *(firmly, not seeking Luthando's approval)* I'll do the talking. If there's any negotiation that has to happen, I'll handle it. *(pause)*

LUTHANDO   Shouldn't we phone her?

AARON   And take away the element of surprise?

LUTHANDO   What if she doesn't come?

AARON   Then we go with Plan B.

LUTHANDO   What is Plan B?

AARON   I'm still working on it.

There's a tense silence for a few moments. Luthando, shaking his head, walks away, and takes out a pack of cigarettes.

AARON   I don't think you should be smoking.

LUTHANDO   It's OK. My father smoked forty a day. And he's seventy-four.

AARON   Good for him. But I still don't think you should smoke.

LUTHANDO   Why?

AARON *(agitated)* Luthando, how would you like to come home and find two people in your house whom you are not expecting, and the place stinks like smoke?

LUTHANDO   But comrade, there's an ashtray ...

AARON   And, Luthando, *(pointing through the side window)* there's a swimming pool.

LUTHANDO   So?

AARON   It doesn't mean you can swim!

LUTHANDO   I don't understand you comrade. We've walked into her house. You've read her newspaper. But it's not OK ...

AARON   If you want to smoke outside, be my guest. Let's show some respect for her space.

LUTHANDO   Comrade ... *(pause, unable to hide his anger)*

AARON *(tersely)* What?

LUTHANDO *(changes his mind)* Nothing.

The doorbell rings. The following conversation takes place in hushed tones.

LUTHANDO   She's here.

AARON   Why would she ring her own doorbell? *(looking through window)* Inspector Abrahams ...

(Luthando registers surprise. Aaron opens the door)

AARON *(charmingly)* Inspector Abrahams ...

ABRAHAMS *(surprised to find Aaron answering the door)* Mr ... Mashaba?

AARON   Matshoba.

ABRAHAMS Correct. I'm sorry ...

AARON   No problem. We haven't seen each other in years.

ABRAHAMS I see you on TV.

AARON   Hopefully, not on *Police File*, Inspector. *(laughter)* Inspector Abrahams, this is Luthando Nyaka.

Abrahams and Luthando stare at each other awkwardly.

ABRAHAMS   Yes, I ...
LUTHANDO *(quickly)* Pleased to meet you, Inspector.
AARON   You know each other?
ABRAHAMS   No, I was going to say I see Mr Nyaka on TV too.
AARON *(playing the game)* TV 2? Really?
   (They all laugh awkwardly)
AARON   How may we help you, Inspector?
ABRAHAMS   Is Mrs Anderson in?
AARON   Ms Anderson.
ABRAHAMS   Correct, yes. Miss Anderson.
AARON   She's not here right now. Was she expecting you?
ABRAHAMS   I told her I will pop around this morning.
AARON   Is it about Matthew?
ABRAHAMS   I'm sorry, no, Mr Matshabo. *(pause)*
AARON   Is anything wrong?
ABRAHAMS   If there is, it would be better for her to tell you.
   (awkward pause) Did Miss Anderson say when she'll be back?
AARON   Actually, we haven't seen her yet. We flew in from
   Jo'burg this morning ... for a conference. We've come to say, 'Hi'
   before it starts.
ABRAHAMS   Oh ...
AARON *(sensing Abrahams' thoughts)* Inspector, you're probably
   wondering how we got in. I remembered where Gabby ... where
   Ms Anderson hides a spare key.
ABRAHAMS   I see.
AARON *(jokingly)* I hope you're not going to arrest us for house-
   breaking.
ABRAHAMS   As you know, Mr Matshabo, we don't interfere in
   domestic affairs unless we receive a complaint.
AARON   I know. I know. I was just ... *(Aaron's cellphone begins
   to ring. He checks the number on the screen)* Excuse me gentlemen,
   I have to take this. Hello? Hello? You're breaking up. Hello? Just
   hold on. I'm going outside to try to get better reception.

*Aaron exits. Abrahams and Luthando are left together, with Luthando
decidedly more uncomfortable than Abrahams.*

ABRAHAMS *(after a few seconds)* Uphila njani, umnumzana Nyaka?
LUTHANDO   Ndiphilile ...

ABRAHAMS   You're very quiet.
LUTHANDO   I don't have anything to say.
ABRAHAMS   How's your father?
LUTHANDO *(awkwardly, constantly looks around to see if Aaron is in earshot. His answers are generally monosyllabic, not really wanting to engage in conversation)* Fine.
ABRAHAMS   He were a good guy. A good cop. Please give him my regards when you see him again.
LUTHANDO   Sure.
ABRAHAMS   He tried to teach me Xhosa when we were stationed together. I weren't a very good student. *(laughs)* You don't miss the Eastern Cape?
LUTHANDO   No.
ABRAHAMS   I was happy when they transferred me to Cape Town. This is a nice place. *(changes tack)* What's the conference about?
LUTHANDO   I don't really know. Comrade Matshoba is speaking. I'm accompanying him.
ABRAHAMS   Are you still doing VIP protection?
LUTHANDO   In a way ...
ABRAHAMS   I read about you in the papers. When you saved Mr Khumalo in that ambush.
LUTHANDO   Was that in the newspapers here also?
ABRAHAMS   I was still in PE then. I don't buy the newspapers. But Major van Rooyen ... you remember Major van Rooyen? Or maybe he was still captain in your time. He phoned me and said I should get the paper. He's retired to a farm near Robertson now. You were on the front page, nogal. Natal was a war zone then. When was that? Four ... five years ago?
LUTHANDO   '93. Before the elections.
ABRAHAMS   Correct. Mr Khumalo wouldn't be a minister today if it wasn't for you.
LUTHANDO *(with false modesty)* I was just doing my job.
ABRAHAMS   Some say Mr Khumalo might be made Deputy President after the next elections ...
LUTHANDO   That would be good for the country.
ABRAHAMS   And what do you do now, if I may ask?
LUTHANDO   Still Security. Deputy Chief of Security. I'm responsible mainly for senior party officials who are not in government.

ABRAHAMS   You don't have a job for me? Former security policeman, now Violent Crimes Unit. There's a ceiling for cops with my history. *(Luthando doesn't respond, pause)* But you've done well for yourself ... *(with a smile)* comrade.

Aaron enters.

ABRAHAMS   I was just telling Mr Nyaka that I think I'll come back later.
AARON   Are you sure?
ABRAHAMS   Yes, no, I don't want to get in the way of your visit with Mrs ... with Miss Anderson.
AARON   I'll let her know that you came by.
ABRAHAMS   Ask her to give me a call when it's convenient. *(gives Aaron a business card)*
AARON   A business card?
ABRAHAMS *(proudly)* We're trying to professionalise the service.
AARON   Wouldn't the money be better spent on catching criminals?
ABRAHAMS   I printed these myself.
AARON   I'm impressed. Our country can do with more patriots like you, Inspector Abrahams.
ABRAHAMS   Thank you Mr Matshabo. Enjoy the seminar. *(deliberately says 'seminar' to see how Aaron responds)*
AARON *(wise to it)* The conference ... Yes, thanks.

Abrahams exits.

AARON   It was Head Office. They want us back as soon as possible. They're very worried about this leaking to the press.
LUTHANDO   How?
AARON   Gabby's best friend is a lawyer. Intelligence says she's probably involved already.
LUTHANDO   What does that have to do with the press, comrade?
AARON   Her ex-husband is Graham Richards. The parliamentary reporter for Independent Newspapers.
LUTHANDO   Shit!
AARON *(pause)* He knows.
LUTHANDO   Richards?
AARON   Abrahams. I'm sure he's involved in the case.

LUTHANDO   You think so, comrade?

AARON   This wasn't just a social call. You heard him say that it wasn't about my son's case. He was the investigating officer.

Lights come up on Gabby and Anna having a drink at Gabby's townhouse in the mid-90s.

ANNA   How long will you be on leave?

GABBY   Just till Tuesday.

ANNA   Isn't it a bit soon into your new job to be taking leave?

GABBY   Someone's got to sort out Matthew's new school. Aaron's away.

ANNA   Again ...

GABBY   It's only a couple of days this time.

ANNA   What was the problem with the co-ed?

GABBY   It's fine. But Bishops offers better sports options.

ANNA   I didn't think Aaron was the private school type.

GABBY   That wouldn't have been Aaron's choice. But that's where my father and my brother went. So I don't mind too much.

Anna's cellphone rings.

ANNA *(answers, businesslike)* Susan, you've done the affidavit? *(pause)* Yes. Leave it on my desk. I'll collect it on my way home. *(ends cellphone conversation)* So how is the new job?

GABBY   It's OK.

ANNA   Just OK? Personal assistant to the great Shadrack Khumalo!

GABBY   To be honest, he's a bit all over the place. He's a good politician. Just not a very good hands-on manager.

ANNA   That's why you're there.

GABBY   I suppose so.

ANNA   Aren't you surprised you got it? I thought it would be a black appointment.

GABBY   Apparently, Khumalo himself insisted on me.

ANNA *(wryly)* And you still maintain that Aaron had nothing to do with your getting the job ...

GABBY   Aaron would never do something like that. Anyway, I told you I applied for the post as Gabby Anderson ...

ANNA   Come on Gabby. Everyone knows that you and Aaron
are connected.

Anna's phone rings. She answers 'Yes?'.
Blackout.
Scene with Anna and Gabby juxtaposed with scenes between Gabby and
Aaron. Lights come up on Aaron and Gabby in Gabby's townhouse.

AARON *(with his jacket off to indicate another time)* What do you
want me to say?

GABBY *(cardigan on)* I just want you to acknowledge it. So we can
deal with it.

AARON *(with a hint of tease)* With what?

GABBY   See? You're in denial. You don't even want to –

AARON   OK, OK, OK. The black-white thing.

GABBY   Yes.

AARON   I'm not even going to go there. It's such ... with due
respect, Gabby, it's such crap!

GABBY   Methinks the gentleman doth protest too much!

AARON   Methinks the lady has constructed a world quite
removed from reality.

GABBY   You know, that's what I used to think. That maybe I was
just imagining these things. That I was imagining that you weren't keen
to take me to social functions after we got back. That I was imagining
that when we did go to functions together, you hardly ever introduced
me as your wife. That maybe I was just imagining that you seemed to
be embarrassed about having a white wife in the new South Africa.

AARON *(whistles nonchalantly, as if he's not listening)* Are you done?

GABBY   We leave the country because it's illegal for us to be
together. Then when we come back and we can live together, you
just about disown me.

AARON   Gabby, your sense of conspiracy is a little ...
overdeveloped.

GABBY   Don't patronise me, Aaron.

AARON   What's happening to us, babe?

GABBY   What's happening to you?

AARON   I don't know what you mean, Gabby. The only thing
that's different is that I'm busier ...

GABBY *(with gentle irony)* Oh, is that all my darling? *(a bit more strongly)* That's pretty damn major, Aaron! We don't talk like we used to. We don't have time to do fun things together ... I feel like I don't really know you anymore. I'm like a single parent to Matthew.

AARON   Gabby, you and Matthew ... I couldn't do what I'm doing now without knowing that you are there.

GABBY   Really?

AARON   Yes, really.

GABBY   You're not just saying that to end this conversation so that we can go to your official little function?

AARON   I mean it.

GABBY *(seductively)* Then let's not go out tonight. Let's cancel the babysitter and order pizza.

AARON   Gabby, don't do this ...

Blackout. Lights come up on Anna and Gabby again in Gabby's townhouse. They pick up on another conversation.

ANNA *(on her cellphone)* For goodness sake, Graham, sort it out. You're their father. *(pause)* So what would you like me to do? *(pause)* No, I'm at Gabby's place. *(pause. Rolls her eyes as she listens, bored)* Graham says hi ...

GABBY *(equally bored)* Hi Graham.

ANNA   Let me speak to Tanya. *(pause)* Graham, just give Tanya the damn phone. *(pause)* Hello darling. I don't think it's a good idea for you and Cheryl to go clubbing tonight. *(pause)* Why? Because Cheryl doesn't have a licence. If your father drops you and picks you up, fine ... OK. OK. Love you. *(pause)* No, I don't need to talk to him. Bye. *(sighs)* If Graham ever has to write his biography, he'll have to call it 'Portrait of a useless man'.

GABBY   That's what you've said about all your men.

ANNA   Maybe. But Graham is the original useless man. I can't believe that I stayed married to him for ten years!

GABBY   Don't you miss having someone?

ANNA   Sometimes. But mostly, I'm too busy running the legal practice and being a single parent to notice.

GABBY   What happened to Stan?

ANNA   I told him to make a new plan.

GABBY   He was quite ... nice.

ANNA   In a Homer Simpson kind of way ...

GABBY   And Jeffrey?

ANNA   He found religion after he crashed my car. *(pause)*
You and Aaron are doing well.

GABBY   It will be twelve years in September.

ANNA   You got one of the good guys.

Blackout. Lights come up on Gabby and Aaron again, this time having a different argument.

AARON   It's just a few days, Gabs. Then we'll go away together.
I promise.

GABBY   I should never have come back here. We should have
stayed in exile.

AARON *(with a suitcase in hand)* You hated Germany.

GABBY   At least there I had a family. I had a husband. My son
had a father.

AARON   Please Gabby, don't make this any harder for me than
it already is.

GABBY *(sharply)* Excuse me. This is not about you.

AARON   I'm sorry. I didn't mean it like that.

GABBY *(bitterly)* It's always been about you, hasn't it? Your job, your
travelling, your meetings. To hell with the rest.

AARON   Gabby, I don't think this is the time ...

GABBY   Oh, but I think it is! I think it's a great time. *(quieter)*
I'm always amazed when you go off to sort out conflicts all over
the country, because you're such a failure at dealing with it in your
own life.

AARON   Gabs, let's deal with this when we both have the time.
Please.

GABBY   You're so busy fixing up everything else, you don't
realise that your own marriage has broken down.

AARON   Gabby, now you're being melodramatic.

GABBY   Is that what you think this is? Melodrama?

AARON   We've been through this so many times. It's my work,
Gabby.

GABBY   We are your family! I am your wife!

AARON   Gabby, everything that we ever dreamed about is
about to happen. As a country. As a region. But these things are not
going to fall out of the sky. We have to work damn hard to get there.
What we do now will determine whether we succeed or not.

GABBY   That's what first attracted me to you.
AARON   What?
GABBY   Your passion. Your commitment.
AARON   So what's the problem now?
GABBY   Now that's what's driving you away from us. There just isn't space for me or Matthew any longer.
AARON   I'm sorry Gabs. I really need to go or I'll miss the plane. I promise to make up for it when I get back. *(he goes over to her to give her a goodbye hug)* It's just a few days, Gabs.
GABBY *(moving away from him)* Go Aaron. Go! Go! Go! Just leave.

Blackout. Scene changes back to Anna and Gabby. They pick up their earlier conversation.

ANNA   When does Aaron get back?
GABBY *(sighs)* I don't know. He said he'll probably have to stay as long as it takes to negotiate the ceasefire.
ANNA   In Angola, that could be weeks.
GABBY   Exactly. *(pause)* So much for our girls' night out!
ANNA   Aaron owes us big time.
GABBY   He was supposed to take Matt to the big soccer game today.
ANNA   Aaron's become the proverbial Mr Fix-it. Why Angola? Don't we have enough of our own problems for him to deal with?
GABBY *(imitating Aaron)* 'Gabby, everything that we ever dreamed about is about to happen. As a country. As a region. But we have to work damn hard to get there'. That's Aaron's most recent speech.
ANNA   I hate to say it. But he has a point.
GABBY   Hey, whose side are you on?
ANNA   Someone's got to do it.
GABBY   But why does it have to be Aaron?
ANNA   You're not taking strain, are you?
GABBY   It wasn't like this when we were in exile. We were a real family then. Mostly what we had was ... each other.
ANNA   It's just a phase we're going through Gabby.
GABBY   So many of the couples we knew in exile split up after they came back. It's bizarre. Like apartheid kept us together. And freedom ... our freedom seems to be driving us apart.

The doorbell rings. Gabby opens it. Inspector Abrahams is at the door.

GABBY   Yes?

ABRAHAMS   I'm looking for a Mrs Matshabo.

GABBY   I'm Mrs Matshoba.

ABRAHAMS *(having expected to see a black person)* Good afternoon
Mrs ... Matshabo? I'm Inspector Abrahams.

GABBY   What is this about, Inspector?

ABRAHAMS *(solemnly)* It's about your son.

GABBY   Matthew?

ABRAHAMS   That is correct.

GABBY *(suddenly very anxious)* Has something happened?

ABRAHAMS   He was at the shopping centre ...

GABBY   Yes, I sent him to buy milk.

ABRAHAMS   Apparently two street kids tried to take his bike. He
resisted ... and they stabbed him.

GABBY   Oh my God! *(Anna comes to support her)* Is he OK?

ANNA   Where is he now?

ABRAHAMS   He's on his way to hospital in an ambulance.

GABBY   Are you sure it's him?

ABRAHAMS   The chemist recognised him and told us where you
lived. I'm sorry to bring you such news.

*Anna embraces Gabby who is in tears. Slow fade as Gabby registers
her extreme anxiety and emotion. Lights come up slowly on Gabby
and Aaron.*

AARON *(quietly)* It's nearly ten months now Gabby ...

GABBY   So?

AARON   How much longer are we going to live in silence?

GABBY   How long does it take for a mother to get over the
death of her child?

AARON   You still blame me for Matthew's death. As if I were
somehow responsible for it.

GABBY *(raising her voice a little)* He would be alive today if you had
been here. That's the same thing.

AARON   I was in Angola.

GABBY   Yes, it was touch and go with the ceasefire. You had to
go immediately. This was a little window for peace. Great! They still
don't have peace in Angola. And I don't have my son.

AARON   Gabby, history is bigger than any of us. Sometimes we have to do things that are at odds with what we really want to do. Especially when there are many lives at stake. It's not easy being caught between the demands of history and the people you love.

GABBY   Oh spare me!

AARON   Gabby, please ...

GABBY   It's not about history! Who do you think you are? God? Sacrificing your son for the sake of humankind ... ?

AARON *(sighs)* OK, Gabby. I surrender ... you win. OK? You win.

GABBY   This is not about winning and losing ...

AARON   I just wish you'd find it in your heart to forgive me.

GABBY   Have you forgiven yourself?

AARON   Gabby, Matthew went to the shop to buy milk. Two kids stabbed him and took his bicycle. It would have happened even if I were here.

GABBY *(angrily)* You promised to spend the day with him. You were going to take him to soccer! But not for the first time, you cancelled on him!

AARON *(quietly)* Children die, Gabby. It's terrible whenever it happens. It's devastating when it happens to be yours. But it happens.

GABBY *(emotionally)* He was my son!

AARON   He was our son! *(pause)* Do you think I haven't had sleepless nights thinking about him? About what could've been if – About what might have been if only ... *(pause)* Life goes on Gabby.

GABBY   So you simply put it all into a little box, and stuck it away somewhere. And threw yourself deeper into your work.

AARON   What would you rather have had me do?

GABBY   I don't know. But it all seems so easy for you.

AARON   Well, it wasn't. It isn't. *(pause)* And I wish you could forgive me ... so we could move on.

Scene shifts to Truth and Reconciliation Commission hearing with Abrahams about to give evidence. Spotlight comes up on Abrahams.

ABRAHAMS *(slowly, in Afrikaans)* Ek sweer om die waarheid to praat. (I swear to tell the truth)

Light comes down slowly on Abrahams. This scene interchanges with Gabby and Anna at Anna's house. Gabby is quiet while Anna speaks to her.

ANNA   Abrahams was here. I told him you were in the bath.
He dropped off the final version of your statement for us to check.
ABRAHAMS   Die hele waarheid, en niks maar die waarheid nie.
(The whole truth and nothing but the truth)
ANNA   I told him you'll be at your place later. He said he'll
pick it up at about eleven.
ABRAHAMS *(still in Afrikaans)* So help my God. *(So help me God)*
ANNA   Would you prefer me to read it?

*Lights fade. Spotlight comes up on Abrahams giving evidence at the
Truth and Reconciliation Commission. This scene alternates with the
reading of Gabby's statement.*

ABRAHAMS   Daar was vyf van ons in die kamer. *(There were five of
us in the room.)*
*(Starts evidence in Afrikaans, and then changes to English to give
the impression that he is essentially Afrikaans-speaking, and which
would have been the language in which he gave evidence at the
Truth and Reconciliation Commission)*
Captain Francois van Rooyen and Captain Mike Naude. Sergeant
Nico Meiring. An askari who we called Tiny because of his big feet.
And myself. Captain Naude ordered Tiny to handcuff Mrs Dlamini
and to tie the handcuffs to a beam above her head. So she was
standing with her arms stretched upwards like this. *(places his
hands in the air as if tied directly above his head)* Captain Naude
and Sergeant Meiring were questioning her about her son, Bongi.
We knew that he had left the country to get military training and
that he and three others were responsible for blowing up electric
pylons in the Despatch area. We wanted to find him.

*Lights fade on Abrahams. Lights come up on Gabby and Anna. Anna
is reading Gabby's statement. After the first few lines, Gabby's voice
takes over the reading.*

ANNA *(reading softer)* There was a history of suggestions, looks, even
touching. *(changes to Gabby's voice reading the statement)*
Sometimes I would threaten to report him, and it would stop for a
while. But then it would start all over again. It was like he couldn't
help himself. I suggested that he go for professional help. After the
farewell cocktail for the Singapore delegation, at about 8pm on

Thursday night, he said that we should go back to the office to collect two files that he needed to take with him to Pretoria the next morning. He told the driver to take us to his car, and then let the driver go. He drove us to the office building and I offered to run up and fetch the files. But he insisted on coming.

Shift to Abrahams at the TRC.

ABRAHAMS   Mrs Dlamini was an active member of the United Democratic Front in the Eastern Cape. She refused to answer any questions. So Captain Naude ordered Sergeant Meiring to turn on a hosepipe. Captain Naude continued to ask her questions while Sergeant Meiring kept wetting her with the hosepipe. She still refused to answer any questions about her son. Then Captain Naude ordered Tiny to start taking off her clothes. First her jersey. Then her dress. Then her slip. And all the time Sergeant Meiring was still wetting her with the hosepipe. Finally she was completely naked. And she was soaking wet. And still she didn't say anything. She didn't even cry like I'd seen so many other women detainees do.

Shift to Anna's house.

GABBY *(reading)* We took the lift to the office on the twelfth floor. He didn't say anything in the lift. Except, he whistled some silly tune. He'd had a couple of glasses of red wine, but I wouldn't say that he was drunk. I put on the light in the secretary's office, then went into his office. He followed me, and I remember thinking it strange that he would close the door behind him. I was bending forward over his desk, looking through the in-tray for the files I had left earlier. And then it happened. So quickly. He came up behind me, and pushed me hard onto the desk. The tray went flying, and I remember feeling pain as my stomach hit the side of the desk. I was completely shocked. He pushed my head down with his one hand, so that I could hardly breathe, and pressed me with all his weight against the desk.

Shift to Abrahams at the TRC.

ABRAHAMS   Captain Naude took the hosepipe and shoved it into Mrs Dlamini's private parts. He then said to Tiny that Mrs Dlamini was now wet. He ordered Tiny to have sex with her. At that stage, Captain van Rooyen and I walked away.

Shift to Gabby and Anna.

GABBY   Then he lifted my dress, pulled down my pants, and entered me from behind. I felt pain, but I was more aware of his grunts as he forced himself into me. When he was done, he picked up the tray and placed it back on the table. He picked up the files from the floor and left.

Shift to Abrahams at the TRC.

ABRAHAMS   Mrs Dlamini was raped repeatedly but she still wouldn't tell us anything. Then one day we told her that we had killed her son in a shoot-out. Then she broke down completely. In fact, she went crazy. We heard that she threw herself under a train a few weeks after she was released.

Shift to Gabby and Anna.

GABBY   I called my friend, Anna Richards. She came to collect me. She took me immediately to the District Surgeon. She wanted me to report the rape at the local police station. But I asked her to contact Inspector Theo Abrahams, a policeman I had met a few years ago, and someone whom I knew I could trust.

ABRAHAMS   At that time, it wasn't appropriate for coloured officers to lodge complaints against their white colleagues. I am thankful for this Truth and Reconciliation process. It allows me to clear my conscience. I am deeply ashamed for being silent. For doing nothing. *(pause)* I know this won't bring her back, but what I want to say to Mrs Dlamini's family ... what I want to say to the country is that I am sorry. Really sorry.

Anna is sitting next to Gabby with her arm around her. Gabby lies her head on Anna's shoulder, and is sobbing.

ANNA   Does it hurt?
(Gabby nods through her tears)
ANNA   Are you still bleeding?
GABBY   A little. ...
ANNA *(herself a bit teary, a mixture of sympathy and anger)* How could he do this? Khumalo ... of all people! I still can't believe it! How could he do it? And to you?
GABBY *(quietly)* Maybe it's my fault ...

ANNA　　　　No! No ways, Gabby! That's what victims often think. That somehow, they were responsible. That's a cliché, Gabby.

GABBY　　　　I feel like a cliché. I never expected that it would happen to me. I know the person who did it. I ... I ... *(weeps again)*

ANNA *(holding Gabby again)* Are you sure you won't stay another night?

GABBY　　　　I need to be in my own space, Anna.

ANNA　　　　This is not something to go through by yourself.

GABBY　　　　Thanks Anna. I don't know what I would have done without you.

ANNA *(deliberately shifting the topic)* What would you like for breakfast?

GABBY　　　　I'm not hungry.

ANNA　　　　You must have something, Gabby. There's fruit, yoghurt, toast, eggs ...

GABBY　　　　I'm really not hungry.

ANNA　　　　You have to eat something before you take your anti-retrovirals.

GABBY *(grimacing at the thought)* Oh no ... !

ANNA　　　　I know. They're horrible. But you have to, Gabby.

GABBY　　　　I have that feeling, Anna. It's like ... Matthew all over again. I don't know if I can do this a second time.

ANNA　　　　When do you see Shireen?

GABBY　　　　Wednesdays.

ANNA　　　　Shall I try to get an appointment with her today?

GABBY　　　　What's today?

ANNA　　　　Saturday.

GABBY　　　　Saturday?

ANNA　　　　I'm sure Shireen will be happy to do an emergency appointment today.

GABBY　　　　It's been three years since Matthew ... three years of weekly sessions with Shireen. And it still hurts, Anna. *(sighs deeply, and begins to sob again)* It still hurts.

ANNA　　　　Let me get you some tissues.

GABBY　　　　There's some in my bag ... *(Anna picks up Gabby's bag and rifles through it)* I feel so ... like ... what's the point, Anna?

Anna pulls out the tissues and hands them to Gabby. Then she pulls out a revolver.

ANNA   What's this?
GABBY *(awkwardly)* It's a gun.
ANNA   Is it yours?
GABBY   Yes.
ANNA   How long have you had it for?
(Gabby shrugs)
ANNA   Since Matthew's death?
GABBY   Yes.
ANNA   Did you have it with you on Thursday?
GABBY *(quietly)* Yes ...
ANNA   But?
GABBY   But it all happened so fast. I couldn't ... I didn't ... think.
ANNA   Jeez, Gabby!
GABBY   I know. It's bizarre. We came back here when apartheid was dying. Now apartheid's dead. My son's dead. My marriage is dead. And I'm carrying a gun.
ANNA   Do you think it's OK for you to have a gun? Now?
GABBY   After what happened? Even more reason to have to it.
ANNA   When we're under stress, our minds play funny tricks on us Gabby.
GABBY   You think I'm going to shoot myself?

Lights fade on this scene. The next scene takes place in Gabby's townhouse, with only Aaron present when the scene opens. Aaron tidies up the newspaper. He crosses to the CD player, and selects a CD, a piece of classical music, which he puts on, using the remote control. He looks through the bookshelf and selects a book. He crosses to the sofa, when his eyes fall on the photographs. He walks across to these, and picks up the one of the ten year-old boy. He stares at it for a while, sighs deeply, puts it down and sits on the sofa to read the book. After a few minutes, there's a key in the door. Aaron turns off the CD player, and Gabby enters.

AARON   Gabby ...
GABBY *(completely surprised)* Aaron ...
AARON   I'm sorry if I scared you ...

Anna enters, talking on her cellphone.

AARON *(his turn to be completely surprised)* Anna ...

ANNA I'll call you back. *(ends conversation)* Well, well, well. If it isn't Mr Fix-it himself.

Both Gabby and Aaron are awkward; Gabby with the presence of Aaron and Aaron with the presence of Anna. Anna takes charge.

AARON Mr Fix-it?

ANNA How dare you Aaron? How dare you just walk into Gabby's house ...

AARON I need to speak to Gabby.

ANNA *(protectively)* I don't think she wants to talk to you right now.

AARON Perhaps Gabby can speak for herself.

ANNA No, I speak for her. She's my client.

GABBY *(a little embarrassed, but delighted that Anna is around)* Anna ...

ANNA *(gently ignoring Gabby)* Why are you here, Mr Matshoba? Is this official business?

GABBY Anna said that we'd be hearing from the party. We didn't ... I didn't expect that they'd send you.

AARON I came down this morning ...

ANNA Of course! When the party's in a tight spot, who do they call? Comrade Aaron Matshoba.

AARON I know that these are not great circumstances ...

ANNA The master of understatement!

AARON Can we talk ... like reasonable people? Please ...

ANNA Reasonable? Shit Aaron! You haven't seen each other ... for how long? Twelve months?

GABBY Longer ...

ANNA Then Gabby arrives home one day – in 'not great circumstances' – and you happen to be in her house. Illegally, I might add.

AARON The key ...

ANNA I don't give a shit about the key! What gives you the right? Do you know what Gabby's just been through?

AARON I have an idea.

ANNA And you talk about being reasonable?

GABBY Anna ...

AARON You're right, Anna. I shouldn't have entered your house, Gabby. It was a misjudgement on my part.

ANNA   Oh, I love it. *(mockingly)* 'I shouldn't have entered
your house.' I shouldn't have entered ... her! It was a 'misjudgement',
your honour.

GABBY   Anna, you're being a little –

ANNA   Hang on, Gabby. Before you start feeling sorry for
him, think about this. He wasn't expecting me to be with you. What
if you had come home alone and he was here? He would have tried
to charm you, persuade you, steamroller you if necessary. Now
things aren't going according to plan, and he has to change tack. 'I'm
so sorry for entering your house'. *(to Aaron)* Am I right?

AARON *(smiles wryly)* Does it matter? You'll believe what you want to.

Bell rings. Gabby goes to answer.

ANNA   I believe what is logical.

AARON   Ever the lawyer.

ANNA *(with a touch of venom)* Ever the party hack.

*Two sets of conversations take place, one between Anna and Aaron
and the other between Abrahams and Gabby. Lighting switches from
one to the other.*

GABBY   Hello, Inspector.

ABRAHAMS   Good morning.

GABBY   I'm glad we got here before you did. I thought we
were late.

ABRAHAMS   I did actually pop in earlier.

GABBY   Oh, I'm sorry. We had to drop off Anna's daughter at a
hockey match along the way.

ABRAHAMS   No problem. Did Mr Matshabo not tell you that I came
around earlier?

GABBY *(with a smile)* I don't think he's had a chance to.

*Lights fade on Abrahams and Gabby who freeze. Light comes up on
Aaron and Anna.*

AARON   I'm going to level with you Anna. The party is very
concerned about what allegedly happened on Thursday night.

ANNA   They wouldn't be concerned if it only allegedly
happened.

AARON   Innocent until proven guilty. Isn't that what the law says?

ANNA   Oh, I know what the law says. And in terms of the law, you couldn't have a more guilty party.

AARON   You're aware of the damage to the country if this goes public.

ANNA   And you're aware of the damage to the party with an election just around the corner.

AARON   Whatever, Anna. Whatever. The point is that there will be major political repercussions.

ANNA   No, Aaron! The point is that a woman has been raped. The point is that this woman, my friend, your ex-wife, Gabby, has a right to justice!

AARON   I agree. A hundred per cent! But life's a little more complex than that. Sometimes ... sometimes justice has to be sacrificed for the greater political good.

ANNA   I don't believe I'm hearing this.

AARON   Anna, you're a lawyer. You represented victims at the TRC. Did you throw up your hands then?

ANNA   That was different.

AARON   Was it? How many perpetrators of human rights abuses were brought to book? How many of the victims whom you represented got justice? None. Not a single one. Justice had to be sacrificed for the greater political good. The TRC was a deal, Anna. It wasn't about justice. You know that.

ANNA   And that's why you're here. To strike a deal. For the good of the nation.

Aaron and Anna freeze. The lights fade on Aaron and Anna, and come up on Gabby and Abrahams who have shifted positions to show development in their conversation.

GABBY   The statement's fine.

ABRAHAMS Are you sure?

GABBY   Anna's happy with it. What happens next?

ABRAHAMS That's up to you. Are you going to lay a charge?

GABBY *(sighs)* The million dollar question. What do you think I should do?

ABRAHAMS A lot of women don't lay charges.

GABBY   So you think I shouldn't lay a charge?

ABRAHAMS   It's not really for me to say ...

GABBY   I know. I just want to know what you think.

ABRAHAMS   It's a very difficult one. There's the trial ... the public
spotlight ... In your case, there will be even more pressure.

GABBY   You don't have to remind me.

ABRAHAMS   We've got the report from the District Surgeon. We've
got your statement. You lay a charge. And we'll arrest the Minister.

Lights fade on them and come up on Aaron and Anna.

AARON   This will be a big case for you Anna.

ANNA   Not the biggest case I've done.

AARON   From a publicity angle, this will be your biggest.

ANNA   Maybe.

AARON   It will be great for your practice.

ANNA   Are you implying that I want Gabby to go through
with the charges so that I can get publicity for my firm?

AARON   I didn't say that.

ANNA   How can you stand there ... Do you still have a
conscience, Aaron? Does Gabby mean nothing to you?

AARON   On the contrary, I'm here precisely to make sure that
Gabby's best interests are served. And I hope that you are as well.

ANNA   I have to say this for you Aaron. You've got balls.

AARON   Anna, have you thought about what a trial will do to
Gabby?

ANNA   This is exactly why rapists get away with ... murder.
It has to stop.

AARON   Khumalo is a powerful man. With great influence and
a large following of people with vested interests in making sure that
he remains in his position. There's strong speculation that he will be
appointed Deputy President after the elections. There are people
whose interests would be hurt if that didn't happen. There are things
beyond the control of the party. I don't want to be dramatic, but
Gabby could face physical danger. Damage to her property. Death
threats. So when I say that I'm here because I care about Gabby,
then you'd better believe it. And not only Gabby. You too, Anna.

ANNA *(with a touch of sarcasm)* Nice speech, Aaron. *(claps in jest)*

Lights fade on Anna and Aaron and come up on Abrahams and Gabby.

GABBY   Anna insisted that I make the statement. But I didn't want to tell the story to just anybody.

ABRAHAMS   We have made some progress in this area. There are now specially trained policeman and women to deal with rape victims.

GABBY   Yes, I know. But I couldn't face the prospect of talking to someone who wouldn't ... *(chokes)* You're the only policeman I know. Thanks for responding to my call.

ABRAHAMS   I'm sorry that it had to be in these circumstances.

GABBY   Does anyone else know?

ABRAHAMS   I had to tell the station commander. It's too big to keep from him.

GABBY   I don't know how they got to know ... *(gesturing towards the living room)*

ABRAHAMS   Mr Matshabo and Mr Nyaka? I thought they weren't down for a conference.

GABBY   Who's Mr Nyaka?

ABRAHAMS   Miss Anderson, you don't want to know ...

Lights fade on them and come up on Aaron and Anna.

AARON   You want to know what's on the table?

ANNA   For academic reasons maybe.

AARON   Anna, you have no right to dismiss what we have to offer out of hand. At least let Gabby hear what's on the table. Let her be part of making the decision.

ANNA   You expect her to make a rational, informed decision in the state that she's in? As her lawyer, it would be completely irresponsible of me to allow it.

AARON   I appreciate that. But time is of the essence. If we don't agree on a course of action in the next few hours, then a tiny window of opportunity to change history will be lost. And we'll reap the whirlwind.

ANNA   How can you be doing this Aaron? Does the constitution mean nothing to you?

AARON   Anna, you know what Gabby has been through ... as a mother, a woman, a person. I don't want her to experience any more suffering. No more humiliation. No more pain.

ANNA   Then we agree on something.

AARON *(going up to Anna, gently taking her hand and talking* *charmingly, gently)* Anna, we agree about lots of things. In your heart you know that what I'm saying makes sense. You're a fantastic lawyer ...

ANNA *(getting sucked in momentarily by the charm)* Don't do this Aaron ...

AARON   Thank you for being there for Gabby, Anna. I really mean that.

Gabby and Abrahams enter. There is a moment of awkwardness as Anna lets go of Aaron's hand.

GABBY   Inspector Abrahams came to collect the ... document, Anna.

ANNA   Yes, it's in my bag. *(reaches inside her bag and retrieves the statement)*

AARON   Hello again, Inspector.

ABRAHAMS   Good morning. *(Abrahams uses the opportunity to walk around and discreetly places his bugs in position)*

ANNA   Thanks Inspector. It's fine. I'll give you a call later.

ABRAHAMS   OK then. Goodbye.

All say goodbye. Abrahams exits. There is an initial, awkward silence after Abrahams leaves.

ANNA   Aaron wants to tell you about a deal they're offering.

GABBY   A deal?

AARON   I have a proposal for you to consider, Gabby.

GABBY *(to Anna)* What do you think?

ANNA   Oh, I think you should at least listen.

AARON   Gabby, I've tried to explain to Anna that this has as much to do with your best interests, as that of anything else.

ANNA   Cut to the chase Aaron.

AARON   You can choose to work in any embassy for a minimum of five years. London, Washington, Paris, Canberra. You name it. Even the consulate in Sydney if you want to be closer to your family.

ANNA   And in exchange?

AARON   In exchange, you don't lay any charges.

ANNA   I thought so.

AARON   You will also have to agree to be silent about what happened. And you won't be able to come back here for at least five years, or until circumstances change that would make it acceptable for you to return. We will ensure that you have a decent job at the embassy of your choice, set you up with accommodation and even pay for professional counselling for up to a year. If you choose an embassy other than Australia, we will pay for an annual ticket for you to visit your family in Australia.

GABBY *(flops into a chair)* Wow!

ANNA   Tell me something, Aaron. If you and Gabby were still married and this had happened, what would you have advised Gabby to do?

AARON   I don't know.

ANNA   If Gabby had laid a charge, and a party delegation came to see her with the same offer you've just made, what would you have advised her to do?

AARON *(sighing loudly)* This is not about Gabby and me.

ANNA   Oh, but it is. You used to be lovers, friends, husband and wife. And now your ex-wife, your former lover, the mother of your child has been raped, and you are standing there, asking her not to charge her rapist. All we want to know is: would you be giving her similar advice if you were still lovers?

AARON   Let's just say that I'm glad not to be in that position.

ANNA   So you're happy to be in the position of telling her not to go through with the charges, because she's your ex-wife.

AARON   That's not what I'm saying. I'd rather not be in this position either.

ANNA   Cut the crap, Aaron. Yes or no. Would you advise Gabby to drop the charges or not?

AARON   What does it matter? It's hypothetical. It makes no difference. What matters, is now.

GABBY   I want to know.

AARON   Why?

GABBY   Just tell me.

AARON   If I said that I'd advise you to charge the Minister, then you would ask why I am doing this now. And if I said that I'd advise you against charging the Minister, it would reinforce your view that the party means more to me than you. Either way, I'd be damned. Let's just say that whatever your choice, I would have supported you.

ANNA   You are the weakest link. Goodbye!

AARON   Sorry?

ANNA   The question wasn't would you support Gabby's choice? If you had to help her make the choice, what would you have advised? That's the question.

AARON   I don't know. It's very hard for me either way.

ANNA   That's such a cop-out.

AARON   So I'm a coward. I'm a bastard. I'm a male prick! But Gabby, this isn't about me. It really is about what's best for you.

GABBY: And you know what's best for me.

AARON   Gabby, I hope that your anger towards me about other things won't influence the way in which you respond to this offer.

GABBY   Don't worry ...

AARON   I just want to put that on the table.

GABBY   I have enough anger to go around. *(pause)*

AARON   Gabby, if you were in our position, what would you do?

GABBY   I don't know.

AARON   But you do know that as a Minister, Khumalo has attracted major foreign investment despite the negative perceptions of political risk. You know that he plays an important role in keeping the lid on political violence in KwaZulu Natal. And you also know that we have an election coming up, and political temperatures are rising again. We cannot afford to lose Khumalo right now.

ANNA   And if we do, then it will all be Gabby's fault.

AARON   No, it will be his fault. He is responsible for his actions. But this is to appeal to you to do something bigger. To consider the greater good.

ANNA   As defined by whom?

AARON   The objective greater good. No one would think that the possible flare up of political violence and the loss of hundreds of lives is in the best interests of the country.

ANNA   Neither is the rape of a woman! *(pause)*

AARON   Anna, if you were standing at the traffic lights, and the green man's flashing in your direction, whose right of way is it?

ANNA   What is this? Twenty questions?

AARON   Indulge me. Please. Whose right of way is it?

GABBY   It's hers. So?

AARON   But there's a taxi coming down the road at eighty kilometers an hour and it's not going to stop, despite the traffic lights being red and the green man flashing in your favour. Would you still cross the street?

ANNA   Of course not.

AARON   But why not? It's your right to cross the street!

ANNA   And your point is? That Gabby can give up her right to seek justice and live. Or she can exercise her right, and risk getting wiped out in the process.

AARON   That's a bit crude.

GABBY   That's what your metaphor implies.

AARON   What I'm trying to say is that sometimes exercising your right is not in your best personal interests.

ANNA   Shit!

GABBY   What?

ANNA   Look at the time. I need to pick up Tanya. You have to come with me, Aaron.

AARON   Why?

ANNA   I'm not leaving you here alone with Gabby.

GABBY   I'll be fine.

AARON   How long will you be?

GABBY   It's OK Anna.

ANNA   Are you sure?

GABBY   Absolutely.

ANNA   Don't agree to and don't sign anything, OK? I'll be back in forty minutes.

AARON *(to Anna)* And don't you say anything to Graham.

ANNA   Forty minutes, Gabby!

Anna exits, leaving Aaron and Gabby alone. They are standing at opposite ends of the room.

AARON   I wouldn't like to face her in court.

GABBY   She is good.

AARON   So ...

GABBY   So ... ?

AARON   Shall we start again? Hello. How are you?

GABBY   Not so great. Thank you for asking.

AARON *(stepping towards Gabby)* Would you mind if I hugged you?

Without answering, Gabby steps towards Aaron and they embrace.
She sobs quietly.

AARON   Shit Gabby. Why you? Why did this have to happen
to you?

Gabby tries to speak, but only sobs louder.

AARON *(still holding her)* Ssshhh. You don't have to say anything.

Aaron leads Gabby gently to the sofa where they sit next to each
other. He still has his arm around her.

AARON   When I heard, I just went completely cold on the
outside. I was shivering. *(pause)* But inside, it was a whirlpool. I
wanted to scream. I wanted to go out and shoot the bastard. And I
wanted to just ... hold you. *(pause)* I've been sitting on the plane for
the last two hours wondering what it would be like to see you.
Wondering what I was going to say to you.

GABBY   And?

AARON   And I couldn't think of anything that wouldn't sound
trite or insincere.

GABBY   What did you come up with?

AARON   I came because I want to help you. I came because,
whatever has passed between us, I still care about you. Deeply.
About what happens to you.

GABBY   That's not so bad.

AARON   You think so?

GABBY   Trite and hollow maybe ...

They share a moment of cathartic laughter.

AARON   Gabs ...

GABBY   Gabs ... that used to be your term of affection.

AARON   They were going to send two of their cowboys. I had to
fight to be part of this delegation. They didn't want me to come.
They said I was too emotionally involved.

Bell rings.

AARON   That's probably Luthando. I asked him to give us
some time together.

Aaron goes to answer the door. Luthando enters.

AARON   Gabby, this is Luthando Nyaka. Luthando ... Gabby.

LUTHANDO *(in a tone which is the opposite of the words)* Glad to meet you.

GABBY   Hi. *(she doesn't accept his hand, but instead, turns back inside)* Excuse me, I need to use the bathroom.

Gabby exits.

AARON   Was the *Kentucky* good?

LUTHANDO   I had *Nandos*. *(pause)* How's it going?

AARON   I think we're making progress.

LUTHANDO   Head office has been trying to reach you.

AARON   I switched off my phone. *(takes out his phone and switches it back on)*

LUTHANDO   That's why they called me.

AARON   What's up?

LUTHANDO   They've been in touch with comrade Khumalo.

AARON   And?

LUTHANDO   He denies anything happened.

AARON   Is that it?

LUTHANDO   He says they were having an affair.

AARON *(angrily)* Bastard!

LUTHANDO   Comrade ...

AARON   What do they want?

LUTHANDO   They still want her to sign the document.

AARON   Why?

LUTHANDO   I don't know. To have more options. But you're right ...

AARON   About what?

LUTHANDO   If they were having an affair, then there's no point ...

AARON   They were not having an affair!

LUTHANDO   With all due respect, comrade ...

AARON   He raped her. Your hero – your comrade Khumalo – the Minister – the bastard *(slowly, emphasising each word through clenched teeth)* he ... raped ... her!

LUTHANDO   Comrade! We all know you're in the camp that doesn't support Comrade Khumalo's appointment as Deputy President.

AARON   You think this is about party politics?

LUTHANDO   I'm just saying – these accusations will damage Comrade Khumalo ...

AARON *(angrily, but quietly)* Luthando, just shut up! *(through gritted teeth)* Just shut the fuck up!

Pause. Aaron paces around. Aaron opens up his briefcase. He takes out the document for Gabby to sign, and a pen. They wait in silence for Gabby to return, avoiding each other's glances. After a while, Gabby enters.

AARON *(calmer)* Gabs, we need to get back to Jo'burg. I know Anna will be back soon. But maybe you could read through this document in the meantime.

GABBY   What is it?

AARON   It spells out the offer and the conditions I spoke *(his cellphone rings)* about earlier. *(checking the screen)* Damn! It's head office. I'm going to have to take it outside. If there's anything there ... *(on phone)* Hello? *(as he exits, he exchanges a tense stare with Luthando)*

Gabby sits down and reads. Luthando shuffles around uneasily. He is deeply offended by Aaron's outburst at him. Then Luthando breaks the ice.

LUTHANDO   You got yourself a good deal, lady. *(pause)* You were lucky to have Comrade Matshoba *(gesturing towards the door)* fighting for you. If it was up to me ... *(shaking his head)* Eish. *(pause)*

GABBY   Please ...

LUTHANDO   Please what? *(pause)* Sign the bloody document, so we can go.

GABBY   I'm not signing anything without my lawyer ...

LUTHANDO   This has got nothing to do with lawyers. You get lawyers involved in this and ... Eish! It's all there ... in black and white. What more do you want?

GABBY   I want what is right.

LUTHANDO   I'm telling you, if you weren't white, this thing would be handled differently. If you were a black woman –

GABBY   Then what?

LUTHANDO   I don't know if I'll ever understand women. But I know I'll never understand white people. We're offering you a deal for the sake of the country. And all you want is your white justice.

GABBY   You don't even know me ... and you talk to me like this?

LUTHANDO   You're giving the opposition ammunition to use against us in the elections! You've been a party supporter all your life but when it comes down to it, white people are all the same. You just want to make a black government look bad ...

GABBY   You're way out of line, Mr Nyaka.

LUTHANDO   You can't resist, can you? Feeding the stereotype that black men can't keep it in their pants ... that all black men are rapists!

GABBY   In twelve years with Aaron, he has shown me nothing but respect.

LUTHANDO   We know that you and the Minister were having an affair.

GABBY *(outraged)* What ...?

LUTHANDO   And now those who don't want Comrade Khumalo to be Deputy President are using dirty tactics to get their way.

GABBY *(shocked)* If you want me to even consider signing this, I think you'd better stop now.

LUTHANDO *(can't help himself)* Your colleagues at the Ministry will testify to the affair.

GABBY   And what deals did you make with them to get their testimony?

LUTHANDO *(angrily)* What's your problem, woman! You can join your family's chicken run to Australia. And with taxpayer support! What more do you want?

GABBY   I want you to leave.

LUTHANDO   Sign the document and I'll go.

GABBY   I told you I'm not signing anything. *(Gabby picks up the document and holds it up to tear it in half)*

LUTHANDO *(outraged)* What are you doing? You tear up that document, and ...

Gabby tears up the document into small pieces. She picks up her bag.

GABBY   Please get out of my house. Now.

LUTHANDO   You crazy white bitch!

GABBY   I'm asking you one more time. Leave!

LUTHANDO *(taking threatening steps towards her)* I told them to let me deal with you ...

GABBY *(unzips her bag, and pulls out a revolver)* I'm warning you! Get out.

LUTHANDO *(arrogantly, smirking)* Are you threatening me?

Throughout this sequence, Luthando steps forward towards Gabby, and she backtracks even though she has a gun. She's reluctant to use it.

GABBY   I have asked you politely to leave ...

LUTHANDO   Pointing that firearm at me ... you've made it personal.

GABBY   I know who you are.

LUTHANDO *(not taking her seriously)* Luthando ... Luthando Nyaka.

GABBY   How many more times do you have to prove your loyalty to the party, Impimpi Nyaka?

LUTHANDO *(looking over his shoulder towards where Aaron exited)* Are you mad?

GABBY   What was it like seeing Inspector Abrahams again? He told me all about you ... Informer Nyaka!

LUTHANDO   The last person who pointed a gun at me ... *(walking towards her)*

GABBY   Please! Please ... Go!

Luthando lunges at Gabby in an attempt to grab her gun. She screams and a shot goes off. Luthando is hit in the shoulder.

GABBY *(shocked at what she's done)* Shit! I'm ... I'm sorry.

Aaron rushes in.

AARON *(shouting from before he enters. Enters with cellphone in hand)* Gabby! *(he shows visible relief that she's not the one hurt)*

GABBY *(in shock)* He ... he ...

LUTHANDO   Comrade ...

AARON *(to Gabby)* Are you OK?

Gabby points at Luthando, but the words can't come out.

AARON *(summing up the situation very quickly, very coolly) (to Gabby)* Ssshhhh. OK, give me the gun. *(he has taken out a handkerchief, and takes the gun from her, barrel first, careful not to get his fingerprints on the gun. Then he holds the gun's butt in his hand with the handkerchief)* Are you OK, Comrade? *(he assumes a position close to where Gabby stood when she shot Luthando)*

LUTHANDO *(in pain)* I'll be OK. The bitch can't shoot ...

Aaron points the gun at Luthando, and shoots him, twice.

GABBY   Aaron!

Aaron hurries over to Luthando, checks his pulse to see that he's dead. With his handkerchief, he takes Luthando's gun out of his holster, and puts it into Luthando's limp hand.

GABBY *(horrified)* Oh my God! Oh my God! Aaron! What are you doing?

AARON *(takes strong hold of Gabby by the shoulders)* He tried to attack you? *(Gabby nods in agreement)* So you shot him in self-defence. *(Gabby nods less now)*

GABBY   You ... you killed him.

AARON   He would have killed you.

GABBY   My God, Aaron ...

AARON   You were lucky to get in first. The bastard! I shouldn't have left him alone with you. Bastard!

GABBY   What's going on Aaron?

AARON   We're managing a situation, Gabby.

GABBY   By killing someone ... ?

AARON   He would have dealt with it by killing you.

GABBY   You scare me.

AARON   When you shot him, did you mean simply to hurt him or to kill him?

GABBY   I don't know.

AARON   But you did shoot him, didn't you.
(Gabby nods) And you could have killed him, right?

GABBY   Maybe.

AARON   And you shot him in self-defence ... not so?

GABBY   I suppose ...

AARON   So does it matter whether he's dead or not?

GABBY   But you just shot him. In cold blood! Why, Aaron? Why?

AARON   Let's just say the world is a better place without 'comrade' Luthando. For here lies a police informer, a thug, a murderer with no conscience. May his victims now rest in peace. *(pause)* It's not legal. It's not constitutional. But no one can say that justice has not been done.

GABBY   Aaron! Listen to yourself!

AARON (grabbing Gabby firmly by the hands) Gabby! The police will
be here soon.

GABBY   What are you going to do?

AARON   We have to agree what to tell them.

GABBY   What ... what are we going to tell them?

AARON   I will say that you shot Nyaka in self-defence. The
evidence is pretty clear-cut. An inquest will be held. They will find
no one criminally liable. And we'll all be able to move on with our
lives. (pause) What will you say?

GABBY   I don't know. I don't know.

AARON   You need to decide quickly. But just remember, Gabs,
(quietly) it's your fingerprints on the weapon.

Gabby sinks into a chair, overcome by the implications of what has
happened and by Aaron's statement. Lights go down but not to black.
Action takes place in full view of the audience, but it is played out to
music and the audience does not hear anything. Aaron pours a drink
and takes it to Gabby. He talks to her, but his words are not heard.
She looks straight ahead of her, not saying anything, like a zombie.
She takes the odd sip from her glass. Aaron takes the newspaper that
he'd been reading earlier and crosses to Luthando. He looks at him,
and then covers his body with the newspaper. Abrahams enters.
Aaron talks to him, explaining what happened. They look at Gabby
who is still looking into space. Abrahams bends down, lifts the
newspaper and checks Luthando's pulse, feeling his neck. Abrahams
listens as Aaron explains, nodding his head at times, but not saying
anything. Aaron takes out his cellphone as he continues explaining.

Lights come up to full, music fades.

AARON   I'm just going to make a phone call, Inspector. If you
need me, I'll be outside.

ABRAHAMS   Fine, Mr Matshabo. (Aaron exits) Quite something,
Miss Anderson. (no response from Gabby) You've had a tough few
days ... You want to tell me what happened?

GABBY   I ... I ... shot him.

ABRAHAMS   He probably deserved it.

GABBY   I suppose you'll need another statement.

ABRAHAMS   A brief one. This looks like a pretty open and shut case of self-defence. *(pause)* Do you mind if I look around?
GABBY   Please ...

Abrahams goes over to where he had planted listening devices earlier, and picks them up. He stands there awkwardly, then looks at Gabby, and speaks in hushed tones so that Aaron cannot hear.

ABRAHAMS   Miss Anderson, I'm going to be honest with you. *(holds up the devices)* These are highly sophisticated listening devices. Part of a bag of tricks I brought with me from my days as a security policeman. Very useful for surveillance work. *(pause)* When I came to collect your statement this morning and saw Mr Matshabo and especially Mr Nyaka here, I was very worried. So when I came back later, I planted these devices and sat in my car just around the corner, where I couldn't be seen, but where I could listen to everything. I thought it was a good idea to keep an eye on you.

Gabby looks straight ahead of her as the implications of what she's hearing sinks in.

GABBY   Then you know everything.
ABRAHAMS   I also have a recording.
GABBY   A recording?
ABRAHAMS *(handing Gabby a micro-cassette tape)* It's all here.
GABBY   You're giving it to me?
ABRAHAMS   You can do with it what you wish.
GABBY   But surely this would be evidence ...
ABRAHAMS   I didn't get the required authority, so the recording would be inadmissible in court. I can't use it. But you can.
GABBY   How?
ABRAHAMS   Send it to the press. Tell Mr Matshabo you have it. Send it to his bosses. Throw it away. *(pause)* That's for you to decide.
GABBY   And you? What will you do?
ABRAHAMS   I don't know. But it feels like old times.

Lights fade on Abrahams and Gabby.
Lights come up on Anna and Gabby at Anna's house in a scene playing itself out the next morning.

ANNA   Did you sleep OK?

GABBY   I don't think I slept at all.

ANNA   Even with the pills?

GABBY   I don't know. Maybe I did. Maybe I just can't distinguish any more between the nightmare that I've lived in the past three days, and the nightmares that I dream at night.

ANNA   It will get better, Gabby.

GABBY   I should have stayed here like you suggested. Then none of this would have happened.

ANNA   Life's full of 'should haves'. We just need to do the right thing when the time comes.

GABBY *(in a subdued, insecure voice, hands over her eyes as if to block the images)* I'm not sure that I can do what you want.

ANNA *(quietly)* It's the right thing to do, Gabby. But don't worry about it now.

GABBY   That's not what my head says.

ANNA   You'll know it in your heart. When you feel stronger.

GABBY   Is that what you think?

ANNA   You know what I think.

GABBY   Tell me again.

ANNA   We have the District Surgeon's report. And your statement. I told Abrahams that we'll come in this afternoon and formally lay charges.

Telephone (landline) rings.

ANNA *(having picked up the cordless phone)* Hi. Yes. Just hold on. *(to Gabby)* It's Aaron. Do you want to talk to him?

GABBY *(with a visible change in her attitude, now more positive)* Yes. *(Anna brings the mobile part of the telephone to her)* Hello? OK, thanks. What? *(a smile breaks on her face)* When? Sure. Yes, of course. OK. Chat to you later. *(she sits there, slightly stunned, but beaming)*

ANNA   What?

GABBY *(takes a deep breath)* I'm leaving for Sydney.

ANNA   What?

GABBY   Tonight.

ANNA *(shocked, and trying hard not to show a little outrage)* Gabby!

GABBY   I'm sorry Anna.

ANNA   You kept this from me ... ?

GABBY I couldn't say anything till I heard from Aaron. We ... I didn't know whether the party would still make good on their offer after Nyaka ...

ANNA You agreed to their offer without telling me?

GABBY It was a decision that I had to take. There and then.

ANNA After all we've been through in the last few days. Together ...

GABBY I'm sorry, Anna. Really. You must feel ... betrayed.

ANNA I'm stunned. Why Gabby? Why? *(doesn't really wait for Gabby to respond)* You're not betraying me. We had a chance ... a chance in a million to put rape on the national agenda. To once and for all strike a blow for all those women, teenagers, girls ... babies that are raped every day in this country. A high profile case like this will not come around every day!

GABBY *(her anger rising)* Anna, please! *(raising her voice)* Please! This is not simply about 'rape'. This is about me. Don't lay a trip on me ...

ANNA *(more conciliatory)* I'm not ...

GABBY You are! You're making me feel guilty about not going through with a trial that could – in your eyes – rescue women from rape in this country!

ANNA If nothing else, it will show just how endemic it is! And then hopefully, something will get done! But we need you to go through with this.

GABBY I haven't asked to be in this position, Anna! I'm no martyr. I don't want to be.

ANNA Maybe, but Gabby ...

GABBY I've felt guilty all my life, Anna. Guilty about being white. Guilty about being able to live abroad when others were going through the hell of apartheid! Guilty about Matthew's death. Sure! I blamed Aaron for not being there on the day, but later I had to accept that maybe I was responsible for sending him to the shop to buy milk in the first place. And then I felt guilty about having divorced Aaron after coming to realise my possible culpability. Since I've come back here, I've felt guilty about being white all over again. Guilty that whatever decision I take, whatever statement I make will be judged in terms of my colour. Not what's right. Or wrong. But because it's a white me doing it. And now ... now you're making me feel guilty about letting down the sisters. I'm tired Anna. I'm tired of feeling guilty all the time!

ANNA *(with a hint of bitterness)* So you're just going to let them get away with it. Khumalo will get off scot free, and when he rapes someone else again, how will you live with the guilt then?

GABBY   Anna ... ! You're incorrigible!

ANNA   So you'll just leave. Again. Everyone who stays can sort out the mess!

GABBY   That's not fair, Anna!

ANNA *(almost pleadingly)* There's an election coming up Gabby. It's a one-in-five-years chance for us to say that things are not OK.

GABBY   Then do it in whatever way you want. Just leave me out of it.

ANNA   They've taken everything from you in the last five years. And you've just made a deal with them to say that it's OK.

GABBY   They? Who's they?

ANNA   You know what I mean ...

GABBY   You're right. You're right Anna. Since coming back here, everything that I've held dear and precious, I've lost. My son. My marriage. My honour. Everything. What should I do, Anna? You want me to fight back. And then what, Anna? Will this be a better place? Will I be happier? More fulfilled?

ANNA   The party will be happy if you don't ...

GABBY   So what? The party's been good to me. I have no desire to hurt it. In exile, my main support came from the party.

ANNA   This is not just about the party. What about the country?

GABBY   That's why I'm going. For the good of the country ... And for my own good. I'm doing what's best for *me*.

ANNA   And for Aaron. *(pause. Their eyes lock on each other's)*

GABBY   Maybe ...

Lights fade slowly. The final sequence returns to the inquest. Spotlight comes up on Aaron, Anna in darkness as before.

ANNA   You heard three shots?

AARON   That's right.

ANNA   And then you ran into the house, calling her name.

AARON   Yes.

ANNA   So in your opinion Mr Matshoba, it was a case of self-defence?

AARON   Ms Anderson certainly had no reason to shoot him. Not that I was aware of anyway. That was the first time that she had even met Mr Nyaka. Knowing both of them quite well, he was a hundred times more likely to initiate or do physical harm to anyone. And he would have needed very little provocation.

ANNA   So in your opinion –?

AARON   In my opinion, the most likely explanation is that Ms Anderson shot Mr Nyaka in self-defence.

Lights fade on Aaron and come up on Abrahams in the witness box at the inquest into Luthando's death.

ANNA   Inspector Abrahams, you were the first on the scene after the shooting at Ms Anderson's townhouse?

ABRAHAMS   That is correct.

ANNA   Could you tell this inquest what you saw?

ABRAHAMS   When I came to the house, Mr Matshabo opened the door for me. Miss Anderson was seated on the sofa. And Mr Nyaka was lying on the ground with a newspaper over his face.

ANNA   So Mr Nyaka was dead by the time you got there?

ABRAHAMS   Yes.

ANNA   And how long had he been dead for?

ABRAHAMS   His body was still warm. I believed that he died within half-an-hour before I got there.

ANNA   We've heard testimony that Mr Nyaka was still holding a gun in his hand?

ABRAHAMS   That is correct.

ANNA   Had any bullets been discharged from his gun?

ABRAHAMS   No. But three rounds from Mrs ... from Miss Anderson's gun had been fired.

ANNA   And they all hit Mr Nyaka?

ABRAHAMS   Yes. One in the right shoulder, and two in the chest.

ANNA   Inspector Abrahams, what was your impression of what happened?

ABRAHAMS   It's difficult to say. But from the scene it was possible to deduce that Mr Nyaka had drawn his gun. It appears that somehow Ms Anderson managed to shoot him first.

ANNA   This inquest needs to find a reasonable explanation for the death of Mr Nyaka and to determine if anyone should be held criminally liable or not. As you know, Ms Anderson is in Australia, but her statement made to you on the day of Mr Nyaka's death states that she acted in self-defence. Could that be a reasonable explanation for the death of Mr Nyaka?

ABRAHAMS   That could be, yes.

Spotlight fades on Abrahams, comes up on Gabby.

ANNA   Under normal circumstances, as she is a key witness, my client would be present at this inquest. But these are not normal circumstances. So I'd like to thank the authorities for allowing her to give evidence by video link to Australia. This inquest is particularly concerned with the events that led to the death of Mr Nyaka.

Lights come up on Abrahams, who is initially surprised and then lets break a wry smile as he prepares to listen to Gabby's evidence.

ANNA   In your own words then, Ms Anderson, please tell us what happened on the morning that Mr Nyaka was shot.

Lights come up on Aaron and Gabby at the same time. Aaron wears an anxious look.

GABBY *(as if she is physically at the inquest, takes in Abrahams and finally Aaron, then looks away from Aaron)* Where shall I start?

Slow fade to black.

The End.

Mike van Graan

Mike graduated from UCT with a BA Hons in Drama. He is a cultural consultant and has held several posts including Director of the Community Arts Project, National Projects Officer for the Congress of S.A. Writers, Director of the Bartel Arts Trust Centre, General Secretary of the National Arts Coalition and currently General Secretary of the Performing Arts Network of S.A. He also writes a weekly column for *The Mail and Guardian.*

His previous plays include: *The Dogs Must be Crazy* and *Some of Our Best Friends are Cultural Workers,* both of which were selected *Hot off the Fringe* at the National Arts Festivals where they premiered in the 90s; *Dinner Talk,* winner of the 1998 Fleur du Cap Award for Best New Script and *Hostile Takeover,* runner-up in both the Jury and Audience Award categories at the 2004 PANSA Festival of Reading of New Writing.

His new play *Some Mothers' Sons* was the Jury runner-up and won the Audience Award at the PANSA Festival of Reading of New Contemporary Writing in November 2005.

www.artslink.co.za/pansa

Playwright's Note

Every time I stand on the side of the road, burning in the hot sun, sticking my index finger out, pointing it up or down or sideways or making whatever hand sign is required to flag down a mini-bus taxi (typically, but not always, a dilapidated *Toyota Hiace* fifteen seater, but can carry up to eighteen people ... or more) I swear to myself this is the last time I travel by taxi, I'm going by bus from now on. No more taxis for me! A few minutes later I'm in a taxi that's speeding along the highway changing lanes miraculously, I swear they move sideways! I'm sitting, fingers clenched, nails digging into my palms, wondering why I bothered having coffee before leaving the house and also, do I really need this kind of adrenalin rush in the morning? Welcome to the debate that rages in my head everyday. If I take the bus, chances are I'll get to work without incident but I'll probably be late. Now, if I take a taxi on the other hand, I'll most probably be on time, but I'll also have one hell of a ride cutting through morning traffic.

Taxis are the most commonly used means of public transport in South Africa and unfortunately, the 'Taxi Industry' is also one of the least-regulated major industries in the country. It is an industry characterised by violent clashes between taxi-owners and taxi associations over routes and also the daily violence that taxi drivers, under pressure to make money for their employers, inflict on themselves, each other and other road users as they speed along South Africa's roads making up the road rules as they go along.

Many people have lost their lives in mini-bus accidents. *Taxi* is about an aspect of South African life that affects us all, whether we travel by taxi or not. The taxi industry is probably one of the most potent headaches of the present government.

Sibusiso Mamba

TAXI

Sibusiso Mamba

First broadcast on BBC Radio 4 on 16th April, 2004
Produced/Directed by Claire Grove.

CHARACTERS

MZEE	Sello Maake ka Ncube
SENZO	Sibusiso Mamba
JAN	Mark Faith
JEMMA	Tracy-Ann Obermann
PETE	Don McCorkindale
DODU	Noma Domezweni
JUDGE	
MARSHALS	
VENDORS	

SCENE 1
INT. DAY – MZEE'S MOVING TAXI

MZEE [V/O] I was alone in my taxi. No *(beat)* I wasn't alone. Not that morning. You see, sometimes I'm alone in the morning. Between half-past six and half past nine … if you take passengers from the north of Johannesburg to the city centre … it is very difficult. There are too many mini-bus taxis and not enough passengers. You want a full taxi? You must drive fast! Hho! *(beat)* Ja … I like to believe I was alone that morning. I wasn't. There was a young man … student from Wits University. He was reading. Lucky boy. Educated. Not like me. I only went up to Standard Three. I was fourteen when I left school. The other children were scared of me. I was big. *(beat)* The morning is the most difficult time if you drive a taxi.

[INTERIOR TAXI.]

MZEE   Wena mfana ... you don't know what you're talking about.

SENZO   HhOK ... explain to me nicely. What did you guys gain
by being on strike yesterday?

MZEE   Don't we have a right to be heard? Like other workers?

SENZO   You're afraid the government will make you give a
better service.

(Mzee laughs)

MZEE   Mara ... you can talk nè?! Service? Ha ha ...

SENZO   You treat us like goats ...

MZEE   Yewena ... *(he laughs)*

SENZO   Serious! This taxi seats fifteen people nè? You put
eighteen.

MZEE   We must make money.

SENZO   Exactly mfethu ...

MZEE   We put extra seats ... what's your problem ...

SENZO   Seats! Ha! Those are not seats ... just a little bit of extra
space for someone with a small bum. Very few people in this country
have a small bum.

(Mzee laughs)

MZEE [V/O] We were on strike the day before. All the mini-bus taxi
drivers around Joburg. Ja! We are not happy. The Transport
Ministry wants to take the taxi industry out of the businessmen's
hands ... and run it themselves. Hhayibo! Are they mad? We are not
civil servants. We'll start paying things like tax and I don't know
what. We'll earn even less than we do now. *(beat)*

On that morning ... I went to see the owner of my taxi ... thinking
he'd be happy to see me ... we were on strike for them too ... He says
to me ... 'I want you to make two extra journeys every day for the
next week ... to make up the earnings lost during the strike.'
Hhayibo! I couldn't believe my ears. Two extra journeys with a full
load of eighteen passengers. It's difficult to make the required seven
journeys a day. Two more? That's not possible.

[INT. TAXI. MZEE HOOTS AT A CAR IN FRONT OF HIM.]

MZEE   Come on wena driva maan!

[HE HOOTS AGAIN.]

Why do these whites drive like they're strolling in their gardens ...?

SENZO   Eish I don't know.

MZEE   You must ask them. Don't you talk to your neighbours?
(Senzo laughs)

MZEE   You should have grown up in the township. These rich
northern suburbs make you soft sonny ...

SENZO   Careful!

[A SUDDEN SCREECH OF TYRES.]

MZEE   Bloody bastard! You're driving kak man.

SCENE 2
INT. DAY – JAN'S MOVING CAR

JAN [V/O] I hate the M1 highway in the mornings. Absolutely chock-a-
block. I wish there was a quicker way to get to Joburg city centre
from the north. The highway is stressful ... crowded. *(beat)* Larry
was a rebellious little boy, eh. Always playing tricks on me.
Sometimes I got angry. But most of the time I just laughed.

[JAN'S MOVING CAR. A RADIO HUMS QUIETLY IN THE
BACKGROUND.]

JAN   Come on now boykie. Larry! That's enough.

[A CHILD GIGGLES IN THE BACKSEAT.]

Son ... I said put your seatbelt back on. Come on now.

[MORE LAUGHTER.]

Listen to me. It's dangerous to drive without a seatbelt ... alright
boykie. *(pause)* There's a good boy. Now keep it on even when Pa's
not looking.

[THE CAR SUDDENLY BRAKES.]

JAN [V/O] This taxi, this blue mini-bus taxi came speeding down the
William Nicol on ramp straight into the highway. The driver didn't
even look to see me approach, he just pulled into my lane ... right in
front of me.

[HE BLOWS HIS HORN FURIOUSLY.]

JAN   Madman! *(beat)* You see son. Lunatics on the road in
the morning. Lunatics! *(pause)*

JAN [V/O] Then he stops. I mean ... right in front of my car on the busy
highway ... So I had to stop. Cars were hooting behind me. He didn't
care. He rolls down his window and makes all these gestures with his
hands and insults me in Zulu or Xhosa ... I don't know.

SCENE 3
INT. DAY – MZEE'S TAXI

[THE TAXI HAS STOPPED. THE WINDOW IS OPEN. OTHER
CARS ARE STILL HOOTING.]

MZEE   Ngizok'phihliza! I'll break you. You saw me coming. I
even indicated. Hhayi maan! Come out of your car!

[V/O] He was in a new 7-series BMW. The ones with a computer
inside. *(beat)* You see ... on the road other motorists have to be
understanding. When a taxi comes, give way maan ... because we are
in a hurry! Time is money. OK?

SENZO   Mfethu please joh ... you are blocking traffic.
MZEE   Bastard is making me angry.

[V/O] Black motorists know that a taxi driver's time is precious ...
even some white motorists too. Sometimes you get stubborn ones.
Like this.

[HE SHUTS THE WINDOW AND DRIVES OFF.]

(to Senzo) These boers. Nx! *(beat)* It's your job to show them.

SENZO   Show them what?
MZEE   Study hard. So you can drive a better car than that.
(beat) To show them who's really running this country.

SCENE 4
EXT. DAY – BREE STREET TAXI RANK

MZEE [V/O] An accident. It can happen at anytime. At any place.
(beat) When you get an accident. A lot of things change.

[TAXI RANK COMES ALIVE. A VERY BUSY PLACE. TAXI

MARSHALS CALL OUT DIFFERENT DESTINATIONS. VENDORS
SELL THEIR WARES. TAXIS PULL IN AND PULL OUT.]

MARSHAL 1   Cresta! Melville! Auckland Park! Hhayi Cresta!
MARSHAL 2   Olivedale Northgate Lanseria! Northern suburbs ...
woza!
MARSHAL 3   Fourways! Diepsloot! Monte Casino! Via Highway!

[THE HUSTLE AND BUSTLE FADES.]

MZEE [V/O] This is where I rank. Bree Street. It's just been rebuilt.
You don't stand all day in the sun any more. It is also very clean.
And everyone knows exactly where they're allowed to park their taxi.
No need to fight about that. Like we used to. You come here you join
your line and wait. Your turn comes. The Marshal tells you, then he
loads eighteen passengers. That is when there is no police. When
there is, only fifteen. Sometimes you can dodge the police. But it's
not easy. *(beat)* Many things they change after an accident.

[TAXI RANK COMES ALIVE AGAIN.]

MARSHAL 1   Where are you going, Madam?
JEMMA   Nowhere right now thanks.
MARSHAL 2 *(he wolf whistles)* Ye Mzee! Here's your woman.
MZEE   Hhe? My woman where?
MARSHAL 1   You can sit in the front with me madam!!
JEMMA   No ... I'm really fine ... thanks ...
MZEE   Jemma?
JEMMA   Hello Mzee ...
MZEE   I'm sorry ...
JEMMA   It's alright. They're just trying to be helpful ... *(beat)* I
need to speak with you ... do you have time?
MZEE   But I said ... I don't want you to write anything about me.
JEMMA   Please just hear me out, Mzee. *(beat)* I spoke to Pete
van Wyck.
MZEE   Who is he?
JEMMA   He's the lawyer the Stewart family have hired ...
MZEE   They have a lawyer? *(pause)*
JEMMA   Yes. *(beat)* Mzee ... Pete said to me ... the police were
wrong to charge you with negligent driving. He says they're going to
try and prove you caused the accident deliberately. If they succeed ...

you'll be charged with culpable homicide. *(beat)* Don't you want to tell your side of the story? *(pause)*

MZEE   No. I don't.

JEMMA   Look ... we're only hearing it from Jan Stewart's family. I am writing an article for *The Saturday Star* ...

MZEE   I said no.

JEMMA   You might be charged with murder Mzee.

MZEE   I don't want to be in your newspaper. Thank you.

(pause)

JEMMA   Here is my card. If you change your mind ...

[PAUSE. JEMMA WALKS AWAY.]

VENDOR 1   Cool ice cream one rand!

VENDOR 2   Loose cigarette fifty cents! *Rothmans! Stuyvesant!*

VENDOR 3   Minty sweets fifty cents!!

MZEE [V/O] Jan Stewart's child got hurt bad in the car ... after three days ... in the hospital ... he died. There was nothing they could do for him.

SCENE 5
EXT. DAY – JAN'S GARDEN, POOLSIDE

[JAN AND PETE HAVE JUST FINISHED LUNCH.
JAN'S TWINS SAMMY AND KERRY ARE SPLASHING ABOUT IN THE POOL.]

JAN [V/O] The twins don't really understand. When you tell a child about death they try to rationalise ... to make sense of it in their own head ... He was three years old. The twins are eight. It doesn't make any sense. Linda's not coping. She just ... well if she didn't have the girls holding her hands tight at Larry's funeral she would have just ... *(he sighs)* I don't know. It makes no sense.

[THE GIRLS SPLASH LOUDLY IN THE POOL.]

JAN   Sammy! Kerry! That's enough girls. Go inside. Mommy has lunch ready now.

[THE GIRLS SPLASH OUT OF THE POOL.]

JAN   Don't make the carpet wet now ...

PETE *(laughing)* They've got so much energy, eh ... *(pause)*
JAN   What other options do we have, Pete?
PETE   We can't do anything but wait. I've put an appeal in
every single newspaper ... we just have to hope he will come
forward.
JAN   There's less than three weeks to go before the trial.
PETE   I know ... but unless we find this passenger, we have no
chance of bringing a culpable homicide charge.
JAN   You mean ... if we find him and he agrees to speak ...
PETE   He's the only hope we have, Jan. Otherwise ... all he'll
get is a suspended sentence for negligent driving.
JAN   It was not negligent Pete. He deliberately stopped his
car in front of mine, opened his window and he threatened me. That
was the start.
PETE   I know ... We just have to prove it.

SCENE 6

MZEE [V/O] My father had two taxis. They used to go from Ntuzuma
township to Durban city centre. When I was thirteen he lost them
both. The bank repossessed them. That was the year I left school.
There was no more money to pay for me. It was difficult for a proud
Zulu man like him to fail to provide for his family. My mother had to
find work. But it paid very little. *(beat)* When my father told me I
couldn't go to school any more he was almost crying. It was OK ... I
never liked school. I wanted to be working. Ja ... and I've been
working every day since then ... and now maybe my son has to stop
school because there is no money for school fees ...

SCENE 7
INT. NIGHT – DUDU'S SHACK. ALEXANDER TOWNSHIP

[MZEE'S SHAVING HIS SON'S HEAD. MACHINE PURRS SOFTLY.
THERE IS PARTY NOISE COMING FROM OUTSIDE THE
SHACK.]

MZEE   How does he look now?
DUDU *(beat)* You must cut more there. Then he must sleep Mzee ...
he has school tomorrow. And the Madam has guests tonight so I

must be at work early in the morning to wash the dishes. I also need
to sleep.

MZEE   Andile, tell your mother you are not sleepy.

DUDU   Finish cutting his hair Mzee please. I'll lay his bed.
(beat) Are you staying tonight?

MZEE   No ... I have to be in Diepsloot.

DUDU   Why?

MZEE   I have to be on the road at half past four ... otherwise I
miss the crowd that comes out of Monte Casino ... that is a quarter
of the day's takings. *(beat)* Diepsloot is ten minutes drive from
Monte Casino. Not like here.

DUDU   Did you speak to the owner of your taxi?

MZEE   I tried. He said I shouldn't even bother to ask for a loan.

DUDU   So what are you going to do?

MZEE   I will borrow some money from a shylock.

DUDU   You won't be able to pay it back, you know that.

MZEE   I have no choice. If Jan Stewart charges me with killing
his child ... I need a lawyer. *(beat)* We also need to pay for Andile's
school. *(pause)*

DUDU   I can't borrow from the Madam Mzee ... I still haven't
paid the loan from last year.

[THE CLIPPERS STOP.]

MZEE   Go and wash your head, my boy.

[HE OPENS THE DOOR.]

MZEE   How is he supposed to sleep with all this noise?

DUDU   Ah ... he's used to it. *(beat)* There is a letter for you from
Damelin College.

MZEE   Hho ... it has finally arrived.

DUDU   Why?

MZEE   I applied for night school.

DUDU   Really? To learn what?

MZEE   To get a school leaving certificate ... then maybe do
business studies after a year ...

DUDU   Hawu! That's very nice!

MZEE   But I need money for registration. So it'll have to wait
until ... well ... it'll all have to wait. *(beat)* Andile ... let's go wash
your head outside in the tap.

SCENE 8
INT. DAY – MZEE'S MOVING TAXI

SENZO   If Kaizer Chiefs win this weekend ... we'll have proved we are the best football team in this country. *(beat)* What are you looking at?

MZEE   The bastard in the BMW ... what's he doing?

SENZO   Talking on his cellphone. If Kaizer Chiefs don't win ...

MZEE   Talking to the police. Look he's reading my number plate.

[THE TAXI BRAKES SUDDENLY.]

SENZO   What are you doing?

MZEE   Put on your seatbelt.

SENZO   Why?

MZEE   Just do it mpinchi ...

SCENE 9
INT. DAY – JAN'S MOVING CAR

JAN *(on the phone)* I'm not racing him, Linda he's driving right in front of me ... I'm on the M1. No ... I'll take a different route ... I'll ... what? Hullo ... lost you for a second ... huh? Larry's fine. No ... he's not sleeping ... traffic's terrible ...

[HE BRAKES SUDDENLY.]

This man's insane! He keeps on slamming his brakes in front of me for no reason. Lunatic! I will ... I will. I'll get off at Grayston Drive ... then take a back route ...

[CAR DRIVES OFF AGAIN.]

I think he wants me to crash into him.

[HE BRAKES SHARP AGAIN.]

Hell's bells! I need to get off this highway. I'll ring you when we get to Braamfontein. Bye darling.

[HE HANGS UP THE PHONE.]

Lunatics! *(beat)* You sitting nicely there boykie?

SCENE 10
INT. DAY – MZEE'S TAXI.

[THE SOUNDS OF BREE STREET STATION. A NUMBER IS
DIALLED ON A PHONE. IT RINGS ON THE OTHER END.]

JEMMA	Hullo Jemma speaking ...
MZEE	Ehh ... Jemma? Hullo ... it is Mzee Dlamini. The taxi
driver.	
JEMMA	Hullo Mzee ... how are you?
MZEE	I am not so fine ... but I am OK ... *(pause)*
JEMMA	What can I do for you?
MZEE	Are you still writing that article for the *Saturday Star*?
JEMMA	Yes.
MZEE	HhOK ...

SCENE 11
INT/EXT. DAY – MZEE'S TAXI/OUTSIDE JEMMA'S HOUSE,
MELVILLE

[MZEE AND JEMMA ARE IN THE FRONT. THE DOORS ARE
OPEN. CHILDREN PLAY IN THE DISTANCE.
JEMMA IS SCRIBBLING AWAY IN A NOTEBOOK.]

MZEE   Your neighbour there ... she's still peeping. Do taxis not
come to this side Melville?
JEMMA   Agh ... don't mind her ... she's nosy. *(beat)* OK ... you
make six hundred and thirty rands a day if you make seven trips?
MZEE   Seven full loads with eighteen people in the taxi.
JEMMA   Why does the owner expect seven hundred rands from
you?
MZEE   You must not ask about the owner ... *(pause)*
JEMMA   Ok ... why do you hand in seven hundred rand then?
MZEE   The passengers pay five rands if they go to Monte
Casino or Fourways Mall. But if they go to Diepsloot they pay six
rand. And most people go to Diepsloot.
JEMMA   How long does it take? To drive to Diepsloot? From town?
MZEE   Not more than half of an hour. Sometimes less.
JEMMA   Mzee that's quite a distance to cover in under half an hour.
MZEE   Maybe ... maybe ...

JEMMA What happens if you don't make the seven hundred rand?

MZEE You get into debt so you have to make it up another day.

JEMMA So what happens if you make more than seven hundred rand then? *(Mzee laughs)* You keep it?

MZEE *(laughing)* What do you think? *(beat)* Ja ... but you see ... most owners are very clever ... they make sure you always owe them money for something ...

JEMMA Like?

MZEE Oh ... anything that breaks ... the engine ... or if the clutch plate is burnt out.

JEMMA Do you pay for the servicing of the taxi then?

MZEE No, he does ... but I pay for anything extra ... like if I have a accident and the kombi needs a new bumper.

JEMMA Who pays for petrol?

MZEE He gives me an allowance for that every week.

JEMMA Does your boss have other taxis?

MZEE *(beat)* Hhe ... you don't listen, nè?

JEMMA I am not going to write anything about him ... I just want to know ...

MZEE *(beat)* You have enough for an article now ...

JEMMA No ... no Mzee I don't. I need more personal stuff from you ... this isn't enough ...

MZEE Another time. I must go to Bree Street or I'll lose my place in the queue.

JEMMA Can I come into town with you?

MZEE That will be three rands and fifty cents ...
(Jemma counts coins. Mzee laughs) I'm joking. I'll give you a lift.

JEMMA No I'll pay. There. Exactly three rand fifty.

MZEE No ... maan! I don't want your money.

[HE STARTS THE CAR. DOORS SHUT. CAR DRIVES OFF.]

SCENE 12
EXT. DAY – BREE STREET STATION

MZEE [V/O] My father became difficult after a while. Drank a lot, borrowed money from shylocks and gambled on horses. My mother left him and I left with her. We lived in KwaMashu township ... I found a job on a train ... cleaning third class compartments. Got my driver's license at age nineteen. Then asked one of my father's friends to give me a job driving a taxi. He said, 'Yes'. *(beat)* Fifteen years I've been driving. First in Durban ... then the last twelve years in Joburg. *(beat)* Yesterday ... Jemma's article came out in *The Star*. The other taxi drivers are shaking my hand and wishing me good luck in court. The owner is not happy. He says if another article comes out ... he'll get a new driver. Maybe he should ...

SCENE 13
INT. DAY – JAN'S MOVING CAR

JAN [V/O]We were close to leaving the M1, close to Grayston Drive off-ramp. But the madman didn't stop harassing me. He'd appear out of nowhere ... pull in, in front of me, and brake sharply. *(beat)* He should've been charged with murder from the start.

[HE DIALS A NUMBER ON HIS MOBILE PHONE. THE PHONE RINGS ON OTHER END.]

PETE *(message)* Hullo this is Pete van Wyck sorry not to be here right now ...
JAN   Shoot!

[HE HANGS UP. TURNS ON RADIO.]

JAN [V/O] A week and a half to the trial. We still haven't found him. The only passenger in the taxi that morning. *(beat)* Negligence? It was not negligence. Negligence implies a mistake.

[HIS MOBILE PHONE RINGS. HE ANSWERS.]

JAN   Hi Pete ... sorry I missed your call earlier ...
PETE *(on distort)* No worries. Where are you?
JAN   Just leaving Randburg. I have to fetch the girls from school.
PETE   Come into my office as soon as you can.
JAN   Oh ... eh ... why?
PETE   That young man ... the passenger. He's on his way here.

SCENE 14
INT. DAY – PETE'S OFFICE.
JAN AND PETE ARE WAITING.

PETE   No Jan ... that's not the answer, eh ...

JAN   Linda's not coping Pete. Everything in the house reminds her of Larry ... everything.

PETE   But where would you go? London's saturated with South Africans already. Australia? New Zealand?

JAN   I don't know. It's just a thought. Linda and the girls need a change you know.

PETE   I ran away January 1990.

JAN   It wouldn't be running away. This is home.

PETE   Ja ... *(beat)* ... well ... London just wasn't for me, eh. 1997 I was back here ...

JAN   1990 was an exciting time, Pete. Mandela had been released from prison and we were all celebrating ... and ...

[THE INTERNAL LINE BUZZES. PETE ANSWERS.]

PETE   Ja, Belinda. *(beat)* Send him through. Thanks. *(he hangs up)* He's here.

SCENE 15
EXT. NIGHT – OUTSIDE JEMMA'S HOUSE

[MZEE'S TAXI PULLS UP. STOPS. HE GETS OUT. RINGS THE BUZZER AT THE GATE. A DOG BARKS INSIDE THE HOUSE.]

JEMMA *(on intercom)* Hullo?

MZEE   Jemma?

JEMMA   Ja? Who's this?

[DOG BARKS THROUGH INTERCOM.]

MZEE   It's me ... Mzee.

JEMMA   Oh!

[SHE HANGS UP THE BUZZER. OPENS THE DOOR. DOG RUSHES OUT AND BARKS VICIOUSLY AT MZEE.]

MZEE   Fuseki! Hhayi fuseki smaku 'ska missus! Mgodoyi!

JEMMA   Trixie! Trixie! Mum can you come get Trixie!

[TRIXIE BARKS]

Sorry Mzee. Come on Trixie! Back in the house. Come on!

[SHE RUNS DOG BACK INTO THE HOUSE. SHUTS THE DOOR. RETURNS TO THE GATE.]

Agh ... sorry man. She gets over-excited sometimes.

MZEE   And barks at black people?

JEMMA   Mzee ... come on ...

MZEE   You must teach your dog ... this is the New South Africa ...

JEMMA   What's wrong with ...

MZEE   ... blacks and whites are living together in peace ... wabona?

JEMMA   What's going on Mzee?

MZEE   Why are you on that side of the gate?

[METAL GATE IS OPEN. THEN SHUT.]

JEMMA   Happy? *(pause)*

MZEE   Your dreadlocks are nice.

JEMMA   Thanks.

MZEE   Do you want to come for a drive?

JEMMA   Now? *(beat)* I'm in the middle of cooking supper ...

MZEE   You don't trust me.

JEMMA   Don't be ridiculous.

MZEE   At night.

JEMMA   That isn't true.

MZEE   I lost my ranking permit today.

JEMMA   What?

MZEE   The marshals at Bree Street suspended me.

JEMMA   Why?

MZEE   I've been driving around alone all day. Thinking.

JEMMA   About −?

MZEE   Maybe I don't want to be a taxi driver anymore. *(beat)* I've lost a day's takings. I must go and tell the owner. Maybe he will shoot me. I don't know. *(beat)* Come to Alexandra township. You can meet my wife and child. Write about them if you want.(pause)

JEMMA   Give me five minutes.

SCENE 16
INT. NIGHT – MZEE'S MOVING TAXI

JEMMA   It doesn't make sense. Why would they take away your permit?

MZEE   They say it takes too long for my taxi to get full. Ever since the article ... some passengers refuse to get into my taxi. They say they'll wait for the next one. They don't want to drive with a child-killer. That is what they say to the marshals.

[CAR STOPS]

We are here ... come ...

JEMMA   Mzee we're on the highway. Why've you stopped?

MZEE   We're going to the bridge over there ... come ...

[HE OPENS HIS DOOR.]

JEMMA   You can't park on the hard shoulder!

MZEE   I've got the hazard lights on ...

[HE EXITS. SHUTS HIS DOOR. SILENCE. JEMMA OPENS HER DOOR.]

JEMMA   Mzee! *(she leaves car)* Wait!

[WINDY NIGHT. TRAFFIC ON THE HIGHWAY. MZEE WALKS AHEAD. JEMMA TRYING TO KEEP UP.]

MZEE   I think the steps to the bridge are there. Let's cross the road.

JEMMA   Mzee ... there's too many cars ...

MZEE   Take my hand. *(beat)* Ready?

JEMMA   Uhm ... OK.

[THEY RUN ACROSS THE ROAD. A CAR HORN SOUNDS LOUDLY.]

This is so dangerous!

MZEE   Hhokay here are the steps ...

SCENE 17
EXT. NIGHT – M1 PASSENGER BRIDGE

[THE WIND BLOWS STRONGER. TRAFFIC IS A DISTANT HUM.]

JEMMA   It's cold up here.

MZEE   Just look at it ...

JEMMA   What?

MZEE   The road ... wabona Jemma ... has a mind of its own. It can decide for itself what's going to happen. You make friends with it ... know it like a best friend ... then you try to be good to it. Sometimes it's like ... it gets so angry ... it wants blood. *(beat)* You see the bend there ... by the big sign saying Grayston Drive?

JEMMA   Ja ... ? *(pause))*

MZEE   That's where it happened.

JEMMA   What happened?

MZEE   Jan Stewart was behind me in the fast lane. In his BMW. Maybe I was driving too slowly for him.

JEMMA   And then ... ? *(beat)*

MZEE   Then I heard a loud crash. Another car ... an *Isuzu* four by four hit Jan's *BMW* from behind.

JEMMA   What were you doing at that moment? *(beat)* Why were you charged with –

MZEE   Look at that corner Jemma ...

JEMMA   I can see it ... I just want to know how you ended up with a charge of negligent driving when Jan Stewart was hit from behind by another car?

MZEE   I think because I put on my brakes very quickly.

JEMMA   Why?

MZEE   Because I didn't want to skid on that bend.

JEMMA   OK. So why were you ... ? OK ... *(beat)* What happened to the people in the *Isuzu* bakkie? *(beat)* Mzee they crashed into Jan's car ... so why were you charged? It doesn't make any sense ...

MZEE   The police said I pulled into Jan's lane too quickly without proper indication! *(pause)*

JEMMA   Did you?

MZEE   I don't know, Jemma. I was in a hurry ...

JEMMA   Mzee ... did you realise that there was a child in Jan's car?

MZEE   Yes ... but I didn't know there'd be an accident.

JEMMA Maybe the *Isuzu* was following Jan too closely. Shouldn't they have been charged with something ... ?

MZEE It was early morning. Everyone follows too closely.

JEMMA Do you think your negligent driving charge is fair?

MZEE Many taxi drivers have been faced with that one. For me it is the second time.

JEMMA So maybe you were negligent?

MZEE Yes, the first time maybe. But not this new one.

JEMMA Why?

MZEE Because ... *(beat)* I have a son too you know.

SCENE 18
INT. DAY – PETE'S OFFICE

JAN It's not because Mzee's a taxi driver Senzo ... I have nothing against taxi drivers. I just can't stand aggressive driving.

SENZO I hear you Mr Stewart ...

JAN Linda and I – we used to travel in kombis, when we were at university. It's different nowadays. Most of you have cars. We lived in Melville and we took taxis all the time. To rallies and demonstrations. In the 80s if you were white and demonstrating you were probably a communist and anti-government agent. Once, a whole taxi load of us got arrested on the way to a demo in the FNB stadium near Soweto. *(beat)* I have travelled in a lot of taxis in my time, Senzo. *(pause)*

SENZO Maybe I'm just not clear what you'd like me to do.

PETE You were sitting in the front seat, ja?

SENZO I've told you all that Mr van Wyck ...

PETE No need to get stressed, Senzo. You're not on trial here ...

SENZO It sort of feels like I am.

JAN Not at all Senzo. We're grateful you are here.

PETE All I'm asking is if he said anything about Jan? How angry was he?

SENZO He wasn't in more of a mood than other drivers I've travelled with.

PETE You said he was cursing white people ...

SENZO I didn't say cursing ... don't put words in my mouth.

JAN Pete ... please ...

SENZO   I said he asked me why whites drive like they're strolling in their gardens ...

PETE   What did he mean by that?

SENZO   He said they drive too slowly on the highway.

PETE   Did he say Jan was driving too slowly? *(beat)* Did he threaten Mr Stewart at any point ...? *(pause)*

SENZO   He leant out the window and asked why Mr Stewart refused to let him into the lane ... why he'd hooted at him.

JAN   He wasn't just asking nicely though Senzo ...

SENZO   No. He was aggressive.

PETE   So, he was angry?

SENZO   Maybe ... *(pause)*

PETE   This is the way I'd be asking you questions in the court Senzo. *(beat)* Are you prepared to go through with it?

SENZO   I can only tell my experience of the journey. Nothing else.

JAN   And that is all we ask ...

PETE   So we'll meet next week for a proper briefing. Is that alright?

SENZO   Ja ... that's cool. *(beat)* I need to get home.

JAN   Where do you live?

SENZO   Near Fourways Mall.

JAN   So do I. *(beat)* Do you want a lift?

SENZO *(pause)* Ja ... cool. *(beat)* Thanks.

SCENE 19

INT. DAY – INSIDE DUDU'S SHACK

[DUDU IS HUMMING VERY SOFTLY TO HERSELF. SHE IS ZIPPING UP BAGS SHE'S PACKED. A CAR PULLS UP OUTSIDE. DOORS OPEN AND SHUT. THEN A KNOCK ON THE CORRUGATED-IRON DOOR.]

DUDU   Who is it?

MZEE   It's Mzee ...

[DUDU WALKS TO THE DOOR. OPENS IT. PAUSE.]

Dudu ... this is Jemma.

JEMMA   Hullo ...

[THEY ENTER THE ROOM. DOOR IS SHUT. PAUSE.]

Nice meeting you finally ...

DUDU   Yes Madam ... do you want a cup of tea?

JEMMA   No ... please ...

DUDU   I'm sorry there's no coffee ...

JEMMA   Please don't call me Madam, Dudu ...

MZEE   Where's Andile ...?

DUDU   He's not here ... *((pause)*

MZEE   Jemma's the woman from the newspaper.

DUDU   Mmh ... I know. I see your picture in *The Star*.

MZEE   She'd like to speak with you and ask you some questions for another article she's writing about me.

DUDU   Mmhh ...

MZEE   Where's Andile? Jemma wants to meet him.

DUDU   Why did you not come yesterday, Mzee? You said you were coming.

JEMMA   Sorry, it was my fault actually. We were gonna take pictures for the article ... but the photographer was late. I'm sorry about that.

DUDU   You have a cellphone, Mzee. You could have called me at work to tell me. *(pause)*

MZEE   What's inside the bag?

DUDU   Clothes.

MZEE   Whose clothes?

DUDU   Andile's ...

MZEE   Where is he going?

DUDU   He is gone already.

MZEE   Gone where?

DUDU   They chased him away from the school because we haven't paid the fees. So I took him to my mother in Pietersburg.

MZEE   When?

DUDU   Yesterday. *(pause)*

MZEE   And when were you going to tell me this?

DUDU   You should have been here yesterday. *(pause)*

MZEE   And the other suitcase? Whose is that?

DUDU   Mine. I am taking the six o' clock *Greyhound* bus.

MZEE   To?

DUDU   Pietersburg also ... *(pause)*

MZEE   Well, you can go! OK? You can just pack all your things
and go and never come back. But you can't send my son away and
not tell me! That is not done! *(beat)* Jemma, stay right where you are.
This is Andile's mother. I am sorry you cannot meet Andile today
because she thinks me not worthy of being told when she sends my
son to the Northern Province! *(beat)* You speak to her Jemma ...
please ... if you want to ask her questions ... go ahead ... here she is ...

[DOOR IS OPENED. THEN SLAMMED SHUT. SILENCE]

JEMMA   Dudu ...
DUDU   Yes Madam.
JEMMA   Please don't call me Madam. Jemma. That's my name.
Call me Jemma. *(beat)* Would you like to talk to me?
DUDU   Why must I like it? *(pause)*
JEMMA   Well ... because ... um ... what I mean is ... is it OK to ask
you a few things about yourself and your life with your husband?
(pause) Do you want me to leave? *(pause)* Can I ask one question?
DUDU   Ask. But I must catch the six o'clock bus.
JEMMA   Has Mzee ever been physically aggressive towards you
or Andile?
DUDU   No.
JEMMA   OK. *(beat)* Why are you leaving for Pietersburg? Do you
realise Mzee might be locked up if they find him guilty? *(pause)*
OK ... look ... you may not like me but I am the only one who is
trying to tell Mzee's side of the story and although that might not
help him in court ... it'll at least make the rest of the country aware
that Mzee is just a husband and a father, doing his best to get
through the day and make ends meet. So if you want to help him ...
talk to me. You want me to be accurate, don't you? *(beat)* How is
Mzee's relationship with his son? *(pause)* OK ... I am sorry to bother
you in your home. You must be wondering who the hell I think I am.
I apologise ... Please put your bags down for just one second ...

[PAUSE. DUDU WALKS TO THE DOOR. OPENS IT.]

DUDU   Goodbye Madam.
JEMMA   Dudu ... I ...

[THE DOOR SHUTS]

SCENE 20
INT. DAY – MZEE'S TAXI

[THE CAR IS MOVING. THEN IT STOPS.]

JEMMA   Has she ever done this before? Left you like this?
MZEE   No ...
JEMMA   So why now?
MZEE   I don't know. *(beat)* Maybe she's not able to deal with the pressure. Maybe she's worried about the trial. Maybe she doesn't like the idea of newspaper articles. I don't know. Or she's just had enough of Jo'burg and living in a shack in Alexandra township.
JEMMA   Is there something else? Something you haven't told me?
MZEE   Like what?
JEMMA   I don't know ... just ...
MZEE   About what?
JEMMA   Mzee ... your trial is in a week. If you want me to write about you again ... you have to be straight with me.
MZEE   I have been straight with you.
JEMMA   I don't want any unpleasant surprises in that court room.

SCENE 21
EXT. DAY – M1 HIGHWAY. THE ACCIDENT

[A CAR HORN SOUNDS OVER AND OVER.
TYRES SCREECH. THERE IS A LOUD CRUNCHING CRASH.
GLASS SHATTERS.]

SENZO   Mzee, stop the car! Stop the car. Oh God ... oh Nkos'yami ... Awubheke manj' ukuthi kwenzekaleni!!

SCENE 22
INT. DAY – MZEE'S TAXI M1 HIGHWAY

MZEE [V/O] Accidents happen so quickly. One minute you are in control and the next minute ... it all has changed. *(beat)* Senzo got out of the taxi and ran to help. Me? I just couldn't even think ...

SCENE 23
EXT. DAY – M1 HARDSHOULDER

[A SIREN WAILS IN THE DISTANCE. A CACOPHONY OF
SHOUTING VOICES. A CHILD CRIES HYSTERICALLY THEN IT
ALL FADES TO JUST THE SOUND OF A RUNNING CAR
ENGINE.]

JAN [V/O] I was trapped. Caught in my seatbelt. I couldn't move.
There were people around the car. I don't know where they'd
appeared from. All trying to open the doors. To try and get Larry
out. *(beat)* There was a face by the window. A young black man with
glasses and dreadlocks. Senzo. He was saying something to me.
Shouting and gesticulating. It dawned on me. He was telling me to
open my door. I'd been holding the handle all along.

SCENE 24

MZEE [V/O] When I was twenty my mother died. She had been
suffering with her kidneys for a long time. *(beat)* I left Durban a
week after the funeral. My father didn't need me there. He was still
angry, I think, that I had gone to live with my mother. It was 1990
when I got to Jo'burg. Yoh! That was an exciting time. Before long I
had a job. Driving. The Black Taxi Association had just been formed.
Many black people were getting loans from the bank to buy taxis.
Everything was looking good. Nelson Mandela had just come out of
prison. That was also the year that I met Dudu. *(beat)* If these
children who were too young to vote in 1994 knew how it felt to
stand in that queue. The longest queue I've ever seen! But we were
happy! We were singing! We were dancing! All the way to the voting
boxes. We were voting for the very first time. I was dreaming of
having my own fleet of taxis! And I've been dreaming and working
and working and dreaming and ... *(beat)* How can these youngsters
understand what it feels like to have all that hope leave you? You
don't know that hope is going. Until it is gone.

PETE *(beat)* Well it'll be simple. Jan will go up to the stand and speak. Then I'll call you ... and ask you questions that will lead to you telling the court about that morning in the taxi. Like you told it to us. OK?

SENZO   Ja ... that's ok.

PETE   Good. *(beat)* I'm glad you're here. It means a lot to Jan and Linda.

[A CAR PULLS UP.]

Here they come.

[JAN AND LINDA COME OUT OF THE CAR AND WALK UP THE STAIRS.]

JAN   You go on inside darling ... I'll meet you in a second.

[LARGE DOORS SWING OPEN. AND THEN SHUT. JAN APPROACHES PETE AND SENZO.]

Morning, gentlemen. Crisp autumn, eh.

SENZO   Morning, Mr Stewart. Sorry I missed the briefing yesterday.

JAN   Agh ... no worries you are here now.

PETE   How's Linda?

JAN   Not good. She didn't sleep at all last night. *(beat)* Listen Senzo ... my wife's not being rude not talking to you, eh. It's just ... she's finding all this incredibly difficult. I hope you understand.

SENZO   I do.

JAN   I'm going inside.

PETE   We'll come in with you.

SENZO   I need to finish my cigarette.

PETE   Alright ... see you in there.

[LARGE DOORS SWING OPEN AND THEN SHUT. MZEE WALKS UP THE STAIRS.]

MZEE *(calling from the bottom)* Heita Senzo ... !

[HE GETS NEARER]

I said heita. Did you hear?

SENZO   Ja ... I heard you ...

SCENE 25
EXT. DAY – OUTSIDE WITS UNIVERSITY

SENZO   I drove with Jan Stewart the other day. In his new car. The *BMW* was a write-off. Did you know that?
MZEE   No ... I didn't know that.
SENZO   He's in a lot of pain. And anger. And frustration.
MZEE   I made a mistake, Senzo. I didn't mean to hurt anyone
SENZO   But you wanted him to crash into you. So you could teach him a lesson or two about respect. You taxi drivers think you own the roads. Right?
MZEE   No we're also afraid of the road.
SENZO   I'll be late for my lecture ... I have to go.
MZEE   Mfethu listen ... I am just asking you ...
SENZO   ... to bend the truth at the hearing.
MZEE   No. *(beat)* It is your decision what you say. But I didn' meant to hurt Jan's child. It was an accident. And I'm sorry.

SCENE 26

JAN [V/O] Brotherhood. Sisterhood. The spirit of humanity and togetherness. That is what our flag stands for. Senzo's decent ... bright. He's of the generation that never really experienced the old South Africa. He'll tell his story just as he told it to Pete and me *(beat)* But ... I've been in a court room before. With four other members of the ANC. And we learnt about how to protect our own

SCENE 27
EXT. DAY – STAIRS OUTSIDE MAGISTRATE COURTROOM.
RANDBURG

PETE   We waited all day, Senzo. If you can't make an appointment. You call. It's courtesy.
SENZO   Mr van Wyck, I said I'm sorry ...
PETE   We wondered if you'd changed your mind about testifying.
SENZO   I wouldn't be here now.

[LARGE DOORS SWING OPEN AND THEN SHUT.]

MZEE [V/O] Just like that? That's all he says. 'Ja ... I heard you ...' Then he goes inside. Cold. Like how white people talk to us sometimes. For people like Senzo life is on a plate for them in this country. Everything is there in equality. Senzo ... Jemma ... they have it so easy ...

[JEMMA APPROACHES.]

JEMMA   Mzee!
MZEE   Hi.
JEMMA   Why didn't you tell me your wife was back?
MZEE   What do you mean?
JEMMA   I just saw her around the corner, with your little boy. I thought she'd gone to Pietersburg?
MZEE   She has.
JEMMA   There! There she is. *(beat)* I should go get myself ready before the other journalists get here. See you inside.

[LARGE DOORS SWING OPEN AND THEN SHUT. MZEE WALKS DOWN THE STAIRS.]

MZEE   Dudu! I didn't know you were in Johannesburg.
DUDU   We came yesterday. To finish packing our things.
MZEE   Let's go inside.
DUDU   No ... we have to catch the bus at ten o'clock. *(beat)* Andile ... say hullo to Baba. Now you're hiding behind my legs! Nangu baba. You've been saying you want to see him.
MZEE   Hullo my boy ...

[MZEE LIFTS ANDILE INTO HIS ARMS.]

Yo! You are so heavy now. Granny's feeding you too much in Pietersburg, hhe? Tell your Gogo not to make you fat! Heh heh. *(beat)* Can't you stay for a little while?
DUDU   We have to get back. *(beat)* I came here to give you this.
MZEE   Dudu ...
DUDU   I know it's very little ... but I thought maybe if you have good luck today ... it will pay for your registration at night school.
MZEE   Where did you get it?

DUDU   I left the house where I was working. When I told the
Madam I was going she said she'd been saving some of my salary for
me. Every month for seven years. Eish. So I paid her the money I
owed her from last year and I have this left.

MZEE   A new start eh ...

DUDU *(beat)* Come to Pietersburg soon. Please.

SCENE 28
INT. DAY – MAGISTRATE'S COURTROOM, A LARGE ROOM

JAN   When the *Isuzu* hit us we went into the railings on the
side of the highway ... then we stopped. I couldn't move ... couldn't
see Larry. I was stuck in the seatbelt. I knew he'd taken his off again.
I should have looked earlier, you know. Just to make sure he hadn't.

[JAN STARTS TO CRY.]

He was lying on the floor ... in between the front and back seats.
Screaming. Glass everywhere ... by the time I was free of the
seatbelt. Larry was quiet. He had cried too much.

[JAN SOBS. PAUSE.]

PETE   Thank you Mr Stewart. That will be all.

[JAN GETS UP AND WALKS TO HIS SEAT.]

Your honour ... we'd like to call up to the stand ... Mr Senzo Mnisi ...
who was the only passenger in the taxi ...

[SENZO WALKS TO THE STAND. WE HEAR HIM BEING SWORN
IN.]

SCENE 29
EXT. DAY – OUTSIDE WITS UNIVERSITY CAMPUS

MZEE   OK Senzo ... OK ... OK! I wanted it. I wanted him to
crash into the back of the taxi. OK? OK? So he learns never to
compete ...

SENZO   He was not competing Mzee ...

MZEE   He was being stubborn!

SENZO   He was driving minding his own business!

MZEE   No. He was on the phone to the police after I shouted at him ... making trouble. So yes, I wanted to hit him. *(beat)* He could have lost me my job so yes, I wanted to hit him. ... he thinks he's a better person than me. So yes, I wanted to hit him.

SENZO   That's all? You were just going to hit him?

MZEE   Yes! *(pause)*

SENZO   Is that why you took your gun out from under your seat? *(pause)* Hhe? I may be a softy from the suburbs Mzee ... but I saw you take out a gun ... hide it under your jacket ... and you were planning to use it ...

MZEE   Yes ... *(beat)* Yes. *(beat)* Yes! I was planning to use it. Yes! He made me angry. You're making me angry. Everything in this country makes me angry. I have waited melayti ... for things to be better ... for my life to start ... but no. No ... I must wait ... and wait ... and I am angry. Every time I get onto the road ... I am angry ... every time I get in the taxi I am angry ... angry when I see young people like you who have no idea what it's like to have nothing. To sleep with an empty stomach after a long day at work. I am angry when bastards like Jan pretend we are not human beings ... when they look at us as if we smell of faeces! Everyday I wake up and I wish I hadn't. I wish I could sleep and never wake up. Because I am tired maan! I am tired of seeing the look on my wife's face that tells me that we need to find money. For school fees. For food. For paraffin. For rent ... I am tired of living in a shack where water drips on your bed when it's raining. You know ... you hope ... you hope and hope ... and nothing! You pray, nothing! You beg God to make your life better ... nothing! Ja! I wanted to hurt him. I was going to hit him with that gun ... I was ... I ... *(he is out of breath)* I'm tired Senzo! Mfethu ... everyday I am tired ... every night I am tired. Tired of the road. Tired of carrying a gun for my own protection. I am sick and tired! *(beat)* I didn't want that little boy to die ... no ... I wanted to hurt his father. Yes! Yes! I did ... but not the boy ... not the little boy ... he'd done nothing ... nothing ... at all ...

[MZEE IS OVERCOME.] LONG PAUSE.]

SENZO   What did you do with the gun?

MZEE   Hhe?

SENZO   After the accident. Where was the gun?

MZEE *(beat)* I hid it under the carpet.

SENZO	And now?
MZEE	I still have it. *(beat)* I can't even sell it ...
SENZO	Why?
MZEE	Other people sell them cheaper.

SCENE 30
INT. DAY – BACK INTO THE COURTROOM

PETE   I'm sorry Mr Mnisi ... can you repeat that please ...?

SENZO   I said ... I said that I do not remember at any point during the journey, the taxi driver saying he wanted to hit Mr Stewart.

PETE   And when he wound down the window shouting at Mr Stewart, those were not violent threats?

SENZO   They were insults ... in Zulu ... he insulted Mr Stewart yes ...

PETE   And what did he say about white drivers?

SENZO   He just said they drive like they're strolling in their gardens ...

PETE   Really?

SENZO   Yes ... really ...

SCENE 31
INT. DAY – CORRIDOR OUTSIDE THE COURTROOM

[THERE ARE PEOPLE WALKING ABOUT IN THE CORRIDOR. JAN, PETE AND SENZO ARE TALKING AS QUIETLY AS THEY CAN.]

JAN   How could you lie like that, Senzo!?

SENZO   I said I'd talk about the journey. And I did.

PETE   Jan ... please ... please ... just calm down ...

JAN   You stood there under oath and you protected him! You are not even worth spitting on ... you ... you ... you ... *(kaffir is what he wants to say. He spits on Senzo)*

PETE   Come on ... we're going back inside. Come on!

SCENE 32
INT. DAY – MAGISTRATE COURTROOM. A JUDGE IS SPEAKING

JUDGE   Believe me ... I can fully understand and sympathise with the emotions that can surround a tragic event of this nature. Mr Stewart and Mr van Wyck ... I'm sorry ... I cannot find reason to accept the charge you are putting forward.

[THERE IS NOISE IN THE COURT ROOM. THE JUDGE RAPS HER HAMMER. SILENCE.]

Mzee Dlamini please rise. *(beat)* You are hereby charged with reckless, careless and negligent driving on the M1 highway on April 8th of this year. Report to this court next Wednesday same time to hear your sentence. *(beat)* I am very sorry about your loss Mr and Mrs Stewart. May the good Lord be with you and your family. *(beat)* Court is adjourned.

[COURT ADJOURNS NOISILY]

JAN [V/O] Linda ... she just crumpled ... right there ... in my arms ... she completely crumpled. And we sat in that courtroom after everyone had gone. Me holding her. And her crying. In my arms. The security guard allowed us you know. And then we got up ... didn't say a word to each other ... and we walked out into the crisp clean sunshine of an autumn day ... *(beat)*
Well ... this country's our home. You know. We also fought for it to be where it is today. *(beat)* But Linda and the girls ... they need a change. So ... we are going away ... just ... for a while.

SCENE 33

MZEE [V/O] The judge gave me a suspended sentence and a fine. She said that if the police charge me again ... they will take away my license. *(beat)* I don't have a gun anymore. I buried it.
I went to Pietersburg the day after the trial. Dudu and Andile were very happy to see me. Dudu's mother didn't say a lot. Andile's going to school in Pietersburg ... it is good. She asked if I had registered for night school ... I told her I had the timetable already. Tuesday and Thursday seven o'clock to nine o'clock ... and you must do a lot

of homework. If I pass ... then next year I can do a business course. I am still driving the taxi. I also have another job ... security guard at Fourways shopping centre ... three nights a week. It will pay my fine ... and later it will pay for my schooling. When I qualify I will stop driving. For sure. A new job. A new start with my family. *(beat)* I saw Senzo at Bree Street a month ago ...

SCENE 34
EXT. DAY – BREE STREET STATION

MZEE   Thank you Senzo ...
SENZO   Ushuk'thini? *(What do you mean?)*
MZEE   I mean ... I thank you for your ... for not kicking a man when he was down.
SENZO   The kicking will be done by the great judge up there in the sky. And by your conscience.
MZEE   My conscience mfowethu ... *(beat)* Ja ... ja ...

[FADE OUT OF BREE STREET STATION.]

MZEE [V/O] After an accident ... things change ...

The End.

Sibusiso Mamba

Sibusiso is an actor/writer who was born in Swaziland in 1978. He comes from a family of four and a large extended family. He trained at the Royal Academy of Dramatic Art in England. He has performed in theatre, radio, television and film both in England and South Africa. He's also written plays for the National Theatre Studio, Chalkfoot Theatre Arts and BBC (Radio 4, World Service).

Sibusiso writes for television in South Africa and works as an actor whenever and wherever he can. He lives in Johannesburg with his partner, Manuela.

Useful links

www.aardklopfees.co.za
www.africacentre.org.uk
www.artscape.co.za
www.artsmart.co.za
www.baxter.co.za
www.capeheart.org.za
www.capetownfestival.co.za
www.cca.ukzn.ac.za
www.kknk.co.za
www.litnet.co.za
www.markettheatre.co.za
www.mothertongue.co.za
www.nafest.co.za
www.playhousecompany.com
www.powerofculture.nl
www.rhodes.ac.za
www.saswa.org.za
www.showbusiness.co.za
www.siyandatheatrelaboratory.com
www.southafricahouse.com
www.statetheatre.co.za
www.theatreonthebay.co.za
www.tmsa.org.za
www.ukarts.com
www.voiceofafricaradio.com

aurora metro press

Founded in 1989 to publish and promote new writing, the press has specialised in new drama, fiction and work in translation, winning recognition and awards from the industry.

New drama
Harvest by Manjula Padmanabhan **ISBN 0-9536757-7-7 £6.99**

I have before me a remarkable document... by Sonja Linden
ISBN 0-9546912-3-7 £7.99

Warrior Square by Nick Wood **ISBN 0-9546912-0-2 £7.99**

Under Their Influence by Wayne Buchanan
ISBN 0-9536757-5-0 £7.99

Trashed by Noël Greig **ISBN 0-9546912-2-9 £7.99**

Lysistrata – the sex strike by Aristophanes, adapted by Germaine Greer and Phil Willmott **ISBN 0-9536757-0-8 £7.99**

Anthologies
Six plays by Black and Asian women writers
ed. Kadija George **ISBN 0-9515877-2-2 £11.95**

Black and Asian plays introduced by Afia Nkrumah
ISBN 09536757-4-2 £9.95

Seven plays by women, female voices, fighting lives
ed. Cheryl Robson **ISBN 0-9515877-1-4 £5.95**

Mediterranean plays by women
ed. Marion Baraitser **ISBN 0-9515877-3-0 £9.95**

Eastern Promise, *7 plays from central and eastern europe* eds. Sian Evans and Cheryl Robson **ISBN 0-9515877-9-X £11.99**

Theatre Centre: plays for young people introduced by Rosamunde Hutt
ISBN 0-9542330-5-0 £12.99

www.aurorametro.com